THE
RITES
OF
PASSAGE

THE
RITES
OF
PASSAGE

Second Edition

Arnold van Gennep

Translated by
MONIKA B. VIZEDOM and GABRIELLE L. CAFFEE

With a New Introduction by DAVID I. KERTZER

THE UNIVERSITY OF CHICAGO PRESS
Chicago and London

The University of Chicago Press, Chicago 60637
The University of Chicago Press, Ltd., London
Introduction © 2019 by David I. Kertzer
Translation © 1960, 1988 by Monika B. Vizedom and Gabrielle L. Caffee
Published 2019
Printed in the United States of America

28 27 26 25 24 23 22 21 20 19   1 2 3 4 5

ISBN-13: 978-0-226-62935-3 (cloth)
ISBN-13: 978-0-226-62949-0 (paper)
ISBN-13: 978-0-226-62952-0 (e-book)
DOI: https://doi.org/10.7208/chicago/9780226629520.001.0001

Library of Congress Cataloging-in-Publication Data

Names: Gennep, Arnold van, 1873–1957, author. | Vizedom, Monika B.,
    translator. | Caffee, Gabrielle L., translator.
Title: The rites of passage / Arnold van Gennep ; translated by
    Monika B. Vizedom and Gabrielle L. Caffee ; with a new introduction
    by David I. Kertzer.
Other titles: Rites de passage. English
Description: Second edition | Chicago ; London : The University of Chicago Press,
    2019. | Includes index.
Identifiers: LCCN 2018057481 | ISBN 9780226629353 (cloth : alk. paper)
    | ISBN 9780226629490 (pbk. : alk. paper) | ISBN 9780226629520 (e-book)
Subjects: LCSH: Rites and ceremonies.
Classification: LCC GN473 .G513 2019 | DDC 392—dc23
LC record available at https://lccn.loc.gov/2018057481

♾ This paper meets the requirements of
ANSI/NISO Z39.48-1992 (Permanence of Paper).

CONTENTS

INTRODUCTION

David I. Kertzer

Few books in anthropology have had as much influence as Arnold van Gennep's *Les rites de passage*, originally published in France in 1909. Yet, it was only with the publication of the English-language edition of the book in 1960 that this influence began to be fully felt. Even now, well over half a century since the translation was published, hundreds of scholarly publications in a vast array of disciplines refer to the book every year. Nor has the book's impact been limited to academic circles, for few concepts from the scholarly literature have entered into popular parlance as fully as van Gennep's "rites of passage." The notion that an individual's life consists of a series of transitions, structured by the society one lives in, and that these consist of three stages—separation from the old role, a liminal period between roles, and then the assumption of the new role—has become so commonplace that relatively few who use the phrase are aware of its origin.[1]

Considerable credit for launching the book into the academic stratosphere is due to Solon Kimball, the American anthropologist who proposed publication of an English-language edition to the University of Chicago Press, oversaw its translation from the French, and wrote the introduction to the volume. In that introduction, Kimball set out to describe the intellectual climate in which van Gennep worked, summarize the book's main ideas, and assess its influence on the social sciences. The huge influence that the book has had since Kimball attempted that task would itself justify this new introduction, but it is not the only reason. Kimball's brief introduction left much to be desired in placing van Gennep and his book in historical context, and recent work has brought to light tensions within French academic life, unmentioned by Kimball, that had a great effect on van Gennep's career. Inevitably, too, Kimball presented van Gennep's text in accordance with the theoretical preoccupations of Kimball's

[1] Deep thanks to my colleagues John Bowen, Caroline Brettell, Paja Faudree, Jessaca Leinaweaver, and Daniel J. Smith for their valuable comments on an earlier draft of this introduction. Thanks, too, to Priya Nelson at the University of Chicago Press for leading the effort to produce this new edition of van Gennep's classic book.

time, which makes his introduction now seem dated. Finally, there are some aspects of the translation itself that bear scrutiny, particularly the renderings of van Gennep's text that themselves have had a significant influence on scholarly uses of the book.

Arnold van Gennep

Arnold van Gennep remains a strangely shadowy figure. Victor Turner, who has done much himself to spread the influence of *Rites of Passage*, introduces him as a "Belgian ethnographer," yet van Gennep was born in 1873 in Germany, his father a descendant of French immigrants to Germany, his mother of Dutch descent.[2] At age six, van Gennep moved to France, where he would live most of the rest of his life. On graduating from lycée in Grenoble, he went to Paris, where he studied Arabic and history at the École des Langues Orientales and religious studies at the École Pratique des Hautes Études. There were no courses in anthropology taught in France at the time.[3]

In 1897, van Gennep moved to Poland, where he taught French at a high school before returning to Paris four years later to accept a position as head of translations for the Ministry of Agriculture. While working at the ministry he continued his studies at the École Pratique. His two-part thesis became his first two books: *Tabou et totémisme à Madagascar* in 1904 and, two years later, *Mythes et légendes d'Australie*, an annotated collection of Australian myths and legends translated into French. Both were based entirely on library sources.[4]

---

[2] Turner uses the "Belgian ethnographer" term in his *Drama, Fields, and Metaphors* (195) and refers to van Gennep as a "Belgian folklorist" in his chapter in the edited volume *Secular Ritual* (36). The source of Turner's confusion is unclear, but given the influence that his publications have had on the spread of van Gennep's fame, his mistake has subsequently been repeated widely, in publications ranging from the *Australian Journal of Outdoor Education* (see Beames, "Overseas Youth Expeditions") to the *Harvard Business Review* (see Pontefract, "Leadership in Liminal Times").

[3] Zumwalt, *Enigma of Arnold van Gennep*, 12; Belmont, *Arnold van Gennep,* 2–11.

[4] Zumwalt, *Enigma of Arnold van Gennep*, 13; Belmont, *Arnold van Gennep*, 4; Belier, "Arnold van Gennep and the Rise of French Sociology of Religion," 144. Van Gennep began his thesis under the direction of the prominent historian of religion Léon Marillier, but due to Marillier's death completed it under his former fellow student Marcel Mauss. See Sibeud, "Un ethnographe face," 91.

In these years immediately preceding his work on *Rites de passage*, van Gennep began to craft the odd professional position that would be his lot in life. Frustrated in his attempts to gain a university post, he nonetheless became a well-known figure in the emerging fields of anthropology and folklore studies. Not only were his publications becoming recognized in both France and Britain, but he was entering into relationships with some of the major figures in anthropology on both sides of the channel. In 1908 he founded and became editor of the *Revue des études ethnographiques et sociologiques* (Journal of ethnographic and sociological studies), the first issues of which featured contributions from James Frazer and Andrew Lang. A decade earlier, van Gennep had prepared a French edition of Frazer's book on totemism. Indeed, van Gennep was becoming one of the prominent authorities on anthropological topics in France through his regular pieces on ethnography and folklore in the *Mercure de France*, the most prestigious publication in France aimed at offering the results of recent scholarship to a broad reading public. He would continue these columns, begun in 1906, for over three decades.[5]

It was while writing *Rites de passage* in 1908 that van Gennep decided to quit his job at the ministry to devote himself full-time to his scholarly activities. Living in spare circumstances at his home outside Paris, he would support himself and his family for most of the rest of his life through the modest income afforded by his writings and translations.[6]

Van Gennep undertook his only non-European fieldwork in two separate two-month field trips to the French colony of Algeria in 1911 and 1912. At the end of his second trip, he moved to Neuchâtel, Switzerland, to accept the only university faculty position he would ever have. Three years later, in the midst of the First World War, he was dismissed, apparently due to his criticism of the Swiss government for what he regarded as its pro-German position.[7] Following

5 Sibeud, "Un ethnographe face," 92; Zumwalt, *Enigma of Arnold van Gennep*, 13.

6 Thomassen, "Hidden Battle," 177.

7 Centlivres, "L'ethnologie à l'Université de Neuchâtel." One of the more curious manifestations of van Gennep's anomalous position in lacking a regular academic position is that in its 2012 publication of the Italian edition of *Rites of Passage* (as *I riti di passaggio*), the publisher's back cover biosketch of van Gennep identifies him as "professor of ethnology at the University of Neuchâtel," a position he held for only three years, ending in 1915.

his return to France, van Gennep took a position with the French Ministry of Information, but he remained there only until 1922, when he resigned to accept an invitation to go on a lecture tour of North America. Remarkably, he gave eighty-six lectures throughout the United States and Canada, including at many of the major American universities.[8]

Exhausted and jobless upon his return, van Gennep briefly tried chicken farming in the south of France before settling back into his modest quarters at Bourg-la-Reine, outside Paris. There, where he remained for the rest of his long life, visitors would be struck by the contrast between his outsized scholarly productivity and reputation—he had by this time published fifteen books and over 160 articles—and his impoverished circumstances. Recalling a colleague's comment about the "shame" he felt at seeing a man of van Gennep's brilliance living in such penurious straits, British anthropologist Rodney Needham railed against the "professional neglect of a man of van Gennep's capacities," which he deemed an "academic disgrace."[9]

Shortly after the 1920 publication of *L'État actuel du problème totémique* (The current state of the totemism problem), van Gennep turned away from traditional anthropological topics to devote himself exclusively to French folklore studies. He would become one of the most influential figures in the development of the academic study of folklore in Europe, although by the study of folklore he simply meant, as he put it, "the ethnography of European rural populations, nothing else." Indeed, one of the principles by which he often organized his French folklore studies was the series of life course transitions he had examined in *Rites de passage*.[10]

---

[8] Zumwalt, *Enigma of Arnold van Gennep*, 14; Thomassen, "Hidden Battle," 178.

[9] Needham, introduction to *The Semi-Scholars*, x–xi; Thomassen, "Hidden Battle," 17.

[10] Van Gennep in a 1914 article, cited by Belmont, *Arnold van Gennep*, 71. His use of the rites of passage concept in his French folklore studies began shortly after publication of his book, with the 1910 publication of the three-part "De quelques rites de passage en Savoie."

Senn called van Gennep "the first modern folklorist of France." He explained: "At a time when the field of folklore was in disrepute with the literary folklorists, when ethnologists and sociologists such as Marcel Mauss denied its claim to an autonomous field of study, and when folklorists still argued over its purview, van Gennep was the primary theorist and collector of folklore whose work not only maintained interest in the subject, but provided specific models of gathering, collating and interpreting folklore." Senn, "Arnold van Gennep: Structuralist and Apologist," 229.

Zerilli, writing in Italy's foremost journal of folklore studies, noted that while van Gennep was well known through his work on rites of passage, he was "perhaps even more appreciated,

Van Gennep, Durkheim, and Mauss

To understand the intellectual and academic environment in which van Gennep was working at the time he wrote *Rites de passage*, it is necessary to examine his relation to Émile Durkheim—the towering figure of anthropological and sociological studies in Paris at the time—and the group of disciples that Durkheim was gathering around him. In his introduction to *Rites of Passage*, Kimball offers few glimpses into this relationship, having little to say about Durkheim other than to remark that his 1912 classic, *The Elementary Forms of the Religious Life*, published three years after van Gennep's book, while "in the same tradition of French sociology as van Gennep," makes no mention of him. This, adds Kimball, is especially curious as Durkheim's book focuses on Australian totemism, a subject on which van Gennep had previously published. Perhaps, Kimball speculates, Durkheim's failure to cite van Gennep was due to the fact that the two men had different objectives in their work, with Durkheim more interested in developing an "encompassing theory" of religion "while van Gennep's objective was more limited."[11]

Kimball's characterization of relations between van Gennep and Durkheim is both misleading and incomplete. In fact, at the time of *Rites de passage*, the two men were working on similar problems: totemism, taboo, myth, and ritual, especially those forms found in what were regarded as the most "primitive" societies.[12] These were issues receiving great attention among other European scholars of the time, ranging from the vast quantity of works by best-selling British anthropologist James Frazer to the influential psychoanalytic publications of Sigmund Freud.

Yet there was also something quite distinctive in the theoretical orientation that van Gennep shared with Durkheim and which would become a hallmark of French anthropology: a concern for

especially in Italy, for his celebrated *Manuel de folklore français contemporain* . . . a fundamental, and we can even say monumental, work." In his introduction to the Italian edition of *Rites of Passage*, the prominent Italian anthropologist Francesco Remotti made a similar point. Indeed, van Gennep published nine volumes of that manual for the study of folklore over the last two decades of his life, the final volume appearing only after his death. Zerilli, "Etnografia e etnologia," 143; Remotti, "Introduzione," viii; van Gennep, *Manuel de folklore*.

11 Kimball, introduction to *The Rites of Passage*, xii.
12 Belmont, "Arnold van Gennep (1873–1957)," 19.

social structure and classification. At the beginning of the century, Durkheim, with Marcel Mauss, had published the highly influential essay "De quelques formes primitives de classification" (Of some primitive forms of classification) in *L'Année sociologique*. In it, they examined systems of classifications of people and things in relation to the social structure.[13] Van Gennep would later share this interest. Indeed, the image of individuals and groups passing from one social category to another lies at the heart of *Rites of Passage*. Durkheim's failure to cite van Gennep's work, then, cannot be attributed simply to differences in their intellectual interests.

If van Gennep was intentionally excluded from the French university system, Durkheim bore no little responsibility. Fifteen years older than van Gennep, Durkheim had occupied the first academic position in sociology in France at the University of Bordeaux in 1887,[14] and in 1898 he founded *L'Année sociologique*, France's first social science journal, which would play a major role in the establishment of sociology and anthropology in France. In 1902, Durkheim was appointed to the Faculty of Letters at the Sorbonne in Paris, where, four years later, he was given a chaired professorship. From that post, he exercised considerable influence over French faculty appointments in sociology and related disciplines. That van Gennep himself was well aware of this influence, and perhaps even exaggerated it, is evident from his later remark that Durkheim had laid siege to faculty positions in his field and that anyone not a member of Durkheim's group was a "marked man."[15]

Durkheim's snubbing of van Gennep has not gone unnoticed. The influential British anthropologist E. E. Evans-Pritchard, in his own critical review of Durkheim's theory of totemism, remarked that he need not offer a detailed critique since one was already "to be found in van Gennep's devastating criticisms." Van Gennep's critique, Evans-Pritchard added, was "all the more vigorous and caustic in that Durkheim and his colleagues excluded and ignored him."[16]

[13] Remotti has previously made note of this point. See Remotti, "Introduzione," xiv–xv.

[14] The existing position at the time Durkheim took it up was simply in education, but at his insistence, the name of the position was changed to add "social science," so that he was appointed as "Chargé d'un Cours de Science Sociale et de Pédagogie." Pickering, *Emile Durkheim*, 101.

[15] Cited in Belmont, *Arnold van Gennep*, 2.

[16] Evans-Pritchard, *Theories of Primitive Religion*, 67. Here Evans-Pritchard was referring

That van Gennep returned the favor, mercilessly skewering Durkheim's *Elementary Forms*, can be seen in the review he wrote of the book in the *Mercure de France*.[17] Durkheim focused his book on Australian aborigines, whom he took to represent the most primitive—and hence simplest—form of social organization, and he paid special attention to their religious system, which he identified with totemism. It was an attempt to capture what lay at the heart of all religious systems. Van Gennep's review could not have helped bring him into the master's good graces, as is evident in his first paragraph:

> As I have myself, over the years, inspected the same documents as Mr. Durkheim, I consider myself entitled to declare their theoretical worth to be rather less than he seems to suppose. Indeed, he treats them in much the same manner as religious commentators treat their sacred texts, marshaling vast erudition to illuminate them, but never wondering whether three-quarters of the raw material is even trustworthy. I should like to hope this volume might attract a few new adepts to ethnography, but I fear that . . . it will only drive them away.[18]

Van Gennep kept up his attack on Durkheim for his uncritical use of ethnographic sources:

> The surfeit of references to documents written by sundry informants, police officers, random colonists, obstreperous missionaries, and so forth, is simply futile, as there are entire pages of Mr. Durkheim's book where the conscientious ethnographer is obliged to append a question mark to each line: "Really? How reliable is this informant? How reliable is the document and what does it actually say?" . . . In ten years, his entire systematization of the Australian material will have been utterly rejected, along with the multiple generalizations constructed on the flimsiest foundation of ethnographic facts I have ever observed.[19]

in particular to van Gennep's 1920 book, *L'État actuel du problème totémique*.

[17] Van Gennep's review of *Les formes élémentaires de la vie religieuse* originally appeared in *Mercure de France* in 1913. I quote here from the English translation published in *HAU: Journal of Ethnographic Theory* 7, no. 1 (2017): 576–78.

[18] Van Gennep, review of *Les formes élémentaires*, 576.

[19] Van Gennep, review of *Les formes élémentaires*, 577.

It is worth noting that reliance on such nonscholarly sources was common at the time, and, ironically, van Gennep's *Rites of Passage* is open to the same criticism he leveled against Durkheim, as we shall see.

Van Gennep's critique of Durkheim's work was in many ways ahead of its time, both theoretically and methodologically. Many of the early anthropologists—and not only anthropologists, as Sigmund Freud's book *Totem and Taboo* makes clear[20]—looked to the Australian aborigines as embodying Europeans' contemporary ancestors, that is, the simplest forms of society and culture that were assumed to have characterized an earlier general stage in human social evolution. Working in the wake of Darwin's discoveries, they viewed the technologically simple, nonliterate societies of the world as somehow stuck at an earlier form of society, a stage through which all more advanced societies had passed. Van Gennep demurred, again criticizing Durkheim:

> The idea he has extracted from this ensemble of primitive man . . . and "simple" societies is simply misguided. The better one is acquainted with Australian societies, and the less one focuses on the development of their material culture and social organization, the more one remarks that they are very complex, very far from the simple or primitive, and indeed very evolved along their own lines.[21]

Van Gennep was likewise prescient in finding fault with Durkheim's theory for ignoring the role of the individual. Bronisław Malinowski would take up this critique in his own way in the twenties and thirties, and by the end of the century it would be identified with the concept of "agency"—the notion that individuals are not simply the products of their culture but also, by their actions, help change it:

> Mr. Durkheim's well-established personal proclivity for identifying and foregrounding the collective (or social) element leads him to neglect the generative role of particular individuals in creating certain institutions and beliefs, which I had myself underlined in *Australian myths and legends*, and which he willfully dismisses as

[20] Freud's *Totem and Taboo* was originally published in 1913 in German. The English translation appeared in 1918.

[21] Van Gennep, review of *Les formes élémentaires*, 577.

nugatory. . . . Having no feel for life, no feel for biology or ethnography, he transforms living phenomena and beings (*vivants*) into scientifically desiccated plants arranged as in a herbarium.

From there to outright denial of the reality of the individual and the dynamic part played by individuals in the evolution of civilizations is a short leap that Mr. Durkheim eagerly makes.[22]

Durkheim died five years after the publication of *Elementary Forms*. Through most of van Gennep's career, the man most responsible for carrying on the Durkheimian project of establishing a science of anthropology and sociology in France was thus not Durkheim himself but his nephew and intellectual heir, Marcel Mauss. Practically the same age as van Gennep, Mauss had been a fellow student at the École Pratique in Paris. It was Mauss who became the guiding force behind *L'Année sociologique* following his uncle's death, and much of his work was published in its pages.[23]

Van Gennep's relations with Mauss were complicated. The men became rivals, yet early on their relationship was apparently quite close. Mauss provided comments on a draft of van Gennep's first book, *Tabou et totémisme à Madagascar*, and van Gennep subsequently offered thanks in the book's preface to "my friend Marcel Mauss." In *Rites de passage* van Gennep wrote positively of some aspects of Mauss's work.[24] Yet though they would both spend most of their lives not far from each other in the Paris area, their career paths diverged, as Mauss solidified his position at the center of the institutional devel-

[22] Van Gennep, review of *Les formes élémentaires*, 578.

Van Gennep continued to offer critical comments on Durkheim well after Durkheim's death. In an article on methodology in folklore studies published in 1934, for example, van Gennep offered an unflattering view of Durkheim's construction of a universal theory of religion based on the study of Australian aborigines: "When one thinks that Durkheim and others based universal theories on tribes comprising no more than twenty to a hundred individuals, one is assailed by qualms. In Savoy I have been dealing with three million people. At that rate I could have invented a hundred universal theories just by concentrating on the exceptions alone." Quoted in Belmont, *Arnold van Gennep*, 56–57.

[23] Fournier, *Marcel Mauss*, 2.

[24] For example, see van Gennep, *Rites de passage*, 155 (hereafter *RDP*), in reference to Hubert and Mauss's 1904 essay in *L'Année sociologique* on a theory of magic. Thomassen notes that van Gennep's lengthy discussion of systems of exchange in *Rites de passage* offered some of the key ideas later taken up by Mauss in his own classic essay in *L'Année sociologique*, later published in English translation as a book, titled *The Gift* (1954). Yet if Mauss was inspired by *Rites de passage*, he does not acknowledge it. Thomassen, "Hidden Battle," 189; Mauss, "Essai sur le don."

opment of anthropology in France, while van Gennep was forced to work outside the world of the universities altogether.[25]

Rites of Passage

"My rites of passage," van Gennep reflected some years after its publication, "is like a part of my own flesh, and was the result of a kind of inner illumination that suddenly dispelled a sort of darkness in which I had been floundering for almost ten years."[26] The darkness in which he was struggling, it seems, was caused by the welter of theories on the nature of ritual appearing in the works of the pioneering late nineteenth-century anthropologists in Britain, France, Germany, the United States, and beyond. No one had been more influential in spreading such theories, which were rooted in a fascination for the exotic rites of the newly colonized world, than James Frazer, whose Golden Bough, first published in 1890, had become a best seller. Many of these writings were organized by what were taken to be types of ritual: fertility rites, rites linked to rain and crops, initiation rites, funeral rites. Few of these theorists had actually observed the rites they examined, relying instead on the flood of descriptions coming in from European travelers, colonial administrators, missionaries, and the like.

The unusually ambitious scope of van Gennep's book is evident from its original title page, which bore the ponderous subtitle: "Systematic study of the rites of the doorway and the threshold, of hospitality, adoption, pregnancy, delivery, birth, childhood, puberty, initiation, ordination, coronation, engagements and marriage, funerals,

[25] Thomassen, "Émile Durkheim," 235–36. As late as 1932, van Gennep was writing Mauss to ask for his help in gaining an academic position in Paris, seeking, he said, to have "something stable for [his] old age." Quoted in Fournier, *Marcel Mauss*, 300. If in the earlier part of his career van Gennep was hardly anomalous as a respected scholar unemployed by any university, museum, or research institute, by the latter decades of his life this scholarly path was becoming increasingly rare.

[26] Van Gennep in a 1914 article on *The Golden Bough*, quoted in Belmont, *Arnold van Gennep*, 58. Although van Gennep could be highly critical of the work of other scholars, he always retained a respectful tone in *Rites of Passage* in his treatment of Frazer and his *Golden Bough*, referring to the work frequently. Frazer's *Totemism* was the first of many anthropological works van Gennep translated into French, from English, German, and Italian authors. Zumwalt, *Enigma of Arnold van Gennep*, 102.

xvi

the seasons, etc."[27] Yet while the book at its heart offered something very new, it in many ways reflected the larger intellectual traditions of the anthropology of its time. In his foreword, van Gennep writes that the new interpretation he offered was "consistent with the progress of science," and this faith in science—and this view of the nature of anthropological work as scientific—was certainly a widely shared tenet of early twentieth-century anthropologists (xlv).[28] The pages of the book are littered with citations to the work of the major anthropologists of the late nineteenth and early twentieth centuries, from Edward Tylor's *Primitive Culture* and Frazer's *Golden Bough* to William Robertson Smith's *Religion of the Semites* and Edward Westermarck's *The History of Human Marriage*. While van Gennep would be critical of Durkheim, he seems to have drawn from Durkheim in dividing the social world into two spheres: the sacred and the profane.[29] And although van Gennep did not always approve of the use of cultural details removed from their ethnographic context, *Rites de passage* is in fact typical of the time in following just such an approach.

"A host of ethnographers and folklorists," writes van Gennep, "have demonstrated that among the majority of peoples, and in all sorts of ceremonies, identical rites are performed for identical purposes." His goal, he tells us, is different: "Our interest lies not in the particular rites but in their essential significance and their relative positions within ceremonial wholes—that is, their order" (191).

Van Gennep opens the book by noting the universality of rites of passage in the life course: "The life of an individual, regardless of the type of society, consists in passing successively from one age to

[27] The subtitle does not appear in the 1960 English edition of the book.

[28] All citations to *Rites of Passage* are to the present edition, with page numbers given in the text. Any references to the English edition of *Rites of Passage* will hereafter be abbreviated as *ROP*.

[29] Van Gennep speaks of the separation into sacred and profane in the very first page of his opening chapter, and on the second page writes (here I use my translation): "As we move downward on the scale of civilization (taking this word 'civilization' in its broadest sense), one notes a greater predominance of the sacred world over the world of the profane" (*RDP*, 2). Later, he refers to the separation between sacred and profane as one of the two primary divisions "characteristic of all societies irrespective of time and place" (the other being the separation of the sexes) (*ROP*, 189). Although it is Durkheim's 1912 book, *The Elementary Forms of the Religious Life*, that is most responsible for the centrality of this sacred/profane distinction in subsequent theorizing on religion, Durkheim had already employed this dichotomy in his study of incest in the opening article of the first volume of *L'Année sociologique* (1897).

another and from one occupation to another."[30] He goes on to note "a wide degree of general similarity among ceremonies of birth, childhood, social puberty, betrothal, marriage, pregnancy, fatherhood, initiation into religious societies, and funerals." Yet rather than limit use of his rites of passage scheme to such individual life course transitions, he sees a much broader application. Such rites, he argues, are also to be found accompanying the regular passages that take place in time and season: rites of the full moon, festivals celebrating seasonal changes, and New Year's celebrations (3–4).

All these rites of passage, van Gennep observes, have a three-part structure: rites of separation, rites of the margin, and rites of incorporation. The first involve rites that mark the separation of the individual from his or her previous role, the second a period that Victor Turner would later dub "betwixt and between," in which the individual, while no longer in the old role, has not yet entered the new one. It is through the third set of rites, those of incorporation, that the individual reintegrates into society in the new role.

Some Misunderstandings

Two points are worth noting, for, although van Gennep is careful to stress them, they are sometimes misunderstood. First, as he states early in the book, "It is by no means my contention that all rites of birth, initiation, marriage, and the like, are only rites of passage." He maintains that these rites have multiple purposes. Marriage rites, for example, are also likely to include rites aimed at ensuring the couple's fertility. Pregnancy ceremonies, he tells us, are likely to include rites aimed at protecting mother and child from evil forces and ill health. Funeral ceremonies may primarily attempt to protect survivors from the wrath of the soul of the deceased (11, 41, 192–93). In short, a complete anthropological study of these rites would include analysis that goes beyond their characteristics as rites of passage.

Second, van Gennep does not argue that each particular sequence of rites of passage develops all three stages of the rites to the same extent. In some sequences, he tells us, it is the phase of separation that is emphasized, in others the phase of the margin—what he refers

[30] *RDP*, 3. Translations of the French are my own.

to as the *marge*—and in yet others it is rites of incorporation. The rite of baptism, for example, is, in van Gennep's view, principally a rite of incorporation (53–54).

It might be expected that a book on rites of passage would be organized by the various common transition points in an individual's life, and indeed chapters 4 through 8 do follow this expected course, from pregnancy and childbirth to funerals. Neither of van Gennep's first two chapters after his introduction, however, deal with such transitions. The first of these, titled "Le passage matériel," focuses on the rites involved in passing from one place to another. In such transitions, he points out, the land between two territories is often accorded a kind of sacrality, a sacrality that he identifies with the *marge*—that is, the middle stage of rites of passage. The *marge*, then, is found in not only the transition between roles, but the transition between places as well.

In the 1960 English edition of the book, "Le passage matériel" is translated as "The Territorial Passage." This is not quite exact. What van Gennep has in mind are not only passages from one country to another, or from one tribe's or kinship group's lands to another, but also much more limited movements. In this context, he gives special attention to rites of entry into a house.[31]

The chapter that follows similarly considers rites of passage that have nothing to do with individual life course transitions. "Individuals and Groups" examines those rites that surround the arrival of strangers. Van Gennep detects a "surprisingly uniform pattern" in ceremonies to which such visitors are subjected (27). Again he identifies a three-stage pattern. He refers to the initial phase here as the "preliminary" stage (28). In this first stage, separation from the previous state may be marked by such symbolic means as the wholesale departure of villagers into nearby hills or forest, or by their closing themselves in behind their doors. He refers to the subsequent phase of the rites as "the period of *marge*." This consists "of such events as an exchange of gifts, an offer of food by the inhabitants, or the provision of lodging" (28). Finally, in the third stage, the ceremonies end by rites of incorporation, as enacted through a formal entrance, a common meal, or exchange of handshakes. Van Gennep cites the

[31] *RDP*, 24.

classic anthropological case of the potlatch of Native Americans of the northwest coast as an example of such rites (30).[32]

Life Course Transitions

With chapter 4, dedicated to pregnancy and childbirth, van Gennep begins his analysis of life course rites. He takes pregnancy and childbirth to form a single system of rites of passage, and he argues that they should therefore be studied as a whole. Rites of pregnancy, he tells us, are primarily rites of the *marge*, as women in this period remain in a marginal state. Rites following childbirth, then, are principally rites of incorporation, that is, rites "intended to reintegrate the woman into the groups to which she previously belonged, or to establish her new position in society as a mother, especially if she has given birth to her first child or to a son" (41).

Van Gennep turns in the following chapter to rites of passage involving the newborn child and young children. Again he argues that these involve a sequence of rites of separation, rites performed in the period of the *marge*, and then rites of incorporation into the new role. As throughout the book, his chapter draws on examples from around the world, discussing within only fifteen pages a dizzying range of examples from Africa, Australia, Borneo, Samoa, South Asia, China, and native North America.

The comparative great length of chapter 6, "Initiation Rites," reflects the central place that rites of transition into adulthood have in the book. Van Gennep begins by criticizing the widespread tendency to label such rituals "puberty rites," pointing out that they may or may not coincide with the physiological attainment of puberty (66). Rather, he suggests, they should be viewed as rites of separation from the asexual world, which are followed, after a period in the state of the *marge*, by rites of incorporation into the "world of sexuality" (67).

Van Gennep's discussion of rites of incorporation into the new social identity offers a colorful example of the way he casts what had been seen as a wide variety of rites from around the world into a single framework: "Cutting off the foreskin is exactly equivalent to

[32] See also *RDP*, 38–39.

pulling out a tooth (in Australia, etc.), to cutting off the little finger above the last joint (in South Africa), to cutting off the ear lobe or perforating the ear lobe or the septum, or to tattooing, scarifying, or cutting the hair in a particular fashion." He then adds the clitoridectomy, or the excision of the clitoris, to this list as an example of a rite of passage that marks girls' passage to the world of sexuality, and he devotes considerable attention to the rite in these pages (65–74).

While this kind of analysis can appear to be a classic example of the quest for the exotic in early anthropology, the chapter in fact represents a significant step in advancing anthropology beyond a simple division of the world into the "savage" and the "civilized." The chapter makes the case that what contemporary scholars had regarded as very different rites of initiation found in more "complex" societies should be placed analytically in the same category as these "primitive" rites. Hence the chapter includes an extensive discussion of the evolution of Christian baptism, along with accounts of the enthronement of kings.[33]

Van Gennep pursues this view further in his next chapter, as he examines marriage and betrothal. He faults previous work for its narrow focus on individual rites in isolation, rather than as part of a larger structure. Here he argues for examining together "the marriage ceremonies of any civilized or semicivilized people, whether they be in Europe or Africa, Asia or Oceania, antiquity or the present" (117). Previously, many scholars had interpreted those ritual features found in European society that were also found in "primitive" societies as survivals, no longer serving any useful purpose in the more "advanced" society. Now van Gennep called on them to recognize that similarities among rites in these very different kinds of societies were due to deeper commonalities.

After in the following chapter applying his scheme to funeral ritual and then offering a somewhat catchall chapter on other kinds of rites of passage, van Gennep comes to his conclusions. What differentiates his work from the vast outpouring of publications on ritual in previous decades, he argues, is his focus on the structure

[33] "It becomes readily apparent," he tells us, "that the conceptual scheme proposed is also applicable to enthronement ceremonies," to which he adds ceremonies undergone by individuals entering Roman Catholic or Orthodox Catholic religious orders or the priesthood (106–14).

of groups of rites, rather than on individual rites themselves. In rites that seem so different in focus, he has discovered a common order: "Their positions may vary, depending on whether the occasion is birth or death, initiation or marriage, but the differences lie only in matters of detail. The underlying arrangement is always the same. Beneath a multiplicity of forms, either consciously expressed or merely implied, a typical pattern always recurs: *the pattern of the rites of passage*" (191). Here we see a kind of structural analysis that would prove influential in later developments in French anthropology, most notably through the works of Claude Lévi-Strauss.

Van Gennep calls attention to a second finding as well. In these rites, he tells us, he has detected a pattern "whose generality no one seems to have noticed previously" (191). They all tend to include a period of *marge*, a time that may acquire a certain autonomy of its own. Here he gives as examples the case of betrothal, not married yet no longer single, and the case of novitiates preparing to enter religious orders or the priesthood.[34] This observation would serve as a springboard for major developments in anthropology over a half century after van Gennep's writing, taken up in different ways by both Mary Douglas and Victor Turner.

The Initial Reception

Van Gennep's book was met by withering criticism in the pages of *L'Année sociologique* in a review written by Marcel Mauss himself. Nicole Belmont's characterization of the review, in her biography of van Gennep, as "fairly uncomplimentary" is an understatement. More on the mark is her charge that the review showed "bad faith," for, in addition to well-founded criticisms, it offered others based on what seem to be willful misinterpretations of van Gennep's text.[35]

Van Gennep was not content, wrote Mauss, to limit his scheme of rites of passage to religious initiation ceremonies, as, Mauss suggested, he should have. Rather, charged Mauss, he "sees everywhere only passages, with [stages of] separation, *marge*, and incorporation."

[34] The original is found in *RDP*, 275. The 1960 English translation is found on p. 191, which, however, translates *marges* as "transitional periods." See my discussion below regarding problems with this translation.

[35] Belmont, *Arnold van Gennep*, 62–64.

Suggesting that van Gennep was proposing a "law," he then argued that van Gennep believed that this law "dominates all religious representations . . . it is the origin of theories of reincarnation . . . of philosophies from that of [ancient] Greece to that of Nietzsche, etc. In the end, this work embraces practically all the questions that the science of religion can pose."[36] Van Gennep would have reason to be upset at Mauss's review, for he nowhere in the book characterized his rites of passage as a "law," and he repeatedly stated that there were many aspects of ritual that his rites of passage schema did not address. Nor did he claim to be offering an explanation for the history of philosophies of any kind.

If Mauss voiced a criticism that rings true today, it is with van Gennep's method—common to anthropology of the time—of employing examples plucked willy-nilly from ethnographic contexts from Borneo to the Congo. "The method employed," wrote Mauss, "is that prevalent in the anthropological school. Rather than focus analysis on some typical facts that one can study with precision, the author takes a kind of ramble through all of history and all ethnography. . . . He makes use of all rituals, those of China, of Islam, of Australia, of America, of Africa, of the Catholic Church, etc. We have often spoken of the disadvantages of these scattershot reviews."[37]

British scholars greeted the book much more warmly, and their reviews—in major journals—testify to the fact that van Gennep was already a well-known figure in anthropological circles.[38] "M. van Gennep's book, like everything he writes, is learned, judicious, and methodical," Andrew Lang, then one of the preeminent anthropological scholars of religion in Great Britain, wrote in his review.[39] T. C. Hodson, a South Asian specialist who would later become the first William Wyse Professor of Social Anthropology at Cambridge, judged

---

[36] Mauss, review of *Rites de passage*. Translations of Mauss's review are my own.

[37] Mauss, review of *Rites de passage*. I translate Mauss's final phrase, *"ces revues tumultueuses,"* as "these scattershot reviews," which I think best gets at his meaning, although there does not seem to be a fully adequate English equivalent.

[38] "M. Van Gennep is well known to specialists for his researches in anthropology, folk-lore, and kindred subjects," reported the review in the *Journal of the Royal African Society* (108). "The variety, as well as the extent and thoroughness of his learning, is shown in his *Mythes et Légendes d'Australie*, his *Tabou et Totémisme à Madagascar*, and *La Question d'Homère*, to which Mr. Andrew Lang devoted an article in the *Morning Post* a few months ago."

[39] Lang, review of *Rites de passage*, 826.

the book "a substantial and valuable contribution to anthropological literature" and remarked that "its sustained and close argument merits thought and attention from the beginning to the last word of the last chapter."[40]

Although less widely reviewed in the United States, what reception the book did receive was no less enthusiastic. Frederick Starr, the first professor of anthropology at the University of Chicago, opened his review in the *American Journal of Sociology* by calling it an "important and original work." Starr highlighted van Gennep's unusually broad sweep in proposing that a common structure united a wide variety of rites and concluded: "To bring all of these into one group and to demonstrate their identity is a synthesis of extraordinary boldness."[41]

The English-Language Edition

Despite the warm reception that *Rites de passage* received in Britain and the United States, it was not until the publication of the English-language edition half a century later, and three years after van Gennep's death, that the book began to have its enormous worldwide impact.[42] Credit for the project of publishing a translation of the book goes to Solon Kimball, who first proposed it to the University of Chicago Press. It was Kimball, too, who arranged for Monika Vizedom, then a graduate student at Columbia, where Kimball was a professor at Teachers College, to translate it.[43]

---

[40] Hodson, review of *Rites de passage*, 30.

[41] Starr, review of *Rites de passage*, 207–8.

[42] In addressing the influence that *Rites of Passage* has had following 1960, I focus on the impact of the newly translated text and so limit my attention in these pages primarily to the English-speaking world. *Rites de passage* continued to have significant influence in the French-speaking world as well, as evident in Pierre Bourdieu's important 1982 essay, "Les rites comme actes d'institution," which begins: "Avec la notion de rite de passage, Arnold Van Gennep a nommé, voire décrit, un phénomène social de grande importance. . . ." For another French example, see Fellous, *À la recherche de nouveaux rites*.

[43] In her translator's introduction, Vizedom writes: "Although Dr. Kimball's name appears on the title page only in connection with his introduction, this translation has been primarily his project, and one which never would have reached completion without his tireless efforts." Gabrielle Caffee is credited on the book's title page with being a cotranslator with Vizedom, but in his introduction Kimball makes clear that the translation is largely Vizedom's work, with Caffee only providing help "in the initial phases of the translation." See 1960 edition of *ROP*, xxii, xviii.

Although Kimball was a prominent anthropologist, it is in some ways surprising that it was he who spearheaded the project. He was not a student of ritual or religion, nor was he known for any previous interest in French theory. While a graduate student at Harvard, he had worked as a research assistant for Lloyd Warner in his community study of Yankee City (Newburyport, MA) and then conducted his dissertation fieldwork in Ireland. Following his graduate work, he spent a decade working for the US Bureau of Indian Affairs. Far from a theorist, he was a pioneer in applied anthropology and the anthropology of education, serving as president of the Society for Applied Anthropology in the mid-1950s.[44]

In offering his rationale for publishing an English edition of van Gennep's book, Kimball explains: "The need for a translation . . . has long been felt by those who were appreciative of the significance of his theoretical formulations. Although his influence has been considerable in some anthropological circles, his contribution, in general, has failed to reach the other social sciences."[45] While perhaps overstating the extent to which van Gennep's book had been read by American anthropologists in its original French, Kimball was prescient in thinking that publication of an English edition would have a major influence on disciplines well beyond anthropology. As for anthropology, Kimball correctly observed that, by the time he was writing, the focus on religious and ritual topics that had so marked earlier anthropological studies had been substantially reduced.[46] While there were some notable holdouts, such as Evans-Pritchard,[47] the functional revolution in anthropology had turned attention to matters of social organization, to economy, politics, and kinship. If in subsequent years anthropologists' attention would turn back to religion and ritual, it would be in no small part due to the influence that publication of the English edition of *Rites of Passage* would have.

Curiously, although she was only a graduate student when she translated *Rites of Passage*, and not a particularly advanced graduate

---

[44] Burns, "Obituary"; Moore, "Obituary." Kimball would later (1970–71) serve as president of the American Ethnological Society. Burns, "Obituary," 153.

[45] Kimball, introduction to *ROP*, v.

[46] Kimball, introduction to *ROP*, xvii.

[47] Evans-Pritchard, *Witchcraft, Oracles and Magic*; Evans-Pritchard, *Nuer Religion*; Evans-Pritchard, *Theories of Primitive Religion*.

student,[48] Vizedom felt free to add scores of her own footnotes to the text. In addition to notes defining or explaining terms that might be unfamiliar to readers, she offered numerous comments giving her own view of the veracity of van Gennep's assertions. In an early note, she remarks that one of van Gennep's ethnographic descriptions "appears to be primarily speculative" (21n1). In response to van Gennep's statement that even in societies where divorce is easy, it is difficult or impossible to get a divorce when the woman has already born children, she offers her own correction: "Current data do not bear out this statement for all societies. Exceptions will be found especially where there are matrilineal or bilateral kinship systems" (49n1). She takes particular issue with a number of van Gennep's characterizations of Jewish rituals. "Van Gennep is in error here," she begins one of these lengthy notes, referring in this case to his description of the Jewish holiday of Passover (40n3). Many more examples could be cited.[49]

Given the impact that publication of the translation has had, and the way its English terms have been employed in thousands of publications since, it is worth calling particular attention to Vizedom's decision to translate the middle stage of rites of passage, which van Gennep referred to as the *rites de marge*, as "rites of transition." The translation is misleading: while stages one and three constitute transitions, this is the one stage that does not. For this reason van Gennep sometimes refers to this second stage as a period, rather than a transition,[50] that is, as a duration of time with unique, often sacred, characteristics. He also uses the term *rites liminaires*, liminal rites, to refer to this stage of the rites of passage.[51] As it would happen, two of

[48] Vizedom would receive her PhD in anthropology at Columbia University in 1963. Zhang, "Recovering Meanings Lost," 127. Thirteen years later she published her own book on rites of passage, *Rites and Relationships*.

[49] It might be thought that Kimball rather than his graduate student wrote these notes, but in the book's first footnote, after offering a seemingly superfluous explanation of what she takes van Gennep to mean in using the term "modern," Vizedom writes: "All further notes by the translator appear in brackets" (1n1). All of the notes in question appear in brackets as footnotes in the text.

[50] E.g., *RDP*, 38, 57, 62. Likewise, van Gennep uses such terms as *le stade de marge* (27) and *l'état de marge* (211) to capture this sense of duration rather than movement.

[51] *RDP*, 14, 27, 62. "I propose to call preliminary rites [*rites préliminaires*] the rites of separation from the previous world, liminal rites [*rites liminaires*] the rites performed during the stage of the marge, and postliminal rites [*rites postliminaires*] the rites of incorporation into the new world" (*RDP*, 27). Zumwalt has previously called attention to the problematic nature

the most influential anthropologists to find their inspiration in van Gennep's work—Mary Douglas and Victor Turner—would base some of their most important work on exactly this concept of a marginal, or liminal, state.[52]

The Reception Given to the English-Language Edition

The stature of the anthropologists who reviewed the University of Chicago Press edition of *Rites of Passage* offers a sense of the importance given to the book's publication. In Britain, Evans-Pritchard reviewed the book for the *Times Literary Supplement*, identifying van Gennep as the author of "several important anthropological treatises and many important books on folklore." He added that, "in spite of his erudition and excellent researches, he never received high academic recognition and was, indeed, cold-shouldered by Durkheim and his colleagues of the *Année Sociologique*, whose writings he subjected to some merciless criticism."[53] Edmund Leach reviewed the book in *Man*, the journal of the Royal Anthropological Institute, together with the newly translated essays in *Death and the Right Hand* by Robert Hertz. "The belated appearance of English translations of these classics of French comparative sociology," wrote Leach, "is thoroughly welcome."[54] Six years later, in his article on "Ritual" for the *International Encyclopedia of the Social Sciences*, Leach offered a comparison that would have been especially pleasing to van Gennep: speaking of the two men's theories of ritual, Leach concluded that "van Gennep's schema has proved more useful than Durkheim's."[55]

of translating *rites de marge* as "rites of transition." Zumwalt, *Enigma of Arnold van Gennep*, 24.

[52] On Douglas and Turner and their use of van Gennep's concept of *marge*, see my discussion below.

[53] Evans-Pritchard, "Ritual Reintegration."

[54] Leach, review of *The Rites of Passage*.

[55] Leach, "Ritual," 522. Leach was much less kind in evaluating Kimball's introduction to *Rites of Passage*. "Professor Kimball," wrote Leach, "offers van Gennep to American College students as an almost unknown author and his comments upon the general climate of anthropological opinion in England and France during the first decade of this century are both naïve and misleading."

In his review, Leach argued that *Rites of Passage* was "really only an elaboration, on a wider canvas, of the ideas contained in Hertz's essay on *Death*." This seems somewhat overstated, although Hertz did recognize the processual nature of rites of transition and wrote of a movement from the status of living member of society to the status of ancestor via an intermediate phase. In this sense his work did presage van Gennep's famous three-stage model. Yet,

In the United States, one indication of the significance of the English edition's publication was the decision of *Science*, the prestigious journal of the American Association for the Advancement of Science, to publish a review, as few books in social anthropology were reviewed in its pages. Just as notable was the anthropologist called on to write the review, Clifford Geertz. Unfortunately, the first sentence of Geertz's review contained three errors: "Although van Gennep, one of the original group of Durkheimian sociologists, lived until 1957, this book, originally published in 1908 but not previously translated into English, is the sole basis for his considerable international reputation as a theorist in the field of comparative religion."[56] As we have seen, van Gennep was decidedly not a part of the original group of Durkheimian sociologists; the book was first published in 1909;[57] and van Gennep's international reputation as a theorist in comparative religion was not based solely on *Rites of Passage*.

In fact, one could argue that in France, at least, his publications on totemism had a greater effect on theories of religion, thanks to the influence they had on Claude Lévi-Strauss. In his classic study *Totemism*, Lévi-Strauss praises van Gennep's interpretative move in highlighting the links between totemism, exogamy, and reciprocity. "This interpretation, which is also our own (see *Les Structures élémentaires de la parenté*)," explains Lévi-Strauss, "seems to us to be still superior to that proposed by Radcliffe Brown." In fact, this linking of exogamy to systems of reciprocity among kin groups, which Lévi-Strauss credits to van Gennep, was central to much of Lévi-Strauss's work on not only totemism but also kinship.[58]

Geertz in his review went on to skewer van Gennep—as Mauss had done a half century earlier—for his uncritical use of a "great variety of material, much of it unreliable, from peoples all over

---

Hertz focused only on a single kind of passage—death—and confined his focus to death rituals in Indonesian societies. Leach, review of *The Rites of Passage*, 173; Hertz, "Contribution à une étude," 49–50.

[56] Geertz, review of *The Rites of Passage*.

[57] Zumwalt noted the widespread reference in American reviews of the book to an original publication date of 1908. Zumwalt, *Enigma of Arnold van Gennep*, 119. It is particularly notable that the estimable British anthropologist E. E. Evans-Pritchard, in his review of the English edition in the *Times Literary Supplement*, makes the same mistake. The error is undoubtedly due to the first sentence of Vizedom's translator's note to the English edition: "Arnold van Gennep published *Les rites de passage* in 1908." See 1960 edition of *ROP*, xxi.

[58] Lévi-Strauss, *Totemism*, 36.

the world" and "his total failure to deal with the social and cultural contexts from which his examples are drawn." Yet, concluded Geertz, despite all these limitations, van Gennep "offers, in his concept of an underlying pattern of withdrawal, isolation, and return which is common to all passage rituals, a valuable theoretical insight into the dynamics of religion in both psychological and sociological terms."[59]

The Influence of *Rites of Passage*

In the decades that followed the English-language publication of *Rites of Passage*, hundreds of anthropological works appeared in the Anglophone world making use of it. None were more influential than the writings of Mary Douglas and Victor Turner, both of whom built on van Gennep's concept of the middle, liminal stage, the *marge*.

In her influential 1966 book, *Purity and Danger*, Mary Douglas draws out theoretical implications from van Gennep's concept of the sacred nature of this liminal stage, giving special attention to the dangerous quality that this state often has. "Danger," she writes, "lies in transitional states, simply because transition is neither one state nor the next." Douglas offers examples from a wide variety of contexts, from the dietary taboos of Leviticus to initiation rites in Africa. "Holiness," she tells us, "requires that individuals shall conform to the class to which they belong." Those people, or those things, that do not fit comfortably into such a class lie at the margins, and the margins are a perilous territory.[60]

The reference to van Gennep in her work is clear: "The person who must pass from one [state] to another is himself in danger and emanates danger to others. The danger is controlled by ritual which

[59] Geertz, review of *The Rites of Passage*, 1801–2. For other reviews of the book by prominent American anthropologists, see Hoebel's 1960 review in *Southwestern Social Science Quarterly* and Spencer's 1961 review in *American Anthropologist*. Spencer's review was very positive, while Hoebel's was more mixed. Hoebel acknowledged that "in its day, this contribution was a major stepping stone in the development of social anthropology: it ordered and placed in proper focus a number of functionally related ritual practices." He concluded that "van Gennep's central thesis was, and to some extent still is, of first-rate importance." Yet, he termed the book "ethnologically crude, artless, and boring," complaining that its author was overly concerned with problems of classification and "given to fragmentary cataloguing of snippets and bits from an anthropological grab bag."

[60] Douglas, *Purity and Danger*, 97, 53, 96.

precisely separates him from his old status, segregates him for a time and then publicly declares his entry to his new status." Among Douglas's insights was the application of this theoretical approach to contemporary secular situations where the lack of rites of passage leaves individuals in a marginal state, and hence regarded uneasily by the larger society. As an example, she writes of the ex-prisoner who, without any ritual means of incorporation into his or her new role in society, remains forever at the margins.[61]

Douglas's work extended van Gennep's concept of the *marge*, applying it to cultural categories more generally, that is, beyond the rites of passage that were the focus of his book. Dirt, for example, is "matter out of place. Where there is dirt there is system. Dirt is the by-product of a systematic ordering and classification."[62] Most famously, she employs this theoretical proposition to offer a new explanation for the hodgepodge of Jewish dietary taboos that have their origin in Leviticus. Those animals it was forbidden to eat failed to conform to the common categories of their kind: creatures that lived in the ocean yet crawled and did not swim; pigs that were four-legged livestock but, unlike cattle, did not chew their cud.

Victor Turner was likewise drawn to the same elements of van Gennep's work that Douglas was building upon—van Gennep's concepts of the liminal and rites of passage. Turner opens his now classic essay "Betwixt and Between: The Liminal Period in *Rites de Passage*" by crediting van Gennep's influence: "In this paper, I wish to consider some of the sociocultural properties of the 'liminal period' in that class of rituals which Arnold van Gennep has definitively characterized as 'rites de passage.'" Turner goes on to characterize what he calls, drawing on van Gennep, "the period of the margin or 'liminality'" as an "interstructural situation." He thus focuses his work on rites of passage that have a well-developed marginal or liminal phase. These he locates above all in rites of transition to social maturity or to cult membership in small-scale societies.[63]

Turner termed *Purity and Danger* a "magnificent book" and praised Douglas for calling attention to the link between the mar-

---

[61] Douglas, *Purity and Danger*, 96, 97.

[62] Douglas, *Purity and Danger*, 36.

[63] Turner, *Forest of Symbols*, 93–95.

ginal state and a condition of uncleanliness and danger. "From this standpoint," writes Turner, "one would expect to find that transitional beings are particularly polluting, since they are neither one thing nor another . . . and are at the very least 'betwixt and between' all the recognized fixed points in space-time of structural classification."[64] Turner would go on to develop this concept of a liminal phase in a series of publications that helped to turn anthropology away from earlier functionalist approaches toward the symbolic dimension, bringing renewed interest to the study of ritual.[65]

Among the topics Turner explored was the application of van Gennep's theoretical construct, and especially his concept of the *marge*, to the relatively neglected topic of the pilgrimage. Turner opens his book on the subject, coauthored by Edith Turner, with an extensive discussion of van Gennep's text. The Turners then proceed to develop van Gennep's concept of liminality well beyond his original focus on rites of passage, terming the implications of van Gennep's "discovery" to be "truly revolutionary" in freeing social scientists from limited paradigms of the social structural.[66]

Another indication of the spreading influence of van Gennep's book in the wake of its appearance in English was the publication in 1962 of Max Gluckman's influential edited collection, *Essays on the Ritual of Social Relations*. The book carries the dedication: "To the Memory of Arnold van Gennep." In his lengthy introductory chapter, titled "Les rites de passage," Gluckman, one of Britain's most prominent anthropologists at the time, argues that *Rites of Passage* "was one of the most important books written about ritual in the generation before the First World War, and his 'discovery' was to make a greater impression on subsequent work than books which are much better known . . . like Tylor's *Primitive Culture*, Frazer's *The Golden Bough*, and Marett's *The Threshold of Religion*." Van Gennep, according to Gluckman, had made a "remarkable breakthrough," one that improved the quality of subsequent studies of ritual by pro-

[64] Turner, *Forest of Symbols*, 97.
[65] Turner, *Ritual Process*; Turner, *Dramas, Fields, and Metaphors*; Turner, "Variations on a Theme." See also the discussion of this point in Thomassen, "Uses and Meanings." Kapferer argues that van Gennep's work granted Turner "a non-Durkheimian legitimacy" for his processual approach to the study of ritual. Kapferer, "Ritual Dynamics," 37.
[66] Turner and Turner, *Image and Pilgrimage*, 1–3.

viding a proper framework for observation.[67] In his own chapter in the book, Meyer Fortes, an equally prominent British social anthropologist, praises van Gennep's book as "one of the major theoretical achievements of our science."[68]

The number of anthropologists who, since the publication of the English edition of *Rites of Passage*, have made use of van Gennep's framework and his insights in their own ethnographic work is not easily calculable, but there are hundreds of examples. They range from short notes, such as Beidelman's "Ghostly *rites de passage* in East Africa," to edited volumes such as Sally Moore and Barbara Myerhoff's application of van Gennep's framework to nonreligious settings in their *Secular Ritual*, and books focusing on the same series of life course transitions that van Gennep examined, as found in Martha and Morton Fried's *Transitions: Four Rituals in Eight Cultures*.

Arguably the best book-length anthropological study of funeral rites in the decades since the publication of the translation of *Rites of Passage*, Richard Huntington and Peter Metcalf's *Celebrations of Death*, appropriately begins with a section titled "Van Gennep's *Rites of Passage*." The authors offer insight into the influence that van Gennep's book has had on the study of ritual. Before the book, they write, scholars seemed unable "to view ritual as anything other than an anachronism," a view associated with "nineteenth-century rationalism." In contrast, they argue, *Rites of Passage* provided "a radically different assessment of the meaning and function of ritual behavior. . . . Elements of ceremonial behavior were no longer the relics of former superstitious eras, but keys to a universal logic of human social life."[69]

Anthropologists have also built on van Gennep's basic framework by using it to provide insight into political processes in modern state

[67] Gluckman, "Les rites de passage," 1–2, 7–8, 12. Gluckman was not without his criticisms of van Gennep's book, accusing him of following the prevailing methods of piling up ethnographic examples as means of proof and lacking the focus on "functional connections" in society that Durkheim had. See Gluckman, "Les rites de passage," 1, 11. For a rebuttal to Gluckman's negative comments on *Rites of Passage*, see Pitt-Rivers, "Un rite de passage," 115–18. Pitt-Rivers credits van Gennep with moving anthropology beyond the study of rites as magical practices to work that focused on the role of ritual in ordering social relations. Pitt-Rivers, "Un rite de passage," 129n2.

[68] Fortes, "Ritual and Office," 54.

[69] Huntington and Metcalf, *Celebrations of Death*, 9–11.

societies. Here I can cite some of my own work. In an ethnographic study of the battle between the Catholic Church and the Italian Communist Party for people's allegiance in a working-class Italian *quartiere*, it became clear that rites of passage constituted an important battleground. The previous church monopoly of such rites of passage as baptisms, weddings, and funerals had great value for binding people to the church. Realizing this, Communist Party leaders went about creating an alternative system of rites of passage. Funerals offered one example. The city hearse in Bologna, used in funeral processions, had a cross on the roof that screwed off for Communist funerals. In Communist processions, red flags replaced the crosses borne aloft in church funerals. Neither the political implications of rites of passage much less political competition over them are discussed in van Gennep's book, which pays little attention to intrasocietal cultural heterogeneity. Yet his work provided the impetus for developing just such insights.[70]

What may be even more remarkable than the great influence that the book's English-language publication has had on anthropology is the influence it has had on other fields. Tracking references to the text, as well as uses of the concepts that originate in it but do not mention van Gennep, one witnesses the vast array of fields in which scholars have used van Gennep's framework in attempts to shed new light on their subjects.

Among those closest to van Gennep's initial fields of interest are works in folklore and religious studies. "It is probably fair to say," wrote the prominent American folklorist Alan Dundes in 1999, referring to *Rites of Passage*, "that no example of folkloristic analysis has had more impact on the scholarly world than this classic study."[71] The religious studies literature, along with the parallel religious practice

---

[70] I note, with embarrassment, that my lengthy discussion of the subject in a subchapter of that book labeled "Rites of Passage" makes no mention of van Gennep, nor is he even cited in the bibliography. I extended this analysis of the political uses of rites of passage in my later, more general book on politics and ritual, in a section titled "The Battle over Rites of Passage." There, I was relieved to see on checking now many years later, I did credit van Gennep. Kertzer, *Comrades and Christians*, 135–43; Kertzer, *Ritual, Politics, and Power*, 114–19.

[71] The Dundes quote is cited by Zhang in his own reevaluation of the influence that van Gennep's work has had on the discipline of folklore. Dundes, *International Folkloristics*, 100–101; Zhang, "Recovering Meanings Lost," 119.

literature, is filled with references to van Gennep.[72] In the allied field
of the archaeology of religion, van Gennep seems no less omnipres-
ent. Fourteen articles in the 2011 *Oxford Handbook of the Archaeology
of Ritual and Religion* employ the concept of "rites of passage," and
in the separate *Handbook* entry titled "Rites of Passage," the author
observes that van Gennep's book "remains extraordinarily influential as the point of departure for discussions of transition rituals."[73]

A whole essay, if not a book, could be written on the effect that
Rites of Passage has had on the work of historians. Indeed the major
cultural turn in history, begun in the early 1970s, with its emphasis
on popular rituals, was influenced in no small part by van Gennep's
book. This is made clear in Natalie Zemon Davis's seminal 1971
article on charivaris in sixteenth-century France, which contains
twenty-seven references to van Gennep. In that oft-cited article she
shows how these carnivalesque rites, in which unmarried young
men publicly humiliated their older neighbors, became vehicles
for political protest. In looking for the analytical tools necessary to
examine such rites, she found inspiration in van Gennep's book,
as her correspondence with fellow historian Edward Thompson
makes clear.[74]

Van Gennep's influence among historians can also be seen in
the fertile line of historical work that has built on his treatment

[72] To get some sense of the range of works making use of rites of passage in religious
studies and what might be called applied religious studies, see Grimes, *Deeply into the Bone*;
Magida, *Opening the Doors*; Guest, review of *Meeting Jesus at University*; Pike, "Radical Animal
Rights"; Williamson, *Illuminata*; Baum, "Wrestlers on the *Awasena* Path."

[73] Garwood, "Rites of Passage," 261. Unfortunately, Garwood not only picks up the mistake Victor Turner had made of referring to van Gennep as "Belgian," but also gives the original date of *Rites de passage* as 1911, two years after its actual publication.

[74] Davis, "Reasons of Misrule"; see also Walsham, "Rough Music and Charivari." While
Davis makes ample use of van Gennep's *Rites of Passage*, most of the citations to van Gennep's work in Davis's article are to his publications on French folklore. Around the same
time that Davis's work on the carnival was having such a big influence in the development of
historiography, the English-language publication of Mikhail Bakhtin's book *Rabelais and His
World* was having a comparable effect. Indeed, many scholars found that combining Bakhtin's
insights of carnival as time outside normal time and van Gennep's insights—often mediated by
Victor Turner—into the state of liminality offered a fertile theoretical framework to explore in
their own work. These include not only historians (e.g., Scribner, "Reformation"), but scholars
from fields ranging from literary studies (Bristol, *Carnival and Theater*) to folklore (Lindahl,
"Bakhtin's Carnival Laughter"; Santino, "Carnivalesque and the Ritualesque") and sociology (Shields, "The 'System of Pleasure'"). The prominent Brazilian anthropologist Roberto
DaMatta, in his recent reconsideration of the concept of rites of passage, similarly brings
Bakhtin into his critique. DaMatta, "Individuality and Liminality."

of coronation rites as rites of passage. The 1999 edited volume *Rites of Passage in Ancient Greece* offers but one example. "The last three decades," Mark Padilla writes in his introduction to the book, "have been exciting for scholars of Greek literature, religion, and society . . . with a particularly productive 'node' of this interdisciplinarity being the study of initiatory patterns, rites, and social functions." Van Gennep, Padilla observes, "pioneered the anthropology of the subject in his seminal *Les rites de passage*," which, he enthuses, "remains an astonishingly stable and useful paradigm to this day."[75]

The sociological, social services, and social problems literatures are similarly filled with applications of the rites of passage model, and in psychology both life course and developmental studies have made abundant use of the paradigm.[76] In literary criticism, as one observer remarked, van Gennep's categories have had "truly remarkable fortune."[77] Feminist and postcolonial literary theorists, as well as feminist psychiatrists, have been developing van Gennep's framework to advance their own new interpretive paradigms.[78] And scholars in fields from mortality and education studies to management, geography, and disability studies have likewise offered new approaches to their subjects by employing van Gennep's insights.[79]

Indeed, the term that van Gennep put into such widespread use has become ubiquitous well beyond the scholarly world. Examples are everywhere, from the 1980 Booker Prize–winning book by William Golding, *Rites of Passage*, to the latest copies of daily newspapers. Another example is found in Julia Alvarez's *Once upon*

---

[75] Padilla, introduction to *Rites of Passage in Ancient Greece*, 15–16. Among many other examples of the use of *Rites of Passage* in historical study, see Lane, *Rites of Rulers*; Centlivres, "Les rites de passage"; McMullen, "Bureaucrats and Cosmology"; Price, "From Noble Funerals"; May, "Presidential Address"; Pickering, "Chartist Rites of Passage."

[76] For representative examples, see Sande, "Intoxication"; Brown, Brunelle, and Malhotra, "Tagging"; Janusz and Walkiewicz, "Rites of Passage Framework."

[77] Calame, "Le rite d'initiation tribale," 23–24. See also Drewery, *Modernist Short Fiction*.

[78] Dodgson-Katiyo and Wisker, *Rites of Passage*; Brenner, *Women's Rites of Passage*.

[79] Among hundreds of examples, see Willett and Deegan, "Liminality and Disability"; Blumenkrantz and Goldstein, "Seeing College"; Söderlund and Borg, "Liminality in Management"; Winchester, McGuirk, and Everett, "Schoolies Week"; Murphy et al., "Physical Disability." "Here," writes Jenny Hockey, "I want to consider the theoretical insights which such a schema might offer for a social science of mortality today." One might substitute for "social science of mortality" any number of fields and find similar articles. Hockey, "Importance of Being Intuitive," 213.

a Quinceañera: Coming of Age in the USA, a feminist examination of a Latina girl's coming of age rite. The number of Latina girls' responses to Alvarez's survey referring to the celebration as their "right of passage" illustrates the depths to which van Gennep's concept has sunk into the popular imagination.[80] Indeed, designing feminist rites of passage has become something of a feminist cottage industry, marked by such events as the 2018 "Rites of Passage Facilitator Training" held in Byron Bay, Australia.[81] Nor does the popular influence of the book show any sign of diminishing. In 2018, the *New York Times* introduced a new column titled Rites of Passage, described as "essays that explore notable life transitions and events," and invited readers to contribute their own essays on the subject for publication.[82] From the time that the English translation of *Rites of Passage* was published in 1960 through 2014, 699 *New York Times* articles made use of the phrase.

And so the legacy of the man whom Durkheim, at the height of his influence in Paris in 1915, dismissed as unworthy of a university position,[83] a man who survived to old age in reduced circumstances outside Paris surrounded by his books and not much else, lives on through a work written when he was thirty-five years old. The envious reputation he achieved is due in no small part to the publication of the English edition of his now classic book in 1960, three years after his death.

---

[80] The author herself credits van Gennep's work as the source of her use of the concept. The reference to a "right of passage" is found on p. 5.

[81] "Imagine having the support of sisterhood & women's wisdom to help you navigate turning 40 or life changes like becoming a mum, divorce, or menopause." The announcement for the five-day workshop—"We're Reclaiming Our Feminine Rites of Passage!"—was accessed on August 7, 2018, at https://themoonwoman.com/rites-of-passage-facilitator-training/.

[82] "How to submit a 'rites of passage' essay," *New York Times*, July 6, 2018. A search of the *New York Times* database from 1969 to 2013 turned up thirty-four *Times* articles with "rites of passage" in their titles.

[83] Thomassen, "Hidden Battle," 185–87. Thomassen has explored this history, quoting from Durkheim's two letters to Mauss regarding van Gennep's candidacy for a faculty position in Paris. Durkheim appears to have been upset at his nephew, suspecting him of having encouraged van Gennep to apply for the positions.

Works Cited

Alvarez, Julia. *Once upon a Quinceañera: Coming of Age in the USA*. New York: Penguin, 2007.

Bakhtin, Mikhail M. *Rabelais and His World*. Translated by Hélène Iswolsky. Cambridge, MA: MIT Press, 1968.

Baum, Robert M. "Wrestlers on the *Awasena* Path: Wrestling, Fertility, and Rites of Passage among the Diola of Southern Senegal." *Numen* 64, no. 4 (2017): 418–33.

Beames, Simon. "Overseas Youth Expeditions with Raleigh International: A Rite of Passage?" *Australian Journal of Outdoor Education* 8, no. 1 (2004): 29–36.

Beidelman, Thomas O. "Ghostly *rites de passage* in East Africa." *Man* 2, no. 3 (1967): 464–65.

Belier, W. W. "Arnold van Gennep and the Rise of French Sociology of Religion." *Numen* 41, no. 2 (1994): 141–62.

Belmont, Nicole. "Arnold van Gennep (1873–1957)." In Hainard and Kaehr, *Naître, vivre et mourir*, 17–31.

———. *Arnold van Gennep, le créateur de l'ethnographie française*. Paris: Payot, 1974. Translated by Derek Coltman as *Arnold Van Gennep: The Creator of French Ethnography* (Chicago: University of Chicago Press, 1979).

Blumenkrantz, David G., and Marc B. Goldstein. "Seeing College as a Rite of Passage: What Might Be Possible." *New Directions for Higher Education* 2014, no. 166 (2014): 85–94. https://doi.org/10.1002/he.20098.

Bourdieu, Pierre. "Les rites comme actes d'institution." *Actes de la Recherche en Sciences Sociales* 43 (1982): 58–63. Reprinted in *Langage et pouvoir symbolique* (Paris: Le Seuil, 2001), 175–86.

Brenner, Abigail. *Women's Rites of Passage: How to Embrace Change and Celebrate Life*. Lanham, MD: Aronson, 2007.

Bristol, Michael B. *Carnival and Theater: Plebeian Culture and the Structure of Authority in Renaissance England*. London: Methuen, 1985.

Brown, Gregory H., Lisa M. Brunelle, and Vikas Malhotra. "Tagging: Deviant Behavior or Adolescent Rites of Passage?" *Culture & Psychology* 23, no. 4 (2017): 487–501.

Burns, Allan F. "Obituary: Solon T. Kimball, 1908–1982." *Anthropology & Education Quarterly* 14, no. 2 (1983): 148–57.

Calame, Claude. "Le rite d'initiation tribale comme catégorie anthropologique (Van Gennep et Platon)." *Revue de l'histoire des religions* 220, no. 1 (2003): 5–62.

Cannadine, David, and Simon Price, eds. *Rituals of Royalty: Power and Ceremo-*

nial in Traditional Societies. Cambridge: Cambridge University Press, 1987.

Centlivres, Pierre. "Les rites de passage: nouveaux espaces, nouveaux emblèmes." In Hainard and Kaehr, *Naître, vivre et mourir*, 161–73.

——. "L'ethnologie à l'Université de Neuchâtel: 1912–1964." Accessed August 8, 2018, at https://www.unine.ch/files/live/sites/ethno/files/shared/documents/PC-ie-12-64.pdf.

DaMatta, Roberto. "Individuality and Liminarity: Some Considerations Concerning Rites of Passage and Modernity." *Vibrant* 14, no. 1 (2017), http://dx.doi.org/10.1590/1809-43412017v14n1p149.

Davis, Natalie Zemon. "The Reasons of Misrule: Youth Groups and Charivaris in Sixteenth-Century France." *Past & Present* 50, no. 1 (1971): 41–75.

Dodgson-Katiyo, Pauline, and Gina Wisker, eds. *Rites of Passage in Postcolonial Women's Writing*. Amsterdam: Rodopi, 2010.

Douglas, Mary. *Purity and Danger: An Analysis of Concepts of Pollution and Taboo*. London: Routledge, 1966.

Drewery, Claire. *Modernist Short Fiction by Women: The Liminal in Katherine Mansfield, Dorothy Richardson, May Sinclair, and Virginia Woolf*. Burlington, VT: Ashgate, 2011.

Dundes, Alan, ed. *International Folkloristics: Classic Contributions by the Founders of Folklore*. Lanham, MD: Rowman & Littlefield, 1999.

Durkheim, Émile. "La prohibition de l'inceste et ses origines. " *L'Année sociologique (1896–1897)* 1 (1897): 1–70.

——. *Les formes élémentaires de la vie religieuse: Le système totémique en Australie*. Paris: Alcan, 1912.

Durkheim, Émile, and Marcel Mauss. "De quelques formes primitives de classification." *L'Année sociologique (1901–1902)* 6 (1903): 1–72.

Evans-Pritchard, E. E. *Nuer Religion*. Oxford: Oxford University Press, 1956.

——. "Ritual Reintegration." *Times Literary Supplement*, April 15, 1960, 236.

——. *Theories of Primitive Religion*. Oxford: Clarendon Press, 1965.

——. *Witchcraft, Oracles and Magic among the Azande*. Oxford: Clarendon Press, 1937.

Fellous, Michèle. *À la recherche de nouveaux rites. Rites de passage et modernité avancée*. Paris: L'Harmattan, 2001.

Fortes, Meyer. "Ritual and Office in Tribal Society." In *Essays on the Ritual of Social Relations*, edited by Max Gluckman, 53–88. Manchester: Manchester University Press, 1962.

Fournier, Marcel. *Marcel Mauss: A Biography*. Princeton, NJ: Princeton University Press, 2006.

Frazer, James. *The Golden Bough*. Vol. 1. London: Macmillan, 1890.

Freud, Sigmund. *Totem and Taboo: Resemblances between the Psychic Lives of Savages and Neurotics*. Translated and introduced by A. A. Brill. New York: Moffat, Yard, 1918.

Fried, Martha, and Morton Fried. *Transitions: Four Rituals in Eight Cultures*. New York: Norton, 1980.

Garwood, Paul. "Rites of Passage." In *Oxford Handbook of the Archaeology of Ritual and Religion*, edited by Timothy Insoll, 261–84. New York: Oxford University Press, 2011.

Geertz, Clifford. Review of *The Rites of Passage*, by Arnold van Gennep. *Science* 131, no. 3416 (1960): 1801–2.

Gluckman, Max. "Les rites de passage." In *Essays on the Ritual of Social Relations*, edited by Max Gluckman, 1–52. Manchester: Manchester University Press, 1962.

Golding, William. *Rites of Passage*. New York: Farrar, Straus, Giroux, 1980.

Grimes, Ronald L. *Deeply into the Bone: Re-Inventing Rites of Passage*. Berkeley: University of California Press, 2000.

Guest, Matthew. Review of *Meeting Jesus at University: Rites of Passage and Student Evangelicals*, by Edward Dutton. *Journal of Contemporary Religion* 25, no. 2 (2010): 319–21.

Hainard, Jacques, and Roland Kaehr, eds. *Naître, vivre et mourir: actualité de van Gennep: essais sur les rites de passage*: exposition du 28 juin au 31 décembre 1981, Musée d'ethnographie, Neuchâtel, Suisse. Neuchâtel: Musée d'ethnographie, 1981.

Hertz, Robert. "Contribution à une étude sur la représentation collective de la mort." *L'Année sociologique (1905–1906)* 10 (1907): 48–137. Translated by Rodney and Claudia Needham as "A contribution to the study of the collective representation of death," in *Death and the Right Hand* (London: Cohen and West, 1960).

Hockey, Jenny. "The Importance of Being Intuitive: Arnold van Gennep's *The Rites of Passage*." *Mortality* 7, no. 2 (2002): 210–17.

Hodson, T. C. Review of *Les rites de passage*, by Arnold van Gennep. *Man* 11, nos. 16–17 (1911): 29–30.

Hoebel, E. Adamson. Review of *The Rites of Passage*, by Arnold van Gennep. *Southwestern Social Science Quarterly* 41, no. 3 (1960): 371.

Huntington, Richard, and Peter Metcalf. *Celebrations of Death: The Anthropology of Mortuary Ritual*. Cambridge: Cambridge University Press, 1979.

Janusz, Bernadetta, and Maciej Walkiewicz. "The Rites of Passage Framework as a Matrix of Transgression Processes in the Life Course." *Journal of Adult Development* 25, no. 3 (2018), https://doi.org/10.1007/s10804-018-9285-1.

Journal of the Royal African Society. Unsigned review of *Les rites de passage*, by Arnold van Gennep. Vol. 9, no. 33 (1909): 108–10.

Kapferer, Bruce. "Ritual Dynamics and Virtual Practice: Beyond Representation and Meaning." In *Ritual in Its Own Right*, edited by Don Handelman and Galina Lindquist, 35–54. New York: Berghahn Books, 2005.

Kertzer, David I. *Comrades and Christians: Religion and Political Struggle in Communist Italy*. Cambridge: Cambridge University Press, 1980.

———. *Ritual, Politics, and Power*. New Haven, CT: Yale University Press, 1988.

Kimball, Solon T. Introduction to *The Rites of Passage*, by Arnold van Gennep, translated by Monica B. Vizedom and Gabrielle L. Caffee, v–xix. Chicago: University of Chicago Press, 1960.

Lane, Christel. *The Rites of Rulers: Rituals in Industrial Society—The Soviet Case*. Cambridge: Cambridge University Press, 1981.

Lang, Andrew. Review of *Les rites de passage*, by Arnold van Gennep. *Anthropos* 4, no. 3 (1909): 824–26.

Leach, Edmund. Review of *The Rites of Passage*, by Arnold van Gennep. *Man* 60 (1960): 173–74.

———. "Ritual." In *International Encyclopedia of the Social Sciences*, edited by David Sills, 13:520–26. New York: Macmillan, 1968.

Lévi-Strauss, Claude. *Les structures élémentaires de la parenté*. Paris: Presses Universitaires de France, 1949.

———. *Totemism*. Translated by Rodney Needham. Boston: Beacon Press, 1963.

Lindahl, Carl. "Bakhtin's Carnival Laughter and the Cajun Country Mardi Gras." *Folklore* 107 (1996): 57–70.

Magida, Arthur J. *Opening the Doors of Wonder: Reflections on Religious Rites of Passage*. Berkeley: University of California Press, 2008.

Mauss, Marcel. "Essai sur le don." *L'Année sociologique (1923–1924)* 1 (1925): 145–279.

———. Review of *Rites de Passage*, by Arnold van Gennep. *L'Année sociologique (1906–1909)* 11 (1910): 200–202.

May, Dean L. "Presidential Address: Rites of Passage: The Gathering as Cultural Credo." *Journal of Mormon History* 29, no. 1 (2003):1–41.

McMullen, David. "Bureaucrats and Cosmology: The Ritual Code of T'ang China." In Cannadine and Price, *Rituals of Royalty*, 181–236.

Moore, Alexander. "Obituary Solon Kimball (1909–1982)." *American Anthropologist* 86, no. 2 (1984): 386–93.

Moore, Sally F., and Barbara G. Myerhoff, eds. *Secular Ritual*. Assen: Van Gorcum, 1977.

Murphy, Robert F., Jessica Scheer, Yolanda Murphy, and Richard Mack. "Physical Disability and Social Liminality: A Study in the Rituals of Adversity."

Social Science & Medicine 26, no. 2 (1988): 235–42.

Needham, Rodney. Introduction to *The Semi-Scholars*, by Arnold van Gennep, ix–xx. London: Routledge, 1967.

Padilla, Mark W. Introduction to *Rites of Passage in Ancient Greece: Literature, Religion, Society*, edited by Mark W. Padilla, 15–23. Lewisburg, PA: Bucknell University Press, 1999.

Pickering, Paul A. "The Chartist Rites of Passage: Commemorating Feargus O'Connor." In *Contested Sites: Commemoration, Memorial and Popular Politics in Nineteenth-Century Britain*, edited by Paul A. Pickering and Alex Tyrrell, 101–26. London: Routledge, 2004.

Pickering, W. F. S. *Emile Durkheim: Selected Writings on Education*. Vol. 1. London: Routledge, 2006.

Pike, Sarah M. "Radical Animal Rights and Environmental Activism as Rites of Passage." *Journal of Ritual Studies* 27, no. 1 (2013): 35–45.

Pitt-Rivers, Julian. "Un rite de passage de la société moderne: le voyage aérien." In *Les rites de passage aujourd'hui*, edited by Pierre Centlivres and Jacques Hainard, 115–30. Lausanne: Editions L'Âge d'Homme, 1986.

Pontefract, Dan. "Leadership in Liminal Times." *Harvard Business Review*, October 10, 2014, https://hbr.org/2014/10/leadership-in-liminal-times.

Price, Simon. "From Noble Funerals to Divine Cult: The Consecration of Roman Emperors." In Cannadine and Price, *Rituals of Royalty*, 56–105.

Remotti, Francesco. "Introduzione: Van Gennep, tra etnologia e folklore." In *I riti di passaggio*, by Arnold van Gennep, translated by Maria Luisa Remotti, vii–xxix. Turin: Bollati Boringhieri, 2012.

Sande, Allan. "Intoxication and Rite of Passage to Adulthood in Norway." *Contemporary Drug Problems* 29, no. 2 (2002): 277–303.

Santino, Jack. "The Carnivalesque and the Ritualesque." *Journal of American Folklore* 124, no. 491 (2011): 61–73.

Scribner, Bob. "Reformation, Carnival and the World Turned Upside-Down." *Social History* 3, no. 3 (1978): 303–29.

Senn, Harry A. "Arnold van Gennep: Structuralist and Apologist for the Study of Folklore in France." *Folklore* 85 (1974): 229–43.

Shields, Rob. "The 'System of Pleasure': Liminality and the Carnivalesque at Brighton." *Theory, Culture & Society* 7 (1990): 39–72.

Sibeud, Emmanuelle. "Un ethnographe face à la colonisation: Arnold van Gennep en Algérie (1911–1912)." *Revue d'Histoire des Sciences Humaines* 10 (2004): 73–103.

Söderlund, Jonas, and Elisabeth Borg. "Liminality in Management and Organization Studies." *International Journal of Management Reviews* 20, no. 4 (2017): 880–902, https://doi.org/10.1111/ijmr.12168.

Spencer, Robert F. Review of *The Rites of Passage*, by Arnold van Gennep. *American Anthropologist* 63, no. 3 (1961): 598–99.

Starr, Frederick. Review of *Les rites de passage*, by Arnold van Gennep. *American Journal of Sociology* 10, no. 5 (1910): 707–9.

Thomassen, Bjørn. "Émile Durkheim between Gabriel Tarde and Arnold van Gennep: Founding Moments of Sociology and Anthropology." *Social Anthropology* 20, no. 3 (2012): 231–49.

———. "The Hidden Battle that Shaped the History of Sociology: Arnold van Gennep contra Emile Durkheim." *Journal of Classical Sociology* 16, no. 2 (2016): 173–95.

———. "The Uses and Meanings of Liminality." *International Political Anthropology* 2, no. 1 (2009): 5–27.

Turner, Victor W. *Dramas, Fields, and Metaphors: Symbolic Action in Human Society*. Ithaca, NY: Cornell University Press, 1974.

———. *The Forest of Symbols: Aspects of Ndembu Ritual*. Ithaca, NY: Cornell University Press, 1967.

———. *The Ritual Process: Structure and Anti-Structure*. Chicago: Aldine, 1969.

———. "Variations on a Theme of Liminality." In *Secular Ritual*, edited by Sally F. Moore and Barbara G. Myerhoff, 36–52. Assen: Van Gorcum, 1977.

Turner, Victor, and Edith L. B. Turner. *Image and Pilgrimage in Christian Culture*. New York: Columbia University Press, 1978.

Van Gennep, Arnold. "De quelques rites de passage en Savoie." *Revue de l'histoire des religions* 62 (1910): 37–55, 183–215, 323–55.

———. "É. Durkheim: *Les Formes élémentaires de la vie religieuse*." *Mercure de France* 101 (1913): 374, 389–91. Translated by Matthew Carey in *HAU: Journal of Ethnographic Theory* 7, no. 1 (2017): 576–78.

———. *I riti di passaggio*. Translated by Maria Luisa Remotti, with an introduction by Francesco Remotti. Turin: Bollati Boringhieri, 2012.

———. *Les rites de passage*. Paris: Nourry, 1909.

———. *L'État actuel du problème totémique*. Paris: Leroux, 1920.

———. *Manuel de folklore français contemporain*. 9 vols. Paris: Picard, 1937–58.

———. *Mythes et légendes d'Australie*. Paris: Guilmoto, 1906.

———. *The Rites of Passage*. Translated by Monika B. Vizedom and Gabrielle L. Caffee, with an introduction by Solon T. Kimball. Chicago: University of Chicago Press, 1960.

———. *Tabou et totémisme à Madagascar*. Paris: Leroux, 1904.

Vizedom, Monika. *Rites and Relationships: Rites of Passage and Contemporary Anthropology*. New York: Sage, 1976.

Walsham, Alexandra. "Rough Music and Charivari: Letters between Natalie

Zemon Davis and Edward Thompson, 1970–1972." *Past & Present* 235, no. 1 (2017): 243–62.

Willett, Jeffrey, and Mary Jo Deegan. "Liminality and Disability: Rites of Passage and Community in Hypermodern Society." *Disability Studies Quarterly* 21, no. 3 (2001): 137–52.

Williamson, Marianne. *Illuminata: Thoughts, Prayers, Rites of Passage*. New York: Random House, 2013.

Winchester, Hilary P. M., Pauline M. McGuirk, and Kathryn Everett. "Schoolies Week as a Rite of Passage." In *Embodied Geographies: Spaces, Bodies and Rites of Passage*, edited by Elizabeth K. Teather, 59–76. London: Routledge, 2005.

Zerilli, F. M. "Etnografia e etnologia al congresso di Arnold van Gennep (Neuchâtel, 1–5 giugno 1914)." *La Ricerca Folklorica* 37 (1998):143–52.

Zhang, Juwen. "Recovering Meanings Lost in Interpretations of *Les Rites de Passage*." *Western Folklore* 71, no. 2 (2012): 119–47.

Zumwalt, Rosemary L. *The Enigma of Arnold van Gennep (1873–1957): Master of French Folklore and Hermit of Bourg-la-Reine*. Helsinki: Suomalainen Tiedeakatemia, 1988.

AUTHOR'S FOREWORD

Detailed descriptions and monographs concerning magico-religious acts have accumulated in sufficient number in the last few years that it is now possible to attempt a classification of these acts, or rites, that would be consistent with the progress of science. Several types of rites are already well known, and it seemed to me that a large number of other rites could also be classed in a special category. As I propose to show, these rites may be found in many ceremonies. Until the present time, however, neither their close relationship nor its cause has been perceived, and the reason for resemblances among them has not been understood. And, above all, no one has shown why such rites are performed in a specific order.

In dealing with so vast a subject, it was difficult to keep from being submerged by the materials. In this book I have presented only a small fraction of the data I have collected, using selections from the most recent detailed monographs whenever I could, and I have referred the reader as often as possible to the great comparative collections for further facts and bibliographic references. Had I not done this, each chapter would have required a volume. I believe, however, that my demonstration is adequate, and I invite the reader to check it by applying the conceptual scheme of *The Rites of Passage* to data in his own realm of study.

A portion of the contents of this book was communicated, almost in the form of a table, by Messrs. Sidney Hartland, J. G. Frazer, and P. Alphandery to the Congress on the History of Religions held at Oxford last September.

I owe thanks also to my publisher and friend, Mr. E. Nourry, who under a pseudonym is well known among folklorists. He has taken an interest in the growth of this volume, has made documents available to me, and has given me the liberty to look at them at my leisure. Thus the publisher has been a victim of the scholar and friend within him. I hope that, at least, he will not be a victim of the reader.

A. v. G.

CLAMART
December, 1908

I THE CLASSIFICATION OF RITES

Each larger society contains within it several distinctly separate social groupings. As we move from higher to lower levels of civilization, the differences among these groups become accentuated and their autonomy increases. In contrast, the only clearly marked social division remaining in modern[1] society is that which distinguishes between the secular and the religious worlds—between the profane and the sacred. Since the time of the Renaissance the relations between these two realms have undergone all kinds of changes within nations and states. But it is a significant fact that, because of fundamental differences between them, secular and religious groups as a whole have remained separate throughout the countries of Europe. The nobility, the world of finance, the working classes, retain their identities without regard—in theory at least—for national boundaries.

In addition, all these groups break down into still smaller societies or subgroups. We find distinctions between the higher nobility and the landed gentry, between high finance and small moneylending, as well as among the various professions and trades. For a man to pass from group to group —for example, for a peasant to become an urban worker, or even for a mason's helper to rise to mason—he must fulfil certain conditions, all of which have one thing in common: their basis is purely economic or intellectual. On the other hand, for a layman to enter the priesthood or for a priest to be unfrocked calls for ceremonies, acts of a special kind, derived from a particular feeling and a particular frame of mind. So great is the incompatibility between the profane and the sacred worlds that a man cannot pass from one to the other without going through an intermediate stage.

[1] To van Gennep, as to many writers of his time and ours, the term "modern" implies essentially the pattern of industrial society found in western Europe and the United States. All further notes by the translator appear in brackets; the author's original notes are without brackets.

1

As we move downward on the scale of civilizations (taking the term "civilization" in the broadest sense), we cannot fail to note an ever-increasing domination of the secular by the sacred. We see that in the least advanced cultures the holy enters nearly every phase of a man's life. Being born, giving birth, and hunting, to cite but a few examples, are all acts whose major aspects fall within the sacred sphere. Social groups in such societies likewise have magico-religious foundations, and a passage from group to group takes on that special quality found in our rites of baptism and ordination.

At the simplest level of development, too, there are social groups that reach across boundaries. For example, a totem clan is recognized as a single intertribal unit among all the tribes of Australia, and its members look upon one another as brothers for the same reason as do Roman Catholic priests, no matter what country they live in. Bonds of caste, on the other hand, present a more complicated problem, for here differences based on occupational specialization are added to those founded on kinship. While modern societies reduce to a theoretical minimum the distinction between male and female, it plays a role of considerable importance among semicivilized peoples, who rigidly segregate the sexes in the economic, the political, and, above all, the magico-religious sphere. The family, whether conceived on a broader or narrower basis than in our own culture, is likewise sharply defined among semicivilized peoples. Furthermore, while a tribe may or may not form part of a larger political unit, it is in all cases endowed with an individuality comparable in rigidity to the narrow parochialism of the ancient Greek city-states. To all the above-mentioned group distinctions, the semicivilized add still another—one for which our society has no real counterpart—a division into generation or age groups.[1]

The life of an individual in any society is a series of pas-

---

[1] [Writing in Europe in 1908, van Gennep did not know the awareness of age distinctions characteristic of modern American society.]

sages from one age to another and from one occupation to another. Wherever there are fine distinctions among age or occupational groups, progression from one group to the next is accompanied by special acts, like those which make up apprenticeship in our trades. Among semicivilized peoples such acts are enveloped in ceremonies, since to the semi-civilized mind no act is entirely free of the sacred. In such societies every change in a person's life involves actions and reactions between sacred and profane—actions and reactions to be regulated and guarded so that society as a whole will suffer no discomfort or injury. Transitions from group to group and from one social situation to the next are looked on as implicit in the very fact of existence, so that a man's life comes to be made up of a succession of stages with similar ends and beginnings: birth, social puberty,[1] marriage, fatherhood, advancement to a higher class, occupational specialization, and death. For every one of these events there are ceremonies whose essential purpose is to enable the individual to pass from one defined position to another which is equally well defined. Since the goal is the same, it follows of necessity that the ways of attaining it should be at least analogous, if not identical in detail (since in any case the individual involved has been modified by passing through several stages and traversing several boundaries).

Thus we encounter a wide degree of general similarity among ceremonies of birth, childhood, social puberty, betrothal, marriage, pregnancy, fatherhood, initiation into religious societies, and funerals. In this respect, man's life resembles nature, from which neither the individual nor the society stands independent. The universe itself is governed by a periodicity which has repercussions on human life, with stages and transitions, movements forward, and periods of relative inactivity. We should therefore include among ceremonies of human passage those rites occasioned by

[1] [Van Gennep distinguishes between social and physiological puberty (see chap. vi).]

3

celestial changes, such as the changeover from month to month (ceremonies of the full moon), from season to season (festivals related to solstices and equinoxes), and from year to year (New Year's Day). All these rites should, it seems to me, be grouped together, though all the details of the proposed scheme cannot be worked out as yet. The study of ritual has made great progress in recent years, but we are still far from knowing either the function or the manner of operation of every single rite, and we lack the knowledge necessary to construct a definitive classification of rites. The first step toward the development of such a classification was a separation of rites into two kinds, sympathetic[1] and contagious.

Sympathetic rites—those based on belief in the reciprocal action of like on like, of opposite on opposite, of the container and the contained, of the part and the whole, of image and real object or real being, or word and deed—were first considered as such by Tylor.[2] Later many of their varieties were studied in Great Britain by Lang,[3] Clodd,[4] Hartland,[5] and several others; in France this work was done

---

[1] I have purposely retained the term "sympathetic," although Frazer, Hubert, Haddon, and others have accepted a division of sympathetic magic into contagious magic and homeopathic magic. They are therefore obliged to create a special place for dynamistic magic, and to homeopathic they will have to add alleopathic or enantheropathic, etc. (See my report on Frazer's *Lectures on the Early History of the Kingship*, in *Revue de l'histoire des religions*, LIII [1906], 396–401.) The classification made by Henri Hubert and Marcel Mauss, in "Esquisse d'une théorie générale de la magie," *Année sociologique*, VI (1902–3), 62 ff., 66 ff., is likewise too artificial: "abstract and impersonal images based on similarity, contiguity, and opposition" become "three aspects of the same idea"—which is that of the sacred and also that of mana, which in turn is "the genus of which the sacred is a species."

[2] Edward Burnett Tylor, *Primitive Culture: Researches into the Development of Mythology, Philosophy, Religion, Art, and Custom* (2 vols.; 1st ed.; London, 1871. French translation of the 2nd ed.; 1876. 4th ed.; London, 1903).

[3] Andrew Lang, *Myth, Ritual, and Religion* (1st ed.; 2 vols.; London: Longmans, Green, 1891. French translation, 1 vol.; Paris, 1898); *The Making of Religion* (1st ed.; London: Longmans, Green, 1899. 2d ed.; 1900); *Magic and Religion* (London: Longmans, Green, 1901).

[4] Edward Clodd, *Tom, Tit, Tot: An Essay on Savage Philosophy in Folk-tale* (London: Duckworth, 1898).

[5] Edwin Sidney Hartland, *The Science of Fairy Tales* (London: W. Scott, 1891); *The Legend of Perseus* (Grimm Library Nos. 2, 3, 5; 3 vols.; London: D. Nutt, 1894–96), certain chapters.

4

by Réville,[1] Marillier,[2] and several others; in Germany, by Liebrecht,[3] Andree,[4] Koch,[5] Schultze,[6] and others; in the Netherlands, by Tiele,[7] Wilken,[8] Kruijt,[9] and others; in Belgium by Monseur[10] and De Cock; while in the United States they have been investigated by Brinton[11] and several others. Oddly enough, however, none of the researchers who adhered to the animistic school developed a rigorous classification of the beliefs and rites they outlined. Their writings are collections of parallels taken out of context and divorced from ritual sequences rather than attempts at systematization. Here their thinking undoubtedly shows the influence of Adolf Bastian. In his youth, Bastian had discovered the concept of *Völkergedanken* ("folk ideas"), and he adhered rigidly to this notion to the end of his long career. Bastian's influence lies at the very foundation of Tylor's *Primitive Culture*, which for about thirty years after its publication in 1871 provided the framework for all kinds of complementary research, particularly in Russia.[12]

[1] Albert Réville, *Prolégomènes de l'histoire des religions* (Paris: G. Fischbacher, 1881); *Histoire des religions*, Part I: "Les religions des peuples non-civilisés" (2 vols.; Paris: G. Fischbacher, 1883). On the same point of view see Michel Revon, *Le shinntoïsme* (Paris: E. Leroux, 1904– ; also published as a series of articles in *Revue de l'histoire des religions*, vols. XLIX–LII [1904–5]).

[2] Léon Marillier, *La survivance de l'âme et l'idée de justice chez les peuples non-civilisés* (Paris: Imprimerie nationale, 1894); numerous analyses in the *Revue de l'histoire des religions*, up to 1906.

[3] Felix Liebrecht, *Zur Volkskunde: Alte und neue Aufsätze* (Heilbronn: Henninger, 1879).

[4] Richard Andree, *Ethnographische Parallelen und Vergleiche* (Leipzig: Veit & Co., 1878–89).

[5] Theodor Koch, *Zum Animismus der sudamerikanischen Indianer* (International Archives of Ethnography, Suppl. 13 [Leiden: Brill, 1900]).

[6] Fritz Schultze, *Der Fetischismus* (Leipzig, 1871); *Psychologie der Naturvölker* (Leipzig: Veit & Co., 1900).

[7] C. P. Tiele, *Manuel de l'histoire des religions*, French translation from the Dutch by Maurice Vernes (Amiens: Rousseau-Leroy; 2d ed.; Paris: E. Leroux, 1885).

[8] A. Wilken, "Het Animisme bij den Volken van den Indischen Archipel," *Indische Gids* (Amsterdam), Vols. VI, VII (1884–85).

[9] Albertus Christian Kruijt, *Het Animisme in den Indischen Archipel* (The Hague: M. Nijhoff, 1906).

[10] Eugène Monseur, "L'âme pupilline," *Revue de l'histoire des religions*, Vol. XLI (1905), No. 1, and "L'âme poucet," *ibid.*, No. 3.

[11] Daniel G. Brinton, *Religions of Primitive Peoples* (New York: G. P. Putnam's Sons, 1897).

[12] [For the historical context of van Gennep's work and the writings he cites, see the Introduction.]

On the other hand, Mannhardt's work[1] led to a new orientation, although it remained unknown until Frazer[2] demonstrated its fruitfulness. Together Mannhardt and Frazer created a school, to which Smith[3] contributed a new line of approach—study of the holy, the sacred, the pure, and the impure. Among those who were to subscribe to this tradition were Hartland,[4] Crawley,[5] Cook,[6] Harrison,[7] and Jevons[8] in England; Dieterich[9] and Preuss[10] in Germany; Reinach,[11] Hubert, and Mauss[12] in France; and Hoffmann-Krayer[13] in Switzerland. Actually, the Bastian-Tylor school and that of Mannhardt, Frazer, Smith, and their successors were very closely related.

Contemporaneously, still another school was coming into

[1] Wilhelm Mannhardt, *Antike Wald und Feldkulte* (2d ed.; Berlin, 1904); "Mythologische Forschungen aus dem Nachlasse," *Quellen und Forschungen*, Vol. LI (1887).

[2] James George Frazer, *The Golden Bough* (1st ed.; 2 vols.; London: Macmillan, 1890. 2d ed.; 3 vols.; 1900). Of the third twelve-volume edition, published beginning in 1906, the following were available at the time of writing: *Lectures on the Early History of the Kingship* (London: Macmillan, 1905); *Adonis, Attis, Osiris: Studies in the History of Oriental Religion* (London: Macmillan, 1906. 2d ed.; 1907).

[3] W. Robertson Smith, *Lectures on the Religion of the Semites* (London: A. & C. Black, 1889. New ed.; 1907); German translation by Stübe, *Die Religion der Semiten* (Freiburg im Breisgau, 1899). [While Van Gennep made use of the German translation of this work, the translator has drawn directly on the original (3rd ed.; New York: Macmillan, 1917).]

[4] Hartland, *The Legend of Perseus*, certain chapters, and numerous analyses in *Folk-lore* (London).

[5] Alfred E. Crawley, *The Mystic Rose: A Study of Primitive Marriage* (London: Macmillan, 1902).

[6] A. B. Cook, "The European Sky-God" (a series of articles), *Folk-lore*, Vol. XV, Nos. 3, 4; Vol. XVI, No. 3; Vol. XVII, Nos. 1–4; Vol. XVIII, No. 1 (1905–7); and articles in the *Classical Review*.

[7] Jane E. Harrison, *Prolegomena to the Study of Greek Religion* (Cambridge: Cambridge University Press, 1903).

[8] Frank Byron Jevons, *An Introduction to the History of Religion* (London: Methuen, 1896).

[9] Albrecht Dieterich, *Eine Mithrasliturgie* (Leipzig: Teubner, 1903); *Mutter Erde* (Leipzig: Teubner, 1905); and other works.

[10] Konrad Theodor Preuss, "Phallische Fruchtbarkeitsdämonen als Träger des altmexikanischen Dramas: Ein Beitrag zur Urgeschichte des mimischen Weltdramas," *Archiv für Anthropologie*, XXIX (1903), 129–88.

[11] Salomon Reinach, *Cultes, mythes, et religions* (a collection of articles published after 1892; 3 vols.; Paris: Leroux, 1905–8).

[12] Henri Hubert and Marcel Mauss, "Essai sur la nature et la fonction du sacrifice," *Année sociologique*, II (1897–98), 29–138.

[13] Eduard Hoffmann-Krayer, "Die Fruchtbarkeitsriten im schweizerischen Volksbrauch," *Schweizerisches Archiv für Volkskunde* (Basel), Vol. XI (1907).

being—the dynamistic school. Marett[1] in England and Hewitt[2] in America had taken a stand in sharp opposition to the animistic theory. Both pointed out the weakness in the concept of animism previously glimpsed by Tiele[3] (namely, polyzoism or polyzoölatry)[4] and put forward the dynamistic theory. This theory was further elaborated by Preuss[5] in Germany; by Farnell,[6] Haddon,[7] and Hartland[8] in England; and by Hubert, Mauss,[9] and van Gennep[10] in France (among others); and today it continues to draw adherents.

This double stream of theory enables us to assert that in addition to sympathetic rites, and ritual with an animistic basis, there exist groups of dynamistic rites (i.e., rites based on a concept of a power, such as mana, that is not personalized) as well as contagious rites. The rites in this last group are characteristically based on a belief that natural or acquired characteristics are material and transmissible (either through physical contact or over a distance). We should note that sympathetic rites are not necessarily animistic, nor contagious rites necessarily dynamistic. The

[1] Robert R. Marett, "Preanimistic Religion," *Folk-lore*, XI (1900), 162–82; "From Spell to Prayer," *ibid.*, XV (1904), No. 2, 132–65.

[2] J. N. B. Hewitt, "Orenda and a Definition of Religion," *American Anthropologist*, N.S. IV (1902), 33–46.

[3] C. P. Tiele, "Religions," *Encyclopaedia Britannica* (9th ed.), and other works.

[4] [The *Oxford English Dictionary* defines polyzoism as "the property in a complex organism, of being composed of minor and quasi-independent organisms (like Polyzoa)."]

[5] Konrad Theodor Preuss, "Der Ursprung der Religion und Kunst," *Globus*, Vols. LXXXVI (1904), LXXXVII (1905).

[6] Lewis R. Farnell, *The Evolution of Religion: An Anthropological Study* (London: Williams & Norgate, 1905).

[7] Alfred C. Haddon, *Magic and Fetishism: Religions, Ancient and Modern* (London: A. Constable, 1906).

[8] Edwin Sidney Hartland, Address as President of Section H (Anthropology) of the British Association for the Advancement of Science, Seventy-sixth Meeting, York, 1906. Published in *Reports of Meetings* (London: John Murray, 1907), LXXVI, 675–88.

[9] Hubert and Mauss, "Esquisse d'une théorie générale de la magie."

[10] Arnold van Gennep, *Tabou et totémisme à Madagascar: Étude descriptive et théorique* (Paris: E. Leroux, 1904); *Mythes et légendes d'Australie* (Paris: Guilmoto, 1906); "Animisme en dynamisme," *De Beweging* (Amsterdam), 1907, No. 2, pp. 394–96.

four classes are independent, although they have been grouped in pairs by the two schools studying magico-religious phenomena from different points of view.

Secondly, we can distinguish between rites which act directly and those which act indirectly. A direct rite, for example a curse or a spell, is designed to produce results immediately, without intervention by any outside agent. On the other hand, an indirect rite—be it vow, prayer, or religious service—is a kind of initial blow which sets into motion some autonomous or personified power, such as a demon, a group of jinn, or a deity, who intervenes on behalf of the performer of the rite. The effect of a direct rite is automatic; that of an indirect rite comes as a repercussion. An indirect rite is not necessarily animistic. To cite one example, when a central Australian aborigine rubs an arrow against a certain stone, he charges it with a magic power called *arungquiltha*. Later, he will shoot this arrow in the direction of an enemy, and as the arrow falls the *arungquiltha* will follow its course and strike down the enemy.[1] The power is thus transmitted with the help of a carrier, and the rite is accordingly dynamistic, contagious, and indirect.

Finally, we may also draw a distinction between positive rites (or volitions translated into action) and negative rites. The latter, now known as taboos, are prohibitions, commands "not to do" or "not to act." Psychologically, they correspond to negative volitions, just as positive rites are the equivalents of positive volitions. In other words, taboos also translate a kind of will and are acts rather than negations of acts. But just as life is not made up of perennial inaction, so by itself a taboo does not make up a ceremony, let alone a magic spell.[2] In this sense a taboo is not autono-

---

[1] See my *Mythes et légendes d'Australie*, p. lxxxvi.

[2] Regarding taboo as a negative rite, see van Gennep, *Tabou et totémisme à Madagascar*, pp. 26–27, 298, 319; Hubert and Mauss, "Esquisse d'une théorie générale de la magie", p. 129. On taboo as negative magic, see Frazer, *Lectures on the Early History of Kingship*, pp. 52, 54, 56, 59; my review of that book in *Revue de l'histoire des religions*, LIII (1906), 396–401; and Robert R. Marett, "Is Taboo a Negative Magic?" in *Anthropological Essays Presented to E. B. Tylor* (Oxford: Clarendon Press, 1907), pp. 219–34. Because it is easier to enumerate the things that

mous, it exists only as a counterpart to a positive rite. In other words, every negative rite if considered in isolation has its own individuality. But taboos in general can be understood only in relation to the active rites with which they coexist in a ceremony. Jevons, Crawley, Reinach, and several others erred in not having perceived this relationship of mutual dependence.

According to the criteria outlined in these pages, a single rite may fall simultaneously into four categories. When their four opposites are eliminated, there remain sixteen possible ways of classifying any given rite according to the table below:

Animistic rites

Sympathetic rites	Contagious rites
Positive rites	Negative rites
Direct rites	Indirect rites

Dynamistic rites

For instance, a pregnant woman abstaining from eating mulberries for fear that her child would be disfigured is performing a rite which is at the same time dynamistic, contagious, direct, and negative. A sailor who has been in danger of perishing in a shipwreck and as a consequence of a vow offers a small boat to Our Lady of Vigilance (Mary, Star of the Sea) is performing an animistic, sympathetic, indirect, and positive rite. Perhaps additional classes of rites will be discovered, but those listed here already include a considerable number. The difficulty lies only in determining precisely the proper interpretation for each case. Often a single rite may be interpreted in several ways, or a single interpretation may fit several rites whose forms differ greatly. Above all, it is difficult to determine whether a rite is essentially animistic or dynamistic—whether, for example, a certain ceremony designed to transfer an illness has as its object transferring the illness as a quality, or exorcising a

---

one should not do than those which one must or may do, the theorists have found among all peoples extensive series of taboos, prohibitions, etc., and have overrated their importance.

demon or spirit who personified the illness. To cite one concrete example, the rite of passage through or across something (which will be discussed later in greater detail) is open to several interpretations—one animistic and indirect, the other dynamistic and direct. In the attempt to formulate an acceptable systematization of rites, general treatises prove of little help: their authors as a rule include only those elements of a ceremony which serve their purposes. Moreover, their classifications are usually based on external similarities rather than on the dynamics of the rite, and this is particularly true in the work of folklorists.

Most ceremonies of a given kind fall into the same category. Accordingly, most pregnancy rites are dynamistic, contagious, direct, and negative, while most childbirth rites are animistic, sympathetic, indirect, and positive. But it is always just a matter of proportion; an animistic, positive ritual will include a counterpart of dynamistic, and positive or animistic, contagious, and indirect rites. Limitations of space prevent me from indicating in each instance the proper category for every particular rite, but at least I should state that I have not interpreted the many rites analyzed here unilaterally.

Once a classification of ritual dynamics has been established, it becomes relatively easy to understand the basis of characteristic patterns in the order of ceremonies. Yet theoreticians have rarely attempted a classification of these ceremonial patterns. There are excellent works on one or another of their aspects, but only a few carry through a complete set of ceremonies in order from beginning to end, and still fewer are the studies of ceremonial patterns in relation to one another (cf. chap. x).

The present volume is intended to be such a study. I have tried to assemble here all the ceremonial patterns which accompany a passage from one situation to another or from one cosmic or social world to another. Because of the importance of these transitions, I think it legitimate to single out *rites of passage* as a special category, which under further analysis may be subdivided into *rites of separation*, *transition rites*, and *rites of incorporation*. These three sub-categories are not developed to the same extent by all peoples or in every ceremonial pattern. Rites of separation are prominent in funeral ceremonies, rites of incorporation at marriages. Transition rites may play an important part, for instance, in pregnancy, betrothal, and initiation; or they may be reduced to a minimum in adoption, in the delivery of a second child, in remarriage, or in the passage from the second to the third age group. Thus, although a complete scheme of rites of passage theoretically includes preliminal rites (rites of separation), liminal rites (rites of transition), and postliminal rites (rites of incorporation), in specific instances these three types are not always equally important or equally elaborated.

Furthermore, in certain ceremonial patterns where the transitional period is sufficiently elaborated to constitute an independent state, the arrangement is reduplicated. A betrothal forms a liminal period between adolescence and marriage, but the passage from adolescence to betrothal itself involves a special series of rites of separation, a transition, and an incorporation into the betrothed condition; and the passage from the transitional period, which is betrothal, to marriage itself, is made through a series of rites of separation from the former, followed by rites consisting of transition, and rites of incorporation into marriage. The pattern of ceremonies comprising rites of pregnancy, delivery, and birth is equally involved. I am trying to group all these rites as clearly as possible, but since I am dealing with activities I do not expect to achieve as rigid a classification as the botanists have, for example.

It is by no means my contention that all rites of birth, initiation, marriage, and the like, are only rites of passage. For, in addition to their over-all goal—to insure a change of condition or a passage from one magico-religious or secular group to another—all these ceremonies have their individual purposes. Marriage ceremonies include fertility rites;

11

birth ceremonies include protection and divination rites; funerals, defensive rites; initiations, propitiatory rites; ordinations, rites of attachment to the deity. All these rites, which have specific effective aims, occur in juxtaposition and combination with rites of passage—and are sometimes so intimately intertwined with them that it is impossible to distinguish whether a particular ritual is, for example, one of protection or of separation. This problem arises in relation to various forms of so-called purification ceremonies, which may simply lift a taboo and therefore remove the contaminating quality, or which may be clearly active rites, imparting the quality of purity.

In connection with this problem, I should like to consider briefly the pivoting of the sacred.[1] Characteristically, the presence of the sacred (and the performance of appropriate rites) is variable. Sacredness as an attribute is not absolute; it is brought into play by the nature of particular situations. A man at home, in his tribe, lives in the secular realm; he moves into the realm of the sacred when he goes on a journey and finds himself a foreigner near a camp of strangers. A Brahman belongs to the sacred world by birth; but within that world there is a hierarchy of Brahman families some of whom are sacred in relation to others. Every woman, though congenitally impure, is sacred to all adult men; if she is pregnant, she also becomes sacred to all other women of the tribe except her close relatives; and these other women constitute in relation to her a profane world, which at that moment includes all children and adult men. Upon performing so-called purification rites, a woman who has just given birth re-enters society, but she takes her place only in appropriate segments of it—such as her sex and her family—and she remains sacred in relation to the initiated

---

[1] This pivoting was already well understood by Smith (see *The Religion of the Semites*, pp. 427–28 and discussion of "taboo", pp. 152–53, 451–54, etc.). Compare the passage from sacred to profane, and vice versa, among the Tarahumare and the Huichol of Mexico as described by Karl Sofus Lumholtz, *Unknown Mexico: A Record of Five Years' Exploration among the Tribes of Western Sierra Madre* (London: C. Scribner's Sons, 1903), *passim*.

men and to the magico-religious ceremonies. Thus the "magic circles" pivot, shifting as a person moves from one place in society to another. The categories and concepts which embody them operate in such a way that whoever passes through the various positions of a lifetime one day sees the sacred where before he has seen the profane, or vice versa. Such changes of condition do not occur without disturbing the life of society and the individual, and it is the function of rites of passage to reduce their harmful effects. That such changes are regarded as real and important is demonstrated by the recurrence of rites, in important ceremonies among widely differing peoples, enacting death in one condition and resurrection in another. These rites, discussed in chapter ix, are rites of passage in their most dramatic form.

It remains for me briefly to define the meaning of the terms used in this work. *Dynamism* designates the impersonal theory of mana; *animism*, the personalistic theory, whether the power personified be a single or a multiple being, animal or plant (e.g., a totem), anthropomorphic or amorphous (e.g., God). These theories constitute *religion*, whose techniques (ceremonies, rites, services) I call *magic*. Since the practice and the theory are inseparable—the theory without the practice becoming metaphysics, and the practice on the basis of a different theory becoming science —the term I will at all times use is the adjective *magico-religious*.

The result is the diagram overleaf.

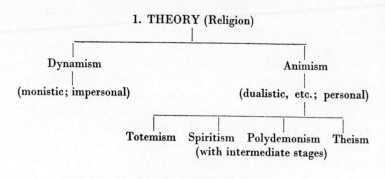

1. THEORY (Religion)

Dynamism

(monistic; impersonal)

Animism

(dualistic, etc.; personal)

Totemism   Spiritism   Polydemonism   Theism
(with intermediate stages)

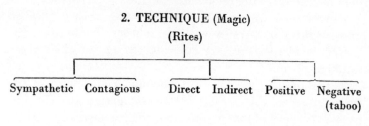

2. TECHNIQUE (Magic)

(Rites)

Sympathetic   Contagious   Direct   Indirect   Positive   Negative
(taboo)

14

II THE TERRITORIAL PASSAGE

Territorial passages can provide a framework for the discussion of rites of passage which follows. Except in the few countries where a passport is still in use, a person in these days may pass freely from one civilized region to another.[1] The frontier, an imaginary line connecting milestones or stakes, is visible—in an exaggerated fashion—only on maps. But not so long ago the passage from one country to another, from one province to another within each country, and, still earlier, even from one manorial domain to another was accompanied by various formalities. These were largely political, legal, and economic, but some were of a magico-religious nature. For instance, Christians, Moslems, and Buddhists were forbidden to enter and stay in portions of the globe which did not adhere to their respective faiths.

It is this magico-religious aspect of crossing frontiers that interests us. To see it operating fully, we must seek out types of civilization in which the magico-religious encompassed what today is within the secular domain.

The territory occupied by a semicivilized tribe is usually defined only by natural features, but its inhabitants and their neighbors know quite well within what territorial limits their rights and prerogatives extend. The natural boundary might be a sacred rock, tree, river, or lake which cannot be crossed or passed without the risk of supernatural sanctions. Such natural boundaries are relatively rare, however. More often the boundary is marked by an object—a stake, portal, or upright rock (milestone or landmark)—whose installation at that particular spot has been accompanied by rites of consecration. Enforcement of the interdiction may be immediate, or it may be mediated by frontier

[1] [It should be remembered that van Gennep wrote in the first decade of the century.]

15

divinities (such as Hermes, Priapus,[1] or the deities represented on the Babylonian *kudurru*). When milestones or boundary signs (e.g., a plow, an animal hide cut in thongs, a ditch) are ceremonially placed by a defined group on a delimited piece of earth, the group takes possession of it in such a way that a stranger who sets foot on it commits a sacrilege analogous to a profane person's entrance into a sacred forest or temple.

The idea of the sanctity of a territory so delimited has sometimes been confused with the belief in the sanctity of the entire earth as the Earth Mother.[2] In China, according to the most ancient documents, the deity was not the earth as such, but each plot of ground was sacred for its inhabitants and owners.[3] It seems to me that the case of Loango,[4] the territory of Greek cities, and that of Rome[5] are all analogous.

The prohibition against entering a given territory is therefore intrinsically magico-religious. It has been expressed with the help of milestones, walls, and statues in the

[1] Here is my interpretation (as yet to be fully demonstrated) of the almost universal association between landmarks and the phallus: (1) There is an association of the stake or the upright rock with the penis in erection; (2) the idea of union associated with the sexual act has a certain magical significance; (3) pointed objects (horns, fingers, etc.) are believed to protect through their power to "pierce" the evil influences, the wicked jinn, etc.; (4) *very seldom* is there the idea of the fecundity of the territory and its inhabitants. The phallic symbolism of landmarks has almost no truly sexual significance.

[2] Several interpretations by Dieterich (in *Mutter Erde*), which I believe to be incorrect, will be discussed with reference to birth and childhood.

[3] "In the ancient Chinese religion there was a god of the soil for each district (no doubt for twenty-five families); the king had a god of the soil for his people and one for his own personal use; the same was true for each feudal lord, each group of families, each imperial dynasty. These gods presided over war, which was created as a punishment; they were fashioned from a piece of wood and associated with gods of the harvest. It seems to me that the earth goddess came later as a result of several syncretisms" (Eduard Chavannes, "Le dieu du sol dans l'ancienne religion chinoise," *Revue de l'histoire des religions*, XLIII [1901], 124–27, 140–44).

[4] Cf. E. Dennett, *At the Back of the Black Man's Mind: Or Notes on the Kingly Office in West Africa* (London: Macmillan, 1906), and Eduard Pechüel-Loesche, *Volkskunde von Loango* (Stuttgart: Strecher & Schroeder, 1907).

[5] Cf. W. Warde Fowler's interesting discussion titled "Lustratio" in *Anthropology and the Classics*, ed. Robert R. Marett (Oxford, 1908), pp. 173–78. My readers will, I hope, accept the view that *lustratio* is nothing more than a rite of territorial separation, cosmic or human (e.g., return from war).

classical world, and through more simple means among the semicivilized. Naturally, these signs are not placed along the entire boundary line. Like our boundary posts, they are set only at points of passage, on paths and at crossroads. A bundle of herbs, a piece of wood, or a stake adorned with a sheaf of straw may be placed in the middle of the path or across it.[1] The erection of a portal,[2] sometimes together with natural objects or crudely made statues,[3] is a more complicated means of indicating the boundary. The details of these various procedures need not concern us here.[4]

Today, in our part of the world, one country touches another; but the situation was quite different in the times when Christian lands comprised only a part of Europe. Each country was surrounded by a strip of neutral ground which in practice was divided into sections or marches.

[1] To the references given by H. Grierson in *The Silent Trade* (Edinburgh, 1903), pp. 12–14, n. 4 (where, unfortunately, the rites of appropriation and the taboos of passage have been confused), add: Dennett, *At the Back of the Black Man's Mind*, pp. 90, 153, n. 192; Pechüel-Loesche, *Volkskunde von Loango*, pp. 223–24, 456, 472, etc.; J. Büttikofer, *Reisebilder aus Liberia* (Leiden, 1890), II, 304; van Gennep, *Tabou et totémisme à Madagascar*, pp. 183–86 (taboos of passage); J. M. M. Van der Burght, *Dictionnaire français Kirundi: Avec l'indication succincte de la signification swahili et allemande augmente d'une introduction et de 196 articles ethnologiques sur les Urundi et les Warundi* (Bar-le-Duc: Société d'Illustration Catholique, 1904), *s.v.* "Iviheko," etc. The custom of planting a stake surmounted with a sheaf of straw to prohibit the entrance into a path or field is very widespread in Europe.

[2] Paul B. du Chaillu (in *L'Afrique sauvage: Nouvelles excursions au pays des Ashongos* [Paris: Michel Levy Freres, 1868], p. 38, from the English; *Journey to Ashango Land* [New York, D. Appleton Co, 1867]), mentions a portal with sacred plants, chimpanzee skulls, etc. (in the Congo). Portals formed by two stakes driven into the ground with a pole running between them, on which hang skulls, eggs, etc., are often found on the Ivory Coast as taboos of passage and protection against the spirits (oral report by Maurice Delafosse); Pechüel-Loesche, *Volkskunde von Loango*, figures on p. 224, 472, etc.

[3] See among others for Surinam, K. Martin, "Bericht uber eine Reise ins Gebiet des oberen Surinam," *Bijdragen tot de Taal-Land en Volkekunde von Nederlands Indie* (The Hague), XXXV (1886), 28–29. Figure 2 shows a statue with two faces which I compared to *Janus bifrons* in an article of the same title in *Revue des traditions populaires*, XXII (1907), No. 4, 97–98. It confirms Frazer's theory in *Lectures on the Early History of the Kingship*, p. 289.

[4] Occasionally in Loango a palisade is erected across the road (Du Chaillu, *L'Afrique sauvage*, p. 133) to prevent diseases from entering the territory of the villages; Büttikofer (*Reisebilder aus Liberia*, p. 304) mentions a barricade of straw matting used to prevent access to sacred forests where initiation rites take place; perhaps the barriers made from branches and from straw matting found in Australia and in New Guinea serve this purpose, rather than simply that of hiding from the profane what is going on there, as is usually thought.

These have gradually disappeared, although the term "letter of marque"[1] retains the meaning of a permit to pass from one territory to another through a neutral zone. Zones of this kind were important in classical antiquity, especially in Greece, where they were used for market places or battle-fields.[2]

The same system of zones is to be found among the semi-civilized, although here boundaries are less precise because the claimed territories are few in number and sparsely settled. The neutral zones are ordinarily deserts, marshes, and most frequently virgin forests where everyone has full rights to travel and hunt. Because of the pivoting of sacredness, the territories on either side of the neutral zone are sacred in relation to whoever is in the zone, but the zone, in turn, is sacred for the inhabitants of the adjacent territories. Whoever passes from one to the other finds himself physically and magico-religiously in a special situation for a certain length of time: he wavers between two worlds. It is this situation which I have designated a transition, and one of the purposes of this book is to demonstrate that this symbolic and spatial area of transition may be found in more or less pronounced form in all the ceremonies which accompany the passage from one social and magico-religious position to another.

·   ·   ·   ·   ·

[1] [Letters of marque originally constituted a license from a sovereign authorizing a subject to seek reprisals against subjects of a hostile state for injuries inflicted by that state. In later times these letters enabled privateers to commit acts against a hostile nation which otherwise would have been considered piracy. In Europe, letters of marque were abolished by the Congress of Paris in 1856. (See *Oxford English Dictionary*.)]

[2] On the subject of sacred zones and bands of neutral territory, see Grierson, *The Silent Trade*, pp. 29, 56–59; and on frontiers and signs of sacred frontiers in Palestine and Assyro-Babylonia, see H. Gressmann, "Mythische Reste in der Paradieser-zählung," *Archiv für Religionswissenschaft*, X (1907), 361–63 n. On the feast of the Terminalia in Rome, see W. Warde Fowler, *The Roman Festivals of the Period of the Republic* (London: Macmillan, 1899), pp. 325–27. It seems likely that the Capitoline Hill was originally one of those neutral zones of which I speak (Fowler, p. 317), as well as a frontier between the city of the Palatine and that of the Quirinal; see also *Roscher's Lexikon*, *s.v.* "Jupiter," col. 668, and W. Warde Fowler in *Anthropology and the Classics* pp. 181 ff. on the subject of the pomerium.

With this introduction we now turn to some descriptions of territorial passages. When a king of Sparta went to war, he sacrificed to Zeus; if the prognostication was favorable, a torchbearer took fire from the altar and carried it in front of the army to the frontier. There the king sacrificed again, and if the fates again decreed in his favor he crossed the frontier with the torchbearer still preceding the army.[1] The rite of separation from one's own land at the moment of entering neutral territory was clearly acted out in this procedure. Several rites of frontier crossing have been studied by Trumbull,[2] who cites the following example: when General Grant came to Asyut, a frontier point in Upper Egypt, a bull was sacrificed as he disembarked. The head was placed on one side of the gangplank and the body on the other, so that Grant had to pass between them as he stepped over the spilled blood.[3] The rite of passing between the parts of an object that has been halved, or between two branches, or under something, is one which must, in a certain number of cases, be interpreted as a direct rite of passage by means of which a person leaves one world behind him and enters a new one.[4]

The procedures discussed apply not only in reference to a country or territory but also in relation to a village, a town, a section of a town, a temple, or a house. The neutral zone shrinks progressively till it ceases to exist except as a simple stone, a beam, or a threshold (except for the pronaos, the narthex, the vestibule, etc.).[5] The portal which symbolizes

[1] See Frazer, *The Golden Bough*, I, 305.

[2] H. Clay Trumbull, *The Threshold Covenant: Or the Beginning of Religious Rites* (New York: Charles Scribner's Sons, 1896), pp. 184–96. I wish to thank Mr. Salomon Reinach for lending me this book, which is difficult to find.

[3] *Ibid.*, p. 186. Trumbull's thesis is that the blood which was shed is a symbol, if not an agent of union.

[4] A collection of these rites has been published in *Mélusine: Recueil de mythologie, littérature populaire, tradition, et usages* (Paris: Gaidoz & Rolland, 1878–1912). A few imply the transfer of a disease, but what are commonly called rites of purification suggest the idea of a transition from the impure to the pure. All these ideas, and the rites to which they correspond, often form a single ceremonial grouping.

[5] For details on the rites of passage pertaining to the threshold, I refer you to Trumbull's *The Threshold Covenant*. Some prostrate themselves before the threshold, some kiss it, some touch it with their hands, some walk upon it or remove their shoes

19

a taboo against entering becomes the postern of the ramparts, the gate in the walls of the city quarter, the door of the house. The quality of sacredness is not localized in the threshold only; it encompasses the lintels and architrave as well.[1]

The rituals pertaining to the door form a unit, and differences among particular ceremonies lie in technicalities: the threshold is sprinkled with blood or with purifying water; doorposts are bathed with blood or with perfumes; sacred objects are hung or nailed onto them, as on-the architrave. Trumbull, in the monograph which he devoted to "the threshold covenant," bypassed the natural interpretation, although he wrote that the bronze threshold of Greece "is an archaic synonym for the enduring border, or outer limit, of spiritual domain."[2] Precisely: the door is the boundary between the foreign and domestic worlds in the case of an ordinary dwelling, between the profane and sacred worlds in the case of a temple. Therefore to cross the threshold is to unite oneself with a new world. It is thus an important act in marriage, adoption, ordination, and funeral ceremonies.

Rites of passing through the door need be stressed no further at this point because several of them will be described in chapters to follow. It will be noted that the rites carried out on the threshold itself are transition rites. "Purifications" (washing, cleansing, etc.) constitute rites of separation from previous surroundings; there follow rites of incorporation (presentation of salt, a shared meal, etc.). The

before doing so, some step over it, some are carried over it, etc. See also William Crooke, "The Lifting of the Bride," *Folk-lore*, XIII (1902), 238–42. All these rites vary from people to people and become more complicated if the threshold is the seat of the spirit of the house, the family, or the threshold god.

[1] For a detailed list of Chinese practices with reference to doors, see Justus Doolittle, *Social Life of the Chinese with Some Account of the Religious, Governmental, Educational, and Business Customs and Opinions with Special but Not Exclusive Reference to Fuhchau* (New York: Harper, 1865), I, 121–22; II, 310–12; Wilhelm Grube, *Zur pekinger Volkskunde* (Berlin, 1902), pp. 93–97. On magical ornamentation pertaining to the door, see Trumbull, *The Threshold Covenant*, pp. 69–74, 323.

[2] I cannot share Trumbull's view that the threshold is a primitive altar and the altar a transplanted threshold, nor can I attribute a greater importance to the presence of blood in rites pertaining to the threshold than to the use of water or simple contact. All these are rites of incorporation or union.

rites of the threshold are therefore not "union" ceremonies, properly speaking, but rites of preparation for union, themselves preceded by rites of preparation for the transitional stage.

Consequently, I propose to call the rites of separation from a previous world, *preliminal rites*, those executed during the transitional stage *liminal (or threshold) rites*, and the ceremonies of incorporation into the new world *postliminal rites*.

The rudimentary portal of Africa is very probably the original form of the isolated portals which were so highly developed in the Far East,[1] where they not only became independent monuments of architectural value (for example, porticoes of deities, of emperors, of widows) but also, at least in Shintoism and Taoism, are used as ceremonial instruments (see description of childhood ceremonies in chap. v).[2] This evolution from the magic portal to the monument seems also to have occurred in the case of the Roman arch of triumph. The victor was first required to separate himself from the enemy world through a series of rites, in order to be able to return to the Roman world by passing through the arch. The rite of incorporation in this case was a sacrifice to Jupiter Capitoline and to the deities protecting the city.[3]

In the instances cited thus far the efficacy of the ritual portal has been direct. But the portal may also be the seat of a particular deity. When "guardians of the threshold" take on monumental proportions, as in Egypt, in Assyro-Babylonia (winged dragons, the sphinx, and all sorts of

---

[1] [This statement appears to be primarily speculative.]

[2] For China, see Gisbert Combaz, *Sépultures impériales de la Chine* (Brussels: Vromant & Co., 1908), pp. 27–33; Doolittle, *Social Life of the Chinese*, II, 299–300. For Japan, see W. E. Griffis, in Trumbull, *The Threshold Covenant*, Appendix, pp. 320–24; B. H. Chamberlain, *Things Japanese: Notes on Various Subjects Connected with Japan for the Use of Travellers and Others* (London: Paul, 1891, p. 356, *s.v.* "torii"); N. Gordon Munro, "Primitive Culture in Japan," *Transactions of the Asiatic Society of Japan*, XXXIV (1906), 144.

[3] For the order of rites of triumph, see Le Père Bernard de Montfaucon, O.S.B., *Antiquités expliquées et représentées en figures* (Paris: F. Delaulne, 1719), 2d ed.; IV, 152–61.

monsters),[1] and in China (in the form of statues), they push
the door and the threshold into the background; prayers
and sacrifices are addressed to the guardians alone. A rite
of spatial passage has become a rite of spiritual passage. The
act of passing no longer accomplishes the passage; a personified power insures it through spiritual means.[2]

The two forms of portal rituals mentioned above seldom
occur in isolation; in the great majority of cases they are
combined. In the various ceremonies one may see the direct
rite combined with the indirect, the dynamistic rite with
the animistic, either to remove possible obstacles to the
passage or to carry out the passage itself.

Among the ceremonies of territorial passage those pertaining to the crossing of mountain passes should also be
cited. These include the depositing of various objects
(stones, bits of cloth, hair, etc.), offerings, invocations of the
spirit of the place, and so forth. They are to be found, for
instance, in Morocco (*kerkour*), Mongolia, Tibet (*obo*),
Assam, the Andes, and the Alps (in the form of chapels). The
crossing of a river is often accompanied by ceremonies,[3] and

[1] Regarding these divinities and the rites pertaining to them, see Eugène Lefebure,
Rites égyptiens: Construction et protection des édifices (Paris: E. Leroux, 1890); for
the Assyrian winged bulls, see p. 62.

[2] Regarding the divinities of the threshold, see (in addition to Trumbull, *The
Threshold Covenant*, pp. 94 ff.): L. R. Farnell, "The Place of the Sonder-götter in
Greek Polytheism," in *Anthropological Essays Presented to E. B. Tylor*, p. 82; and
Frazer, *The Golden Bough*. In China they are ordinarily Shen-Shu and Jü-Lü (see
Jan M. de Groot and Eduard Chavannes, *Les fêtes annuellement célébrées à Emouy*
[Paris, 1886], pp. 597 ff.) but in Peking also Ch'in-Ch'iung and Yü-chih-Kung (see
Grube, *Zur pekinger Volkskunde*). For Japan see Isabella L. Bird, *Unbeaten Tracks in
Japan: Travels in the Interior, Including Visits to the Aborigines of Yozzo and the
Shrine of Nikko* (London: J. Murray, 1905), I, 117, 273; Revon, "Le shinntoïsme,"
pp. 389, 390; Munro, "Primitive Culture in Japan," p. 144, etc.

[3] See among others H. Gaidoz, *Étude de la mythologie gauloise*, Vol. I: *Le dieu
gaulois du soleil et le symbolisme de la roue* (Paris: E. Leroux, 1886), p. 65; I recall
the ceremonies of construction and of the opening of bridges (cf. "pontifex"). As
for rites of passing between or under something, they have been collected in
Mélusine and by almost all folklore students. They should all be discussed again,
but it will be impossible to do so at this time. Therefore I will cite only the following,
taken from Stepan Petrovitch Krašeninnikov, *Histoire et description du Kamtchatka*,
trans. from the Russian by M. de Saint Pré (Amsterdam: M. M. Rey, 1760), I,
130–31, and see p. 136: "Soon afterward, they brought birch branches into the
yurt, according to the number of families represented. Each Kamchadal took one of
these branches for his family, and after bending it into a circle he made his wife and

a corresponding negative rite is found where a king or a priest is prohibited from crossing a certain river or any flowing water. Likewise, the acts of embarking and disembarking, of entering a vehicle or a litter, and of mounting a horse to take a trip are often accompanied by rites of separation at the time of departure and by rites of incorporation upon return.

Finally, in some cases the sacrifices associated with laying the foundation for a house and constructing a house fall into the category of rites of passage. It is curious that they have been studied in isolation, since they are part of a homogeneous ceremonial whole, the ceremony of changing residence.[1] Every new house is *taboo* until, by appropriate

children pass through it twice; as they emerged from this hoop, they began to spin around. Among them this is called being purified of one's faults."

It is apparent from the detailed descriptions by Krašeninnikov that the birch is a sacred tree for the Kamchadals and that it is used ritually in most of their ceremonies. Two interpretations are possible: direct sanctification may occur under the influence of the birch, which is considered *pure*, or a transference of impurity from the people to the birch may take place. The latter seems to be in keeping with the rest of the ceremony: "When all had been purified, the Kamchadals came out of the yurt with these small branches through the *župan*, or the lower opening, and they were followed by their relatives of both sexes. As soon as they were out of the yurt, they passed through the birch circle for the second time and then stuck the little branches in the snow, bending the end towards the east. After throwing all their *tonšič* on this spot and shaking their clothing, the Kamchadals re-entered the yurt by the ordinary opening and not by the *župan*." In other words, they rid themselves of the sacred material impurities which had accumulated in their clothes, and of their most important ritual object, the *tonšič* (which together with "sweet grass," etc., comprises their category of sacra). The branches, which had been endowed with the sacred, are thrown away.

The passage through the sacred arcs automatically removes from the celebrants the sacred characteristics which they acquired by performing the complicated ceremonies that this rite terminates. These circles form the portal which separates the sacred world from the profane world, so that, once they have entered the profane, the performers of the ceremony are again able to use the big door of the hut.

[1] Regarding construction sacrifices, see Paul Satori ("Über das Bauopfer," *Zeitschrift für Ethnologie*, XXX [1898], 1–54), who did not see that a few of them are rites of appropriation. For French rites, see Paul Sébillot, *Le folk-lore de la France* (Paris: E. Guilmoto, 1907), IV, 96–98; and for various theories, see Trumbull, *The Threshold Covenant*, pp. 45–57, and Edvard Alexander Westermarck, *The Origin and Development of Moral Ideas* (London: Macmillan, 1906–8), I, 461. Those rites fall into a wider category which I call the "rites of the first time" (see chap. ix). The charm 43, 3–15, of the Kausikasutra (W. Calland, *Altindisches Zauberrei: Darstellung der altindischen Wunschopfer* [Amsterdam: J. Muller, 1900], pp. 147–48) not only is connected with construction and with entering but also is mentioned in people's and animals' changing of dwellings.

rites, it is made *noa* (secular or profane).[1] In form and dynamics, the lifting of this taboo resembles those pertaining to a sacred territory or woman: there is washing or lustration or a communal meal. Other practices are intended to insure that the house remains intact, does not crumble, and so forth. Scholars have been wrong in interpreting some of these practices as survivals and distortions of an ancient custom of human sacrifice. Ceremonies to lift a taboo, to determine who will be the protecting spirit, to transfer the first death, to insure all sorts of future security, are followed by rites of incorporation: libations, ceremonial visiting, consecration of the various parts of the house, the sharing of bread and salt or a beverage, the sharing of a meal. (In France, a housewarming is given, called literally, "hanging the pothook.") These ceremonies are essentially rites identifying the future inhabitants with their new residence. When the inhabitants—for instance, a betrothed man or a young husband and his family or his wife—build the house themselves, the ceremonies begin at the very start of construction.

Rites of entering a house, a temple, and so forth, have their counterpart in rites of exit, which are either identical or the reverse. At the time of Mohammed, the Arabs stroked the household god when entering and when leaving,[2] so that the same gesture was a rite of incorporation or a rite of separation, depending on the case. In the same way, whenever an Orthodox Jew passes through the main door of a house, a finger of his right hand touches the mezuzah, a casket attached to the doorpost which contains a piece of paper or a ribbon upon which is written or embroidered the sacred name of God (Shaddai). He then kisses the finger and says, "The Lord shall preserve thy going out and thy coming in from this time forth evermore."[3] The verbal rite is here joined to the manual one.

[1] For a typical ceremony, see W. L. Hildburgh, "Notes on Sinhalese Magic," *Journal of the Royal Anthropological Institute*, XXXVIII (1908), 190.

[2] Smith, *The Religion of the Semites*, pp. 461–62.

[3] Trumbull, *The Threshold Covenant*, pp. 69–70, with reference to Syria. [Van Gennep evidently relied on Trumbull for this information. According to *The Jewish*

It will be noted that only the main door is the site of entrance and exit rites, perhaps because it is consecrated by a special rite or because it faces in a favorable direction. The other openings do not have the same quality of a point of transition between the familial world and the external world. Therefore thieves (in civilizations other than our own) prefer to enter otherwise than through the door; corpses are removed by the back door or the window; a pregnant or menstruating woman is allowed to enter and leave through a secondary door only; the cadaver of a sacred animal is brought in only through a window or a hole; and so forth. These practices are intended to prevent the pollution of a passage which must remain uncontaminated once it has been purified by special ceremonies. Spitting or stepping on it, for instance, are forbidden. But sometimes the sacred value of the threshold is present in all the thresholds of the house. In Russia I saw houses in which little horseshoes, used to protect the heels of boots, were nailed on the threshold of every room. In addition, every room in these houses had its own icon.

In order to understand rites pertaining to the threshold, one should always remember that the threshold is only a part of the door and that most of these rites should be understood as direct and physical rites of entrance, of waiting, and of departure—that is, as rites of passage.

Encyclopedia, ed. Isidore Singer (New York and London: Funk & Wagnalls, 1916), the prayer at the door is translated as "may God keep my going out and my coming in from now on and evermore." The inside of the mezuzah contains the words of Deuteronomy 6 : 4–9 and 11 : 13–21, both of which exhort the Jews to love and obey God, and which command them to write God's name on their doors and gateposts. "Shaddai" is written on the outside of the mezuzah, which is touched and kissed in passing through the door.]

III INDIVIDUALS AND GROUPS

A society is similar to a house divided into rooms and corridors. The more the society resembles ours in its form of civilization, the thinner are its internal partitions and the wider and more open are its doors of communication. In a semicivilized society, on the other hand, sections are carefully isolated, and passage from one to another must be made through formalities and ceremonies which show extensive parallels to the rites of territorial passage discussed in the last chapter.

An individual or group that does not have an immediate right, by birth or through specially acquired attributes, to enter a particular house and to become established in one of its sections is in a state of isolation. This isolation has two aspects, which may be found separately or in combination: such a person is weak, because he is outside a given group or society, but he is also strong, since he is in the sacred realm with respect to the group's members, for whom their society constitutes the secular world. In consequence, some peoples kill, strip, and mistreat a stranger without ceremony,[1] while others fear him, take great care of him, treat him as a powerful being, or take magico-religious protective measures against him.

For a great many peoples a stranger is sacred, endowed with magico-religious powers, and supernaturally benevolent or malevolent. This fact has been pointed out repeatedly, especially by Frazer[2] and Crawley,[3] who both attribute the rites to which a stranger is subjected to magico-religious terror in his presence. These rites, they maintain, are intended to make him neutral or benevolent, to remove

---

[1] In the case of organized robbery—of caravans, for example—or of the right of shipwreck, the phenomenon is much more economic and legal than magico-religious; occasionally however, as in the Fiji Islands, the right of shipwreck seems intended to prevent magically dangerous strangers from entering the tribe's territory.

[2] Frazer, *The Golden Bough*, I, 297–304. Trumbull, *The Threshold Covenant*, pp. 4–5 and *passim*, considers only rites of entrance in relation to the blood and the threshold.

[3] Crawley, *The Mystic Rose*, pp. 414, 239, 250 ff.

the special qualities attributed to him. Grierson accepts the same point of view, but he is also interested in the economic and legal position of the stranger, and he cites many references.[1] Westermarck presents even ampler evidence, and also suggests further motives which may affect behavior toward a stranger (e.g., personal feelings, positive or supernatural interest).[2] He rejects Crawley's theory based on the concept of contagion—that rites pertaining to the stranger are but a means of lifting "a taboo of individual isolation"[3] by which everyone is surrounded—and proposes an even narrower one. For him the purpose of the rites is to destroy both the evil eye possessed by all strangers a priori and the "conditional curse" placed upon the host by the stranger's presence.[4] Jevons, on the other hand limits, the significance of these rites to purification of the clothing and belongings of the stranger, excluding the stranger himself.[5]

Each of these points of view is applicable to a series of particular facts, but none of them enables us to understand the dynamics of rites pertaining to the stranger, their patterns, and the parallels between these ceremonial patterns and the order of rites of childhood, adolescence, betrothal, and marriage.

However, if we consult documents which describe in detail the ceremonies to which isolated strangers or groups (such as caravans or scientific expeditions) are subjected, we see, beneath a variety of forms, a surprisingly uniform pattern. The actions which follow an arrival of strangers in large numbers tend to reinforce local social cohesion: the inhabitants all leave the village and take refuge in a well-protected place such as a hill or forest; or they close their

---

[1] Grierson, *The Silent Trade*, pp. 30–36, 70–83.

[2] Westermarck, *The Origin and Development of Moral Ideas*, I, 570.

[3] Crawley, *The Mystic Rose*, p. 172.

[4] Westermarck, *The Origin and Development of Moral Ideas*, I. See especially pp. 586–92 and the truly ignorant conclusions of p. 390.

[5] Jevons, *An Introduction to the History of Religion*, p. 71. It is impossible to understand how clothing or other possessions can be impure, dangerous, and taboo while the user remains unaffected.

doors, arm themselves, and send out signals for a gathering (e.g., fire, trumpet, drum); or the chief, alone or with his warriors, goes before the strangers as a representative of his society, since he is better immunized against this contact than the ordinary inhabitants. Elsewhere, special intermediaries or elected delegates are sent. In addition (though there are exceptions of a political nature, for example), foreigners cannot immediately enter the territory of the tribe or the village; they must prove their intentions from afar and undergo a stage best known in the form of the tedious African palaver. This preliminary stage; whose duration varies, is followed by a transitional period consisting of such events as an exchange of gifts, an offer of food by the inhabitants, or the provision of lodging.[1] The ceremony terminates in rites of incorporation—a formal entrance, a meal in common, an exchange of handclasps.

The length and intricacy of each stage through which foreigners and natives move toward each other vary with different peoples.[2] The basic procedure is always the same, however, for either a company or an individual: they must stop, wait, go through a transitional period, enter, be incorporated. The particular rites may include actual contact (e.g., a slap, a handclasp), exchanging gifts of food or valuables, eating, drinking, smoking a pipe together, sacrificing animals, sprinkling water or blood, anointing, being attached to each other, being covered together, or sitting on the same seat. Indirect contact may occur through a spokesman or through touching simultaneously or one after the other a sacred object, the statue of a local deity, or a "fetish post." This enumeration could be continued indefi-

[1] This may be a "communal house" of young men or warriors, a special place belonging to the chief or a noble, or even a room in a local family's house. In the last case the stranger is often incorporated into the family, and thus into the society.

[2] See some accounts which are compared in my *Tabou et totémisme à Madagascar*, pp. 40–47. In this category might be listed the protocol for the reception of ambassadorial missions, etc., which mark the contact between two groups. Particularly the "welcome" ritual of the central Australians should be noted; see B. Spencer and F. J. Gillen, *The Northern Tribes of Central Australia* (London: Macmillan, 1904), pp. 568–79.

nitely, but space forbids a close examination of more than a few rites.

The rite of eating and drinking together, which will be frequently mentioned in this book, is clearly a rite of incorporation, of physical union,[1] and has been called a sacrament of communion.[2] A union by this means may be permanent, but more often it lasts only during the period of digestion. Captain Lyon has noted that the Eskimo consider a man their guest only for twenty-four hours.[3] Often the sharing of meals is reciprocal, and there is thus an exchange of food which constitutes the confirmation of a bond. When food is exchanged without a common meal, the action falls into the vast category of gift exchanges.[4]

Exchanges have a direct constraining effect: to accept a gift is to be bound to the giver. Crawley perceived this in part,[5] but Ciszewski, in his monograph on fraternal bonds among the Slavic populations of the Balkans and Russia, did not understand it. He considered rites of incorporation "symbolic" and recognized four major ones: eating and drinking together, the act of tying one to the other, kissing one another, and the "symbol of *naturae imitatio*." Leaving aside the last (simulated childbirth, etc.), which is sympathetic in nature, the rites described by Ciszewski in his research may be classified as follows: individual or collective eating in common; simultaneous Christian communion; being tied with a single rope or belt; holding hands; embracing; putting feet together on the hearth; exchanging gifts of cloth, garments, weapons, gold or silver coins, bouquets, garlands, pipes, rings, kisses, blood, Christian sacred objects (a cross, a candle, or an icon); kissing these sacred

---

[1] See Crawley, *The Mystic Rose*, pp. 157 ff., 214, 456 ff.

[2] Smith, *The Religion of the Semites*, pp. 206–10; Hartland, *The Legend of Perseus*, Vol. III, *passim*.

[3] *The Private Journal of Captain G. F. Lyon of the H.M.S. Hecla, During the Recent Voyage of Discovery under Captain Parry* (London: J. Murray, 1824), p. 350.

[4] For bibliographic references, see Grierson, *The Silent Trade*, pp. 20–22, 71; Westermarck, *The Origin and Development of Moral Ideas*, I, 593–94.

[5] Crawley, *The Mystic Rose*, p. 237; he was mistaken in interpreting the lifting of the taboo and the rites of union from a totally individualistic point of view.

objects (an icon, a cross, the Gospels); or pronouncing an oath.[1]

Moreover, it appears from Ciszewski's monograph that in each local ceremony there is a combination of several of these uniting acts and that in all of them there occur one or more rites of exchange. It is this rite which usually occupies the central place—as is also the case in marriage ceremonies, to be examined later. In reality, the rite involves a mutual transference of personality, and its operation is as simple as the mechanics of being tied one to the other, being covered with the same coat or veil, and so forth. Furthermore, although the exchange of blood may be coarser or more cruel than that of a piece of clothing, a ring, or a kiss, it is no more primitive.[2]

We might also add to the kinds of exchanges already listed those which include children (practiced in China, for example), sisters and wives (in Australia), entire garments, deities, or all sorts of sacred objects, such as umbilical cords.[3] Among some North American Indians (such as the Salish) exchange has become an institution called "potlatch," which is held periodically for each person in turn.[4]

---

[1] Stanislaus Ciszewski, *Künstliche Verwandschaft bei den Südslaven* (Leipzig: T. Krakau, 1897). See, respectively, pp. 141, 2, 33, 35, 39, 43–45, 54, 57, 34, 63, 3, 38, 40, 35, 46, 54, 55, 45, 47, 27, 33, 34, 45, 46, 55, 32, 57, 69, 43–45, 43–46, 41, 57, 42, 27, 33, 37, 38, 41–43, 45, 27, 45, 60–69, 37, 56–57, 34, 37, 39, 55, 56. On pp. 41 ff. and 33, Ciszewski cites an interesting instance where the fraternal bond is formed in three stages (small, medium, and large)—which call to mind the stages of initiation and incorporation into age groups.

[2] On fraternal bonds see the inquiry of the *Revue des traditions populaires* and of *Mélusine*; G. Tamassia, *L'affratellamento* (Turin, 1886); Smith, *The Religion of the Semites*, pp. 239–48; J. Robinsohn, *Psychologie der Naturvölker* (Leipzig, 1896), pp. 20–26. According to even Ciszewski's account (p. 94) social fraternal bonds create a stronger relationship than natural consanguinity.

[3] Taplin, *The Narrinyeri* (2d ed.; Adelaide: T. Shawyer, 1878), pp. 32–34. This exchange creates the relationship called *ngiangiampe*, on which Crawley (in *The Mystic Rose*) built his theory of "mutual inoculation between individuals," without seeing that all forms of exchange have exactly the same purpose. On the social significance of fraternal bonds, see Ciszewski, *Künstliche Verwandschaft bei den Südslaven, passim,* esp. p. 29. Fraternal bonds may be permanent or temporary, in which case they may be renewed (see Ciszewski, pp. 7, 45, 49, etc.).

[4] Among others, see C. Hill-Tout, "Report on the Ethnology of the Southeastern Tribes of Vancouver Island, British Columbia," *Journal of the Royal Anthropological Institute*, XXXVII (1907), 311–12.

One of the duties of royalty, among the semicivilized, is redistributing to their subjects the "gifts" obligatorily given. In short, the movement of objects among persons constituting a defined group creates a continuous social bond between them in the same way that a "communion" does.

Among rites of union similar to those creating a fraternal bond may be cited the joint performance of a ceremonial act, such as godparenthood or a pilgrimage. Such a union cannot be broken except by a special rite of separation.

The direct and simple operation of the rite incorporating a stranger is very clear in the ceremony to which Thomson submitted just before his entrance into Masai territory.[1]

On the day after our arrival a Swahili runaway came as a messenger of the chief to make friends and brothers with me. A goat was brought and, taking it by one ear, I was required to state where I was going, to declare that I meant no evil and did not work in *uchawi* (black magic), and finally to promise that I would do no harm to the country. The other ear was then taken by the sultan's ambassador, and he made promise on his part that no harm would be done to us, that food would be given, and all articles stolen refunded. The goat was then killed, and a strip of skin cut off the forehead, in which two slits were made. The M-Swahili, taking hold of this, pushed it on my finger by the lower slit five times, finally pushing it over the joint. I had next to take the strip, still keeping it on my finger, and do the same for the M-Swahili, through the upper slit. This operation finished, the strips had to be cut in two, leaving the respective portions on our fingers; and the Sultan of Shira and I were sworn brothers.[2]

Among the Zaramo, Wazigula, and Wasagala it is the practice to exchange blood. The two individuals sit face to face, the legs of one crossing those of the other, while a third person brandishes a sword above them, pronouncing a curse against the breaker of the fraternal bond. Here the bond is created by simultaneous contact and blood

---

[1] [The ceremony described was performed by Thomson with the Chaga of Shira at a camp adjacent to Masai territory.]

[2] Joseph Thomson, *Through Masai Land* (London: Law, 1885); French translation: *Au pays des Massaï* (Paris, 1886), pp. 101–2. [The original English has been used in the translation.]

exchange, and an exchange of gifts follows.[1] I cite this last instance chiefly to show that it is a mistake to separate rites involving blood arbitrarily from those of incorporation. Actually, these special rites seldom constitute the whole ceremony, which, in the great majority of cases, includes rites of contact, food sharing, exchanges, joining (tying, etc.), "lustration," and so forth.

A combination of the various rites of incorporation by direct contact is very apparent, for instance, in the following customs of the Shammar, an Arab tribe. Layard writes:

Amongst the Shammar, if a man can seize the end of a string or thread the other end of which is held by his enemy, he immediately becomes his Dakheel. If he touch the canvas of a tent, or can even throw his mace towards it, he becomes the Dakheel of its owner. If he can spit upon a man, or touch any article belonging to him with his teeth, he is *Dakhal*, unless, of course, in the case of theft, it be the person who caught him. The Shammars never plunder a caravan within sight of their encampment, for as long as a stranger can see their tents they consider him their *Dakheel*.[2]

Here even sight is contact. Rites of this kind play an important part in ceremonials of the right of asylum.[3] The simple fact of pronouncing a word or a formula like the Moslem salaam also has the effect of creating at least a temporary bond; that is why Moslems look for all sorts of ways to avoid giving a salaam to a Christian.[4]

The various forms of greeting also fall into the category

[1] R. Burton, *The Lake Regions of Central Africa* (London: Longmans, Green, 1860), I, 114, 115.

[2] A. H. Layard, *Nineveh and Babylon: Second Expedition to Assyria, 1848–51* (London: Murray, 1861), pp. 317 ff. Regarding the *dakhīl*, see W. Robertson Smith, *Kinship and Marriage in Early Arabia*, ed. Stanley A. Cook (London: Stack, 1907), pp. 48–49 n. [The rules governing contact apply equally to protector (*dākhal*) and protégé (*dakhīl*); the role assumed depends, of course, on circumstances independent of the ritual.]

[3] On the right of asylum, see Trumbull, *The Threshold Covenant*, pp. 58–59. Albas Hellwig (*Das Asylrecht der Naturvölker* [Stuttgart, 1903]) did not see the magico-religious side or the link between taboo and the rites of incorporation pertaining to the right of asylum among the semicivilized; these have been studied in part from this point of view by Smith (*The Religion of the Semites*, pp. 53–57, 206–8) and Ciszewski (*Künstliche Verwandschaft bei den Südslaven*, pp. 71–86, etc.).

[4] Edmond Doutté, *Merrâkech* (Paris: Comité de Maroc, 1805), I, 35–38.

32

of rites of incorporation; they vary according to the extent to which the person arriving is a stranger to the inhabitants of the house or to those he meets. The various greetings of Christians, still found in archaic forms in Slavic countries, renew each time the mystical bond created by belonging to the same religion, as does the salaam among the Moslems. The reading of several detailed descriptions will show that among semicivilized people these greetings have the following effects: (1) In the case of relatives, neighbors, or members of the same tribe, there is a renewal and reinforcement of membership in a single, more or less restricted group. (2) In the case of a stranger, he is introduced first to a limited group and then, if he so desires, to other restricted groups and at the same time to the society at large. Here again, people clasp hands or rub noses, separate themselves from the outside world by removing their shoes, coat, or headdress, unite by eating or drinking together, or perform prescribed rites before household gods, and the like. In short, a person identifies himself in one way or another with those he meets, if only for the moment. Among the Ainu, for instance, a greeting is intrinsically a religious act.[1] The same ritual sequences may be found in the exchange of visits, which as an exchange also basically has the value of a bond; among the Australians, for example, it is an intertribal custom.

Direct rites of incorporation based on contagion include a number of sexual rites, such as wife exchange. If the rite is unilateral, a woman is loaned (a wife, daughter, sister, relative, wife of the host, or woman of the same class or tribe as the host).[2] Although in some cases the purpose of this

---

[1] For details of these rites see J. Batchelor, *The Ainu: the Hairy Aborigines of Japan* (London: Religious Tract Society, 1891), pp. 188–97; Chamberlain, *Things Japanese*, pp. 333–39, on tea ceremonies; F. Hutter, *Wanderungen und Forschungen in Nord Hinterland von Kamerun* (Brunswick, 1902), pp. 135–36, 417–18; and in general the references to politeness, etiquette, salutation, and hospitality in ethnographic monographs.

[2] For theories and references see: Edvard Alexander Westermarck, *The History of Human Marriage* (London: Macmillan, 1891), pp. 73–75; Crawley, *The Mystic Rose*, pp. 248, 280, 285, 479; *The Book of Ser Marco Polo, the Venetian*, trans. Henry Yule,

loan is to obtain more gifted and powerful children (because of the mana inherent in all strangers),[1] usually the rite is clearly intended to incorporate the stranger into a more or less restricted group of which the woman lent to him is a member. In fact, the loan is an equivalent of a shared meal. Among the central Australians a man and a woman, or two men and two women, are sent as messengers. As a sign of their mission they bring packages of cockatoo feathers and bones for the nose (to be placed in the perforated septum). When the messengers and the men of the camp have discussed the business at hand, the former take the two women a short distance away from the camp and leave. If the men of the visited group accept the negotiations, they all have sexual intercourse with the women; if not, they do not go to join them.

When a party of warriors on an expedition of revenge approaches a camp with the intention of killing some inhabitant, women are similarly offered to them. If they have sexual relations with these women the quarrel is ended, since accepting them is a sign of friendship; to accept the women and continue the vendetta would constitute a serious breach of intertribal custom.[2] In both cases, coitus is clearly an act of union and identification. Its significance conforms with facts I have cited elsewhere,[3] which show that among the central Australian the sexual act is auxiliary to magic and is not a fertility rite. Incorporation into a religiously united group may also be mediated by sacred prostitutes, and where they are explicitly reserved for strangers this role

rev. Henri Cordier (London: J. Murray), I, 214; II, 48 n. 4, 53–54; Murray Anthony Potter, *Sohrab and Rustum* (London: P. Nutt, 1902), pp. 145–52. In Morocco, as among the Kabyles of Algeria, the lending of daughters is customary for "guests of the tent" but not for "guests of the community."

[1] This case falls into the general category of fertility rites; e.g., the loan of women reported in *Ser Marco Polo*, II, 53, is intended to assure good harvests and "a great augmentation of material prosperity."

[2] B. Spencer and F. J. Gillen, *Native Tribes of Central Australia* (London: Macmillan, 1899), p. 98.

[3] *Mythes et légendes d'Australie*, pp. lvi–lvii; on the subject of wife lending in Australia, see Spencer and Gillen, *Native Tribes of Central Australia*, pp. 74, 106–8, 267, and *The Northern Tribes of Central Australia*, pp. 133–39.

may explain their presence. The word "strangers" may here be construed in a wider sense as the equivalent of "non-initiates" or "those who are not worshipers, in particular, of the deity to which the prostitutes are attached."[1]

It would be interesting to isolate the rules which often seem to govern the protocol of receiving a stranger. For instance, the stranger is often lodged in a "communal house" (such as the *lapa* of Madagascar), which may be a "young men's house," a "house of adult men," or a "house of warriors," depending on the peoples.[2] He is thus incorporated into the group that most closely corresponds to his own character as an active and powerful man, not into the society at large. Such hospitality gives the stranger a number of military, sexual, and political rights; it is a widespread custom, especially in Indonesia, Polynesia, and certain parts of Africa. In other regions of that continent the stranger's abode is assigned to him by a sacred personage such as the chief or king. When the ancient rite of incorporation is replaced by the Oriental caravansery and various kinds of tribute, the reception of strangers moves into a purely economic stage.

Up to now we have considered the stranger only from the point of view of those individuals or groups with which he comes in contact. But as a rule he, too, has a home, and it would be surprising if he could leave it without the performance of ceremonies which signify the reverse of the rites of incorporation just discussed. Furthermore, if a man away from home is incorporated by a group with whom he is staying, he should theoretically go through rites of separation when leaving it—and perfect balance has in fact been noted between rites of arrival and the corresponding rites of leave-taking, which include visits, a last exchange

[1] See facts in Edwin Sidney Hartland, "Concerning the Rite at the Temple of Mylitta," in *Anthropological Essays Presented to E. B. Tylor*, pp. 189–202, and books by Dulaure, Frazer, etc.

[2] See H. Schurtz, *Altersklassen und Männerbünde* (Berlin: A. Reiner, 1902), pp. 203–13, especially on the various forms of communal houses and their evolution.

of gifts, a meal in common, a last drink, wishes, accompaniment on the road, and sometimes even sacrifices. Explorers' accounts generally mention observances such as the following:

Among the Moslems, in particular, the religion includes numerous precepts pertaining to travel. The books of the Ahadith and the *adab*[1] dedicate a whole chapter to travelers. . . . In North Africa water is thrown under the steps of the one departing. When, in 1902, we were leaving Mogador for an excursion into the interior, a member of the family of one of my Moslem companions came out of his home at the moment of our departure and threw a pail of water under the feet of my companion's horse.[2]

Perhaps this is a rite of "purification" or a rite "intended to break past or future spells" as Doutté asserts on the basis of Frazer's interpretations;[3] to my mind it is more probably a rite of separation in which the traveler crosses an artificial Rubicon. Rites of separation have been greatly elaborated in China to mark a mandarin's change of province, a departure for a trip, and so forth.[4] It seems to me that all the rites observing departure on a trip or an expedition are intended to make the break gradual rather than abrupt. Incorporation is, as a rule, also carried out in stages.

As for rites on the occasion of the traveler's return, these include the removal of impurities acquired on the voyage

---

[1] The Ahadith are sacred writings of Islam. The *adab al-kātib*, *adab al-wuzarâ'*, and others are strictly distinguished from religious writings but are works of a secular nature dedicated to a cultivation of higher human qualities, or *adab* (see *Encyclopedia of Islam*, ed. M. T. Houtsma and M. Seligsohn [Leiden: Brill, 1908]).

[2] Doutté, *Merrâkech*, pp. 31, 91.

[3] Frazer, *The Golden Bough*, I, 303; see also Grierson, *The Silent Trade*, pp. 33–34, 72–74; Westermarck, *The Origin and Development of Moral Ideas*, I, 589–94.

[4] "When the mandarin is about to leave, all the inhabitants go out on the main roads and line up from place to place, from the city gate through which he will pass up to two or three miles farther. Highly polished tables draped with satin and covered with preserves, liqueurs, and tea can be seen everywhere. Everyone stops the mandarin, and against his wishes he is made to sit, eat, and drink. . . . The most pleasant part is that all the people want something which belongs to him. Some take his shoes, others his cap, some his overcoat, but each one of these things is replaced by others, and by the time he has passed through the mob, he may have changed shoes thirty different times." Le Père Louis LeComte, *Nouveaux mémoires sur l'état présent de la Chine* (3d ed.; Paris: J. Annison, 1700), II, 53–54. For more modern details, see Doolittle, *Social Life of the Chinese*, II, 235–36, 302–3.

(rites of separation) and rites of gradual incorporation, such as certain ordeals and rites of animal intercourse in Madagascar.[1] Such rites are especially prevalent where absences —of the husband, for instance—are regular.

However, the traveler's departure does not completely separate him either from the society to which he originally belonged or from the one he joins during his trip. Therefore, special rules for the conduct of his family while he is absent prohibit all actions which could harm him directly (by telepathy) or by sympathetic means.[2] Hence, too, it is the custom to provide the traveler, at each departure, with a sign of recognition, such as a staff, a letter, or a tessera in ancient Greece,[3] which automatically incorporates him into other groups. This is done among the Votyak when a shaman or *usto-tuno* is called for cases of illness or animal epidemics:

He is brought from far away, so that he knows no one. He is taken from village to village, as he is needed. When he leaves home, he asks the village that has called him for a "pledge" consisting of a piece of wood on which the chief of each family has inscribed his *tamga* (clan and property mark). The *usto-tuno* leaves this piece of wood at home, giving his wife the right to demand that her husband be brought back to her. This formality is repeated each time the *usto-tuno* goes to another village, and the piece of wood bearing the *tamga* of the next village is always placed in the hands of the mistress of the household the *usto-tuno* leaves.[4]

The journeys of Australian messengers among various clans

[1] *Tabou et totémisme à Madagascar*, pp. 249–51, 169–70; on rites of return in general, see Frazer, *The Golden Bough*, I, 306–7; for the return of warriors, see Joseph François Lafitau, *Mœurs des sauvages amériquains comparées aux mœurs des premiers temps* (Paris: Saugrain l'Aîné, 1724), II, 194–95, 260; on the rites of travel in ancient India, see Calland, *Altindisches Zauberrei*, pp. 46, 63–64.

[2] It is the same during the absence of fishermen, hunters, and warriors; see Frazer, *The Golden Bough*, I, 27–35; van Gennep, *Tabou et totémisme à Madagascar*, pp. 171–72; as well as references in William Ellis, *History of Madagascar* (London: Fisher & Co., 1838), I, 167; for Borneo, Florence E. Hewitt, "Some Sea Dayak Taboos," *Man*, VII (1908), No. 12, 186–87.

[3] [A tessera was "a die broken between host and guest and kept as a means of recognition (Attic and Ionic)" (*Oxford English Dictionary*).]

[4] Vasiliev, *Obozrenie iazycheskikh obriadov, sueverii i verovanii Votiakov Kazanskoi i Viatskoï gubernii* (Kazan, 1906), p. 15. See, on this subject, publications on messengers' staffs, etc.

and tribes are also definitely ritualized,[1] as were the procedures regulating merchants' coming and going in Europe and the Far East during the Middle Ages.

The pattern outlined for ceremonies pertaining to strangers and travelers may be found also in adoption rituals. In Rome these included the *detestatio sacrorum*, a set of rites of separation from the patrician class, the gens, the cult of the former household, and the former immediate family; and the *transitio in sacra*, a set of rites of incorporation to the new environment.[2] The Chinese ritual likewise includes relinquishing ties with the former clan and household cult for the sake of the new. The particular rites performed at adoption are identical with those mentioned for other instances of incorporation. They include exchanges (of blood, gifts, etc.), tying, veiling, seating together, real or simulated nursing, simulated birth, and so forth. The rites of separation have been observed much less frequently, but I have noticed that among the southern Slavs there is a rite of separation for persons considered related because they were born during the same month.

Among the Chamar, a caste of tanners and leatherworkers in northern India, in cases of adoption all members of the clan come together, and the parents of the boy say: "You were my son by a deed of evil (*pap*); now you are the son of so-and-so by a virtuous act (*dharm*)."[3] The members of the clan sprinkle the child with rice, and the adopting parent gives a ceremonial meal to all those present. Among some American Indians, the adoption ritual is related to concepts of mana (orenda, manito, etc.) and reincarnation. Naming

[1] Spencer and Gillen, *Native Tribes of Central Australia*, pp. 94, 156, 274; *The Northern Tribes of Central Australia*, pp. 139, 551; A. W. Howitt, *The Native Tribes of South-east Australia* (London: Macmillan, 1904), pp. 678–91.

[2] Charles Daremberg and Edmond Saglio, *Dictionnaire des antiquités grecques et romaines d'après les textes et les monuments* (Paris: Hachette, 1877–1906), *s.v.*: "adoptio," "consecratio," "detestatio," etc.; regarding adoption among the semi-civilized, see Hartland, *The Legend of Perseus*, II, 417 ff.; Frazer, *The Golden Bough*, I, 21 ff.; among the Slavs, Ciszewski, *Künstliche Verwandschaft bei den Südslaven*, pp. 103–9.

[3] William Crooke, "Typical Castes and Tribes . . . of the Aryo-Dravidian Tract: Chamar," *Census of India*, Ethnographical Appendixes (Calcutta, 1903), p. 174.

forms an important part of their ceremonies, because an individual's name indicates his place with reference to the various marriage and clan sections. In addition, those adopted are assigned a fictitious age group, even where a group is involved (the Tuscaroras became "children" to the Oneida; the Delawares were adopted as "cooks" by the League of Five Nations and therefore wore women's dress and changed their economic activity).[1]

The rites performed when a slave or a retainer changes masters also may be explained as rites of passage. As a rite of incorporation, one may cite the violent blow with a stick given by a slave in Loango to a new master he has chosen for himself;[2] another is the ceremony of the Bambunda called *tombika* (or *shimbika*).[3] The change in a slave's status brought about when she gives her master a child is marked by rites of incorporation sometimes reminiscent of marriage ceremonies; these rites are related to those of the right to asylum. Ceremonies of changing clan, caste, or tribe and those of naturalization also include rites of separation, transition, and incorporation. Some of these will later be discussed in detail.

The operation of rites is the same for groups as for individuals. Among rites of separation for groups may be included a declaration of war, either tribal or familial. The European and Semitic rites of the vendetta are well known, so I shall mention the Australian ones, which have also been described in detail.[4] The group charged with implementing revenge is first separated from society and acquires its own individuality; its members do not re-enter society until after the performance of rites which remove that temporary individuality and reintegrate them into the society. The

---

[1] See J. N. B. Hewitt, under "Adoption," in *Handbook of American Indians*, ed. Frederick Hodge (*Bulletin of the Bureau of American Ethnology*, Vol. I [1907], No. 30, pp. 15–16.

[2] Pechüel-Loesche, *Volkskunde von Loango*, pp. 245–46.

[3] References in Albert Hermann Post, *Afrikanische Jurisprudenz*, 2 vols. in *Ethnologischjuristische Beiträge zur Kenntnis des einheimische Rechte Afrikas* (Oldenburg: Schulze, 1887), I, 102.

[4] See Spencer and Gillen, *The Northern Tribes of Central Australia*, pp. 556–68.

purpose of the vendetta is to recreate a social unity of which some aspect has been destroyed; in this sense it resembles certain kinds of adoption and shares a number of elements with rites of passage. The ceremonies performed at the end of a vendetta or a war (peace ceremonies)[1] are identical with rites of friendship[2] and of adopting groups of strangers.

Rites of union with a god or with a group of deities also ought to be mentioned in this chapter. The Jewish Passover (the word itself signifies *passage*) is a rite of passage which, through a process of convergence, has been combined on the one hand with ceremonies of the changing of seasons and on the other with a commemoration of the passage through Babylon and the return to Jerusalem.[3] The ritual of this holiday therefore includes, in combination, several of the kinds of rites of passage studied in this volume.[4]

[1] Regarding these rites, see Hartland, "Rite at the Temple of Mylitta," pp. 250–251; Crawley, *The Mystic Rose*, pp. 377, 239–46; Hutter, *Wanderungen und Forschungen*, pp. 435–38.

[2] And on individual reconciliation in Borneo: "If two men who have been at deadly feud meet in a house, they refuse to cast their eyes upon each other till a fowl has been killed and the blood sprinkled over them; and, when two tribes make peace, after solemn engagements are concluded, a pig is killed the blood of which is supposed to cement the bond of friendship." Spencer Saint John, *Life in the Forests of the Far East* (London: Smith & Elder, 1862), I, 64–65. The word "cementing" should be taken in its material sense, but not symbolically, as is ordinarily done. This rite has nothing to do with the threshold, as Trumbull believed (*The Threshold Covenant*, p. 21).

[3] [Van Gennep is in error here. Passover has no relation to the Babylonian captivity—it is connected with the belief that during the last of the seven plagues in Egypt the houses of the Hebrews were spared by the Angel of Death, and they were exempt from the slaying of the first-born children. The angel knew Hebrew homes by the mark of a lamb's blood on the portal (see Exodus 12, *The Jewish Encyclopedia*, *Universal Jewish Encyclopedia*).]

[4] I do not know whether this very simple interpretation has ever been proposed before. It explains the sequence of the rites of the Jewish Passover and the incorporation into the Christian Easter of the idea of death and resurrection without any borrowing from the rites of Adonis, etc. This holiday has been a ceremonial of passage from its very beginning and bit by bit has attracted and absorbed various elements which are still independent among other peoples.

IV PREGNANCY AND CHILDBIRTH

The ceremonies of pregnancy and childbirth together generally constitute a whole. Often the first rites performed separate the pregnant woman from society, from her family group, and sometimes even from her sex. They are followed by rites pertaining to pregnancy itself, which is a transitional period. Finally come the rites of childbirth intended to reintegrate the woman into the groups to which she previously belonged, or to establish her new position in society as a mother, especially if she has given birth to her first child or to a son.

Of all these rites, those of separation at pregnancy and childbirth have been subject to closest study. Frazer and Crawley[1] have drawn attention especially to the customs of seclusion in special huts or in a special part of the home; to the taboos, which are primarily dietary, sumptuary, and sexual; and to the so-called purification rites, through which in some cases taboos may be lifted, in others reintegration effected. It has been established that at the onset of pregnancy a woman is placed in a state of isolation, either because she is considered impure and dangerous or because her very pregnancy places her physiologically and socially in an abnormal condition. Nothing seems more natural than that she should be treated as if she were ill or a stranger.

Pregnancy ceremonies, like those of childbirth, include a great many rites—sympathetic or contagious, direct or indirect, dynamistic or animistic—whose purpose is to facilitate delivery and to protect mother and child (and sometimes also the father, close relatives, the whole family, or the entire clan) against evil forces, which may be impersonal or personified. These have been studied repeatedly,[2] no

[1] Frazer, *The Golden Bough*, I, 326–27, II, 462; Crawley, *The Mystic Rose*, pp. 213, 414–16, 432; also passages cited further on from Hermann H. Ploss, *Das Weib in Natur und Völkerkunde*, posthumously ed. Max Bartels (Leipzig: Theodor Grieben, 1899. 8th ed.; 1905).

[2] Tylor, *Primitive Culture*, II, 305; Hartland, *The Legend of Perseus*, I, 147–81; Victor Henry, *La magie dans l'Inde antique* (Paris: Dujarric, 1904), pp. 138–44;

doubt because they are at once the most numerous and the most conspicuous. There is no need to deal with them here, and I mention them only to make it clear that I do not mean to lump them all in the category of rites of passage. It is often difficult to discern clearly whether a particular ceremony is a rite of passage, a rite of protection, or a sympathetic rite (with reference to birthmarks, for example).

The order of pregnancy and childbirth rites among the Todas of India runs as follows:[1] (1) When a woman becomes pregnant, she is forbidden to enter the villages or the sacred places. (2) In the fifth month there is a ceremony called "village we leave." At this time the woman must live in a special hut, and she is ritually separated from the dairy, the sacred industry which is the heart of Toda social life. (3) She invokes two deities, Pirn and Piri. (4) She burns each hand in two places. (5) A ceremony marks the leaving of the hut; the woman drinks sacred milk. (6) She goes back to live in her home till the seventh month. (7) During the seventh month "the ceremony of the bow and arrow" establishes a social father for the unborn child (the Todas practice polyandry). (8) The woman returns to her home, performing the appropriate rites. (The last two ceremonies occur only during the first pregnancy, or if the woman has a new husband, or if she wants her future children to have a different father from the one she has previously chosen.) (9) The woman is delivered in her house, in anyone's presence and without special ceremonies. (10) Two or three days later, mother and child go to live in a special hut; the rites performed for the departure from the house, the de-

Walter William Skeat, *Malay Magic* (London: Macmillan, 1900), pp. 320–52; Edmond Doutté, *La société musulmane de Maghreb: Magie et religion dans l'Afrique du Nord* (Algiers: A. Jourdin, 1909), p. 233; Paul Sébillot, *Le paganisme contemporain chez les peuples celto-latins* (Paris: O Doin, 1908), pp. 16–33; A. Riédjko ("Nechistaia sila v sudbakh zhenshchiny-materi," *Etnograficheskoe Obozrenie* [1899], Books I–II, pp. 54–131) has collected many facts, especially from Russia, Siberia, and the Caucasus, which I have summarized under the title "L'action des puissances impures de la vie de la femme-mère" in *Revue de l'histoire des religions*, XLII (1900), 453–64.

[1] W. H. R. Rivers, *The Todas* (London: Macmillan, 1906), pp. 313–33.

parture from the hut, and the return to the house are the same as those marking the woman's previous trip. (11) While in the hut, the woman, her husband, and the child are tainted with the impurity called *ichchil*. (12) Ceremonies are performed to protect them against the evil spirit *keirt*. They return to ordinary life by drinking sacred milk.

From the detailed descriptions of these rites given by Rivers it is evident that they are clearly intended to separate the woman from her surroundings, to keep her on three occasions in a fairly long transitional state, and to permit her reintegration into her usual surroundings only by stages (e.g., she is required to live in two intermediate houses in going from the taboo hut to her usual home).

For details of other separation procedures during pregnancy (seclusion, sexual and dietary prohibitions, cessation of economic activity, etc.) I refer the reader to the work of Ploss, which shows that pregnancy is definitely a transitional period.[1] It is divided into stages corresponding to whatever months are considered important—usually the third, fifth, seventh, eighth, and ninth.[2] The return to ordinary life is rarely made all at once; it, too, is accomplished in stages reminiscent of initiation steps. Thus the mother's transitional period continues beyond the moment of delivery, and its duration varies among different peoples. The first transitional period of childhood, to be discussed in the next chapter, is grafted to its latter stages.

Two documents on North America illustrate this point. Among the Hopi of Oraibi (in Arizona) the moment of childbirth is sacred to a woman. As a rule, her mother is present during labor, and the woman remains at home; but neither

[1] Ploss, *Das Weib in Natur und Völkerkunde*, I, 843–46, 858–77. See also my *Tabou et totémisme à Madagascar*, pp. 20, 165–68, 343. The rites of separation, transition, and incorporation are very clearly defined in Madagascar; the Hova (an *Antaimerina* caste) even consider a pregnant woman *dead*, and after childbirth she is congratulated on being *resurrected* (*ibid.*, p. 165); on this point, see chap. ix of this volume.

[2] Cf. other descriptions of rites among the Hindus and Moslems in the Punjab given by H. A. Rose, "Hindu Pregnancy Observances in the Punjab," and "Muhammadan Pregnancy Observances in the Punjab," *Journal of the Royal Anthropological Institute*, XXXV (1905), 271–82.

her mother, her husband, her children, nor anyone else may be present at the delivery itself. When the child has arrived, her mother returns to assist, if necessary, in the expulsion of the placenta and to bind the baby's umbilical cord. Then her mother places " on an old tray, the placenta, pads, sand, from under the woman, and the little broom, and carries it all to one of the placenta hills (*kiwuchochmo*) of which there are several in close proximity to the village."[1]

For twenty days the young mother is subject to dietary taboos, and if it has been her first pregnancy she may not leave her house before sundown during this time, though she may do so after the fifth day if she has borne other children. On the fifth, tenth, and fifteenth days there is a ritual washing of both mother's and child's head and body; on the twentieth day the woman, her child, her mother, her husband, and other relatives are washed in this manner. On that day the women of the clan name the child, which is then presented to the sun. Then all the family and the women who have named the child partake of a meal to which all the inhabitants of the pueblo are invited by the maternal grandmother, or even by a special crier. From that day on everything in the house goes its usual way for the mother, the child, the family, and the pueblo. Therefore the sequence is: (1) separation, (2) a transitional period with gradual removal of barriers, and (3) reintegration into ordinary life. In the ceremonies of the Muskwaki (commonly known as Fox) the sex group also plays a part; the pregnant woman is separated from other women and, after delivery, is reintegrated into their midst by a special rite. A particular woman who is important in other ceremonies acts as intermediary.[2]

[1] Henry R. Voth, *Oraibi Natal Customs and Ceremonies* (The Stanley McCormick Hopi Expedition, Field Columbian Museum, Chicago, Publication 97, Anthropology Series, Vol. VI, No. 2 [Chicago, 1905]), p. 48.

[2] Mary Owen, *Folk-lore of the Musquakie Indians of North America* ("Publications of the Folk-lore Society," Vol. LI [London, 1904]), pp. 63–65. For good descriptions of the rites of childbirth in South Africa, see, among others, Henri A. Junod, *Les Ba-Ronga* (Neufchâtel: F. A. Hager, 1898), pp. 15–19, and J. Irle, *Die Herero* (Gütersloh, 1906), pp. 93–99.

The frequent confusion of rites of passage with rites of protection may very well explain why the former have not been accorded the importance they merit. Most Bulgarian rites, for example, are intended to shelter the woman, the fetus, and then the child from malevolent powers, to insure their good health, and so forth. This is the case, in fact, among all the Slavs and most European peoples. Nevertheless, the detailed description of these ceremonies given by Strausz[1] makes it possible to isolate rites of separation, transition, and incorporation. I believe that this is true for the rites cited here, although I am not certain that my classification is correct for all of them, or that I have not omitted others that are rites of passage.

From St. Ignatius' Day until the feast of the calends (Koliada) the expectant mother must neither wash her hair, clean her clothes, nor comb her hair after nightfall; she must not leave her house during the ninth month. She must not remove for a whole week the clothing she wears at the time of delivery. A fire is kept burning until the christening, and the bed is surrounded with a rope. Then cakes are baked; the young mother must eat the first piece and share the rest with her relatives, but not a single crumb may leave the house. The relatives bring gifts and all spit on mother and child (obvious rites of incorporation). They come to see her throughout the first week. On the eighth day the baptism takes place. On the fifteenth day the young mother bakes cakes and invites her neighbors and the women of her acquaintance to come and eat; all of them bring flour.

For forty days the young mother is not allowed to leave her house or her courtyard, or to have sexual relations with her husband. On the fortieth day she takes pieces of silver or nuts which have been consecrated in the child's first bath and goes with her child, her husband, and her mother (or an old woman or the midwife) to the church, where the priest blesses them; on the way back the midwife, the mother, and

[1] Adolf Strausz, *Die Bulgaren: Ethnographische Studien* (Leipzig: T. Grieben, 1898), pp. 291–300.

45

the child enter three houses, where presents are given them, and the child is sprinkled with flour. The next morning all the relatives come to call on the young mother, who then sprinkles holy water in all the corners of the house and yard where she has been during the forty days; after this, daily life resumes its ordinary course. In addition to a reintegration into the family and sex group, we have here a reintegration into the Slav *sosiedstvo* or neighborhood—a restricted group which merits a monograph in itself.

The stages of reintegration are even more apparent among the Kota of the Nilgiri Hills. A woman is taken to a very distant special hut immediately after being delivered, and there she remains thirty days. She spends the following month in another special hut, and the third in yet another. Then she spends some time in the house of a relative, while her husband "purifies" the family home with sprinklings of water and dung.[1] The length of this more or less absolute separation ranges among different peoples from two to forty, fifty, and, as in the case cited, one hundred days. It is apparent that the physiological return from childbirth is not the primary consideration, but that instead there is a *social return from childbirth*, just as there is a social parenthood which is distinct from physical parenthood,[2] and a social marriage which is distinct from sexual union. We will see that there is also a social puberty which does not coincide with physical puberty.

This *social return from childbirth* tends, in our society, to coincide with the physical return.[3] This tendency may be noted also in the other institutions enumerated, and it is directly related to a progress in the knowledge about the laws of nature. Our ceremony on this occasion is known as the "churching of women," and, although its character is

[1] Ploss, *Das Weib in Natur und Völkerkunde*, II, 403; for other details, *ibid.*, pp. 414–18.

[2] Van Gennep, *Mythes et légendes d'Australie*, p. lxiii; N. W. Thomas, *Kinship Organizations and Group Marriage in Australia* (Cambridge: Cambridge University Press, 1906), pp. 6–8; Rivers, *The Todas*, p. 547.

[3] For a rite of the physiological return from childbirth, see Rose, "Hindu Pregnancy Observances," p. 271.

more mundane than magico-religious, it is easy to see what it must have been during the Middle Ages—the woman's reintegration into her family, her sex group, and her society.[1]

Furthermore, all rites of passage become more complex in abnormal cases, especially if the mother has given birth to twins. Among the Basoko, in the Congo, the mother is confined to her cabin until the two children are grown; she is allowed to speak only to members of her family; only her mother and father have the right to enter her cabin; any stranger who sets foot in it is sold as a slave; and she has to live in complete chastity. The twins are kept apart from other children, and all dishes and other utensils employed by them are taboo. The house they live in is marked by two posts placed one on each side of the door and overhung with a piece of canvas. The threshold is adorned with many little stakes which are driven into the ground and painted white. These are the rites of separation.

The transitional period lasts until the children are more than six years old. Then comes the rite of reintegration: "During the day, two women were stationed at the door of the house, with their faces and legs painted white—one was the doctor, the other the mother. The festivities commenced by their marching down the street, one beating a drum with a slow measured beat and the other singing. The dancing, singing, and drinking of all the villagers then set in for the night. After the ceremony, the twins were allowed to go about like other children."[2] The ritualistic traversing of territory belonging to the society as a whole and the sharing of food represent well-known types of incorporation whose social significance is clear.

In their components, the rites of pregnancy and childbirth are in many ways analogous to those discussed in

[1] Ploss (*Das Weib in Natur und Völkerkunde*, II, 402–35) gives a description of the signs prohibiting entrance into the room, and so forth, which are of the same order as the taboos mentioned above.

[2] See Paul B. du Chaillu, *Journey to Ashango Land* (New York: D. Appleton Co., 1867), p. 274.

previous chapters, and to others which follow. They include a passage over or across something, joint prayers and sacrifices, and so forth. One notes the role of intermediaries. Here, as in other ceremonies, they are intended not only to neutralize an impurity or to attract sorcery to themselves but to serve as actual bridges, chains, or links—in short, to facilitate the changing of condition without violent social disruptions or an abrupt cessation of individual and collective life.

The first birth has a considerable social importance which is variously expressed among different peoples. Sometimes, as among the Bontok Igorot of the Philippines, and elsewhere, a girl cannot marry until she has borne a child and has thus proved that she is capable of reproduction. Among peoples who do not consider a marriage valid until after a child is born, the rites of pregnancy and childbirth constitute the last acts of the marriage ceremony (as they do among the Todas), and the woman's transitional period stretches from the beginning of her betrothal to the birth of her first child. Becoming a mother raises her moral and social position;[1] instead of being just a woman she is now a matron; instead of being a slave or concubine she is an equal of free women and legitimate wives.

In such cases many polygynous peoples, Moslems among them, perform rites of passage to mark the change from the

[1] Among many peoples the same is true of the father and is indicated, for instance, by technonymy: he loses his name and is called "father-of-so-and-so." Changing the name is one of the rites of baptism, initiation, marriage or enthronement; therefore technonymy also may be interpreted as a rite of passage, a classification into a new group. On technonymy, see among others Crawley, *The Mystic Rose*, pp. 428–35; M. Merker, *Die Masai: Ethnographische Monographie eines ostafrikanischen semiten Volkes* (Berlin: Reimer, 1904), p. 59; Hutton Webster, *Primitive Secret Societies: A Study in Early Politics and Religion* (New York: Macmillan, 1908), p. 90. These scholars did not see the bond between technonymy and other factors pointed out above, a bond which is clear-cut among the Bemba of the Congo, for example: "Until the birth of the first child, the wife never calls her husband by his name; she calls him only by his common name *bwana* (master) or *mwenzangu* (companion). As soon as the father recognizes his offspring, the wife calls her husband by the child's name, preceding it by the word *si-* (father of . . .), and she, herself, receives the name of the newborn child preceded by *na-* (mother of . . .)" (Charles Delhaise, "Ethnographie congolaise chez les Wabemba," *Bulletin de la Société Belge de Geographie* [Brussels: Type-Ethnographie General, 1908], pp. 189–90).

old status to the new one. Even among peoples whose customs make divorce easy, it is impossible or difficult to obtain a divorce from a woman who has borne one or more children.[1] Therefore, rites of pregnancy and childbirth must be viewed as having considerable individual and social importance; rites of protection or those intended to facilitate delivery (often performed by the father), and those involving transference of roles (couvade and pseudo-couvade), should be placed in a category of secondary rites of passage, since they assure to the future mother and father an entrance into a special segment of society, the most important one of all, and the one which constitutes society's permanent nucleus.

Finally, I want to call attention to a particular ritual event among the Ngente, a Lushae tribe in Assam, who hold a three-day feast every autumn in honor of all the children born that year. During the first two days all the adults sit, eat, and drink, but on the third day the men, disguised as women or as Poi[2] (a neighboring group), go from house to house calling on all the mothers of the year, who give them something to drink and small presents, in return for which they dance.[3] This feast is exactly parallel to the annual feasts for the dead, and it presents an interesting instance of fertility ritually celebrated not alone by a restricted family but by the whole society.

[1] [Current data do not bear out this statement for all societies. Exceptions will be found especially where there are matrilineal or bilateral kinship systems.]

[2] [The Poi closely resemble the Chin in culture and perhaps are descendants of Chin immigrants (see van Gennep's source below).]

[3] Drake-Brockmann, cited by Major Shakespear in "Typical Tribes and Castes... (of the Mongoloid Tract Lusheis)," *Census of India*, Ethnographical Appendixes (Calcutta, 1903), Appendix IV, p. 228.

V BIRTH AND CHILDHOOD

Some of the rites discussed in the preceding chapter have to do not only with the mother but also with the child. Among peoples who consider the pregnant woman impure, that impurity is ordinarily transmitted to the child, who is consequently subject to certain taboos and whose first transitional period coincides with the mother's last transition preceding her *social return from childbirth*. The various rites of protection against the evil eye, infections, diseases, all kinds of evil spirits, and so forth, are good simultaneously for mother and child; where they pertain particularly to the child, they do not differ significantly from other practices of the same sort.

Ceremonies for the newborn child again involve a sequence of rites of separation, transition, and incorporation. An opinion encountered by Doutté among the Rahūna of Morocco—and one which may be more widespread than would appear at first—provides a satisfactory explanation for certain practices. Not only is the newborn child considered "sacred," but it is believed that "he can be born only after he has obtained the favor of all those present."[1] This statement expresses a defensive attitude like one the group assumes toward a stranger.

And again, like a stranger, the child must first be separated from his previous environment, which may simply be his mother. I think this necessity accounts for putting a child in the care of another woman for the first few days, a practice which has no relation to the time required for the appearance of milk. The principal separation is expressed in the cutting of the umbilical cord (with a knife of wood or stone, etc.) and in the rites surrounding the portion which dries and falls off by itself at the end of a variable number of days.[2]

Sometimes the instruments used to cut the umbilical cord

[1] Doutté, *Merrâkech*, I, 343, 354.   [2] The Kalduke of the Narrinyeri, etc.

belong to a class of tools appropriate to activities of one or the other sex. In the Punjab if the child is a boy, the cord is cut with a knife or a *janiū* belonging to an old man in the family; among the Oraibi Hopi of Arizona it is cut with an arrow. If the child is a girl, the Punjabi use a spindle, while the Hopi use a stick for piling grain in jars.[1] Through their choice of instruments these peoples definitively establish the sex of the child, and the same is true in Samoa.[2] The cutting of the umbilical cord often seems to be the occasion for family feasts and celebrations, and in these cases the significance of the rite is clearly collective as well as individual.

The umbilical cord itself is handled in a variety of ways: sometimes the child himself saves all of it, along with his hair or his nail parings, to prevent any diminution of his personality or to make sure these exuviae do not fall into the hands of some other person. But sometimes it is placed in the custody of a relative, either to protect the child's personality (in accordance with a belief in an external soul) or to keep alive the relationship between the child and his family, represented by the keeper of his umbilical cord. In other cases, the umbilical cord is buried in a distant place hidden from everyone, or under the threshold, or in the room. In the latter practices I am inclined to see direct rites of assimilation into the kin group. The treatment of the placenta and of the foreskin after circumcision is similar, though varying from people to people. Each of the two operations marks a separation which must be compensated for with at least temporary precautions.

It has been pointed out by the English and German school that some of the rites performed are of sympathetic nature

---

[1] H. A. Rose, "Hindu Birth Observances in the Punjab," *Journal of the Royal Anthropological Institute*, XXXVII (1907), 224; Voth, *Oraibi Natal Customs and Ceremonies*, pp. 47–61. On the *janiū*, or sacred thread, see *Indian Antiquary: A Journal of Oriental Research* (Bombay), 1902, p. 216, and William Crooke, *Things Indian: Discursive Notes on Various Subjects Connected with India* (London: Murray, 1906), pp. 471–73.

[2] G. Turner, *Samoa a Hundred Years Ago and Long Before* (London: Macmillan, 1884), p. 79.

and prepare the child for a better utilization of his limbs, his strength, and his skills. Others, however, are clearly rites of separation from the asexual world or from the world preceding human society, and rites of incorporation into the society of the sexes and into the nuclear or extended family, clan, or tribe. While rites such as the first bath, the washing of the head, the rubbing of the child have hygienic purposes, they seem at the same time to be rites of purification falling into the category of rites of separation from the mother. Such, too, are the rites of passing the child through, across, or under something, and of putting the child on the ground, although Dieterich regarded the last as a rite of incorporation with Mother Earth.[1]

Some of the rites noted by Dieterich do actually pertain to the earth itself, but they are nonetheless rites of separation.[2] Thus the expression *kourotrophos* should be taken literally; the earth is the home of children before they are born—not symbolically as a mother, but physically, as it is the home of the dead.[3] Therefore there are some resemblances in the details of certain birth and funeral rites. If a child dies before the rite of his incorporation into the world is performed and is therefore buried rather than cremated, this is done, in my opinion, in order to return him to his place of origin. Dieterich has cited German beliefs (and identical ones exist in Australia and Africa) according to which the souls to be born (taking the word "soul" in its broadest sense) live under the earth or in rocks. Various peoples also believe that the souls live in trees, bushes, flowers, or vegetables, in the forest, and so forth.[4] The idea that the unborn children first live in fountains, springs, lakes, and flowing water is also prevalent.[5]

---

[1] Dieterich, *Mutter Erde*, pp. 1–21.   [2] See, for details, *ibid.*, pp. 34, 39.

[3] *Ibid.*, pp. 57 ff. Cf. Burton, *The Lake Regions of Central Africa*, I, 115; among the Zaramo of eastern Africa: "In the case of abortion or of a stillborn child, they say: 'He hath returned' that is to say, to his home in earth."

[4] See my *Mythes et légendes d'Australie*, pp. xxxi, xliv–lxvii; for the souls of the Ainu in the willows, see Batchelor, *The Ainu*, p. 235.

[5] Dieterich, *Mutter Erde*, p. 18; Dan McKenzie, "Children and Wells," *Folk-lore*, XVIII (1907), No. 3, 253–82.

Therefore I consider all rites intended to assist the child in entering the liminal (transitional) period as rites of passage. This period lasts from two to more than forty days, depending on the people.

Where there is a belief in transmigration and reincarnation, the rites whose purpose is the separation of the newborn child from the world of the dead and his incorporation into the society of the living, or a restricted group of them, are more systematized than elsewhere. Such is the case among the Arunta, the Kaitish, the Warramunga, and other groups in central Australia.[1] Among the Tshi on the Gulf of Guinea a newborn child is shown various objects which belonged to dead members of the family; his choice among them identifies him with one of his ancestors, and this rite suffices to incorporate him into the family.[2]

The idea of reincarnation most often coexists with a number of other beliefs. The Ainu give the following reason for the liminal period in which mother, father, and child are maintained for the first days after birth: the mother gives the child its body and the father its soul, but this occurs only gradually; the body is acquired during pregnancy, and the soul comes into being during the twelve days following birth, of which the father spends the first six in the hut of a friend and the remainder in his own hut; only on the twelfth day is the child a complete and autonomous individual.[3] This may be an explanation after the fact, but it may also be—and this seems to me more likely—that a number of rites of seclusion and protection of the newborn child are based on the idea that it takes several days of real life for the child to become an individual.

Rites which involve cutting something—especially the first haircut, the shaving of the head, and the rite of putting

---

[1] See, among others, Spencer and Gillen, *Northern Tribes of Central Australia,* pp. 606–8.

[2] Mary H. Kingsley, *Travels in West Africa: Congo Française, Corisco, Cameroons* (London: Macmillan, 1897), p. 493.

[3] See Batchelor, *The Ainu,* p. 240, and for the rites of childbed, naming, etc., pp. 235–37.

on clothes for the first time—are generally rites of separation. Naming, ritual nursing, the first tooth, baptism, and so forth, are rites of incorporation which, according to the Yao of East Africa, "introduce the child into the world,"[1] or, as the Dyaks of Bakarang (British North Borneo) say, "launch the child into the world" like a boat onto the water.[2]

An example of a childhood rite of separation is the following Hindu practice.[3] A hymn is recited, and at its conclusion a talisman of *pūtudru* (a kind of resinous wood) is fastened on the child, with the words: "Take possession of this charm of immortality . . . I bring you breath and life; do not go toward the dark shadows; remain safe; go before you toward the light of the living," etc. This rite is performed on the tenth day, which is the last day of the mother's confinement. The child is given two names, an ordinary one which incorporates him among the living in general, and another which may be known only to his family. On the third day of the third moon, the father presents the child to the moon in a rite which I consider to be a cosmic incorporation. The first outing (at four months) and the first solid food (at six months) are also accompanied by ceremonies. During the third year the ceremony of the first haircut is performed; since every family has a particular hair style by which members are recognized, and which is imposed on the child, this rite—intrinsically one of separation[4]

[1] F. Alice Werner, *The Natives of British Central Africa* (London: A. Constable, 1907), pp. 102–3.

[2] H. Ling Roth, *The Natives of Sarawak and British North Borneo* (London: Truelove, 1896), I, 102.

[3] For these facts, see Hermann Oldenberg, *La religion du Véda* (trans. Victor Henry from *Die Religion des Veda* [Berlin: Besser, 1894]), (Paris: F. Alcan, 1903), pp. 363, 397–98; Henry, *La magie dans l'Inde antique*, pp. 82–83; Calland, *Altindisches Zauberrei*, p. 107.

[4] Oldenberg (*La religion du Véda*, pp. 361–66) notes that the cutting of the hair, the fingernails, etc., is the occasion for frequent ceremonies, and he interprets these as rites of purification or lustration. He is correct in cases where a sacrifice constitutes the transition from the profane to the sacred, but these terms are not applicable to secular passages such as those from one age group to another or from one social situation to another. In these cases cutting off a part of the body, or taking a bath, or changing clothes does not imply any idea of an impurity to be rejected or a purity

54

—is also a rite of incorporation into the family group. Childhood lasts until the performance of the important ceremony (at eight, ten, or twelve years) called "entering school"; this marks the beginning of adolescence.

In modern Punjab, the transitional period (period of impurity) for the mother and child lasts ten days for Brahmans, twelve for Kshatriyas, fifteen for Vaisyas, and thirty for Sudras—the period lengthening with a lesser purity of caste. Confinement in the house, however, lasts forty days, during which the woman and child pass through a series of ceremonies—the most important being the bath—whose purpose is clearly the gradual reintegration of the mother into her family, sex group, and society. The child is incorporated into the family by being named, having his ears pierced, and having his hair cut for the first time when he is one and a quarter to four years old. The rite of *ajīja* among the Punjabi Moslems has been subject to Hindu influences,[1] but it seems to be more significant as a rite of incorporation into the community of the faithful than it is for the rest of Islam.

Childhood ceremonies in Minhow[2] may be outlined as follows: Chinese children of both sexes, up to the age of sixteen, are under the special protection of a deity called "Mother," and ceremonies are identical for boys and girls, even though girls are held socially in lower esteem than are boys.[2] On the third day after birth the child is washed for the first time; sacrifices are made to the "Mother"; food and gifts are sent to relatives and friends. After the bath

---

to be acquired. Also see W. Calland, *Een indogermaansch Lustratie-Gebruik* ("Verslagen een Mededeelingen der Koninkijke Akademie van Wetenschappen" [Amsterdam, 1898]), p. 277, for his interpretation of triple circumcision.

[1] For details, I refer you to articles by H. A. Rose, "Hindu Birth Observances in the Punjab," and "Muhammadan Birth Observance in the Punjab," *Journal of the Royal Anthropological Institute*, XXXVII (1907), pp. 220–60.

[2] See Doolittle, *Social Life of the Chinese*, I, 120–40; on childhood ceremonies in Peking, see Grube, *Zur pekinger Volkskunde*, pp. 3–10; see pp. 8–9 and elsewhere for the ceremonies for placing the child in the hands of a wet nurse; they include the sequence of passage and are analogous to the rite of adoption (being nursed was one means of becoming related); the two families then consider themselves members of the same clan (*pên-chia*).

comes the ceremony of binding the child's wrists with a string of red cotton on which are hung ancient coins and miniature silver toys; the string is two feet long, and the wristbands may be pulled about a foot from each other. They are removed on the fourteenth day and sometimes replaced by two bracelets of red string which are worn several months or a year. The Chinese explanation is that this rite makes the children obedient. Also on the third day a sign intended to ward off unfavorable influences is hung on the door of the room; it is understood by persons not very close to the family as a request not to enter the room. This sign consists of two Chinese characters on a piece of red paper, and a bundle:

This parcel contains two of a certain fruit full of seed used in the manufacture of material employed somewhat like soap in washing, some pith of a rush used for wicking, two chopsticks, one or two onions, two pieces of charcoal, some cat's hair and some dog's hair. A pair of trowsers of the child's father are put on the frame of the bedstead in such a way that the waist shall hang downward, or be lower than the legs. On the trowsers is stuck a piece of red paper, having four words written upon it, intimating that *all unfavorable influences are to go to the trowsers* instead of afflicting the babe. The hair in the package, on the outside of the bedroom door, is to keep the noises which may be made for eleven days by dogs and cats in the vicinity from frightening the babe. The coal is to aid in making it hardy and vigorous. The onions are to cause it to be quick witted and intelligent. The pith is explained as contributing to make it fortunate or successful in life. The two fruits are to aid it in being cleanly and neat.[1]

On the fourteenth day the bundle and the trousers are removed and thanks are given to the "Mother." At the end of the month, mother and child leave the room for the first time, and the barber or some member of the family shaves the child's head for the first time in front of the "Mother" or the ancestral tablets.

All the relatives and friends are invited to a feast, and they bring gifts (usually twenty painted duck eggs and sweet cakes—both decorated with paintings of flowers—and objects which portend good fortune; white paintings

[1] Doolittle, *Social Life of the Chinese*, pp. 121–22.

are forbidden, since white is the color of mourning). The maternal grandmother plays an important role. During the second and third months the parents give gifts (round biscuits) to their friends and relatives in return for the ones they have received at the time of the delivery and at the end of the first month. During the fourth month thanks are offered to the "Mother" in the form of gifts brought or sent by the maternal grandmother; family and guests eat a meal together; then the child is ceremonially placed on a chair for the first time and for the first time is given animal food.

At the end of the year an offering is made to the "Mother" with gifts sent by the maternal grandmother, who theoretically pays all the expenses of the celebration; there is a family meal; several toys representing tools of different occupations are placed before the child, and the one which he picks up first is taken as an indication of his future character, profession, and social status. The child takes an active part in all rites performed before the "Mother" or the ancestral tablets—he is made to move his hands, etc. On every birthday until the sixteenth, when the ceremony of "departure from childhood" is performed, thanks are offered to the ancestral tablets and to the "Mother." When the child begins to walk a member of his family approaches him from the back, carrying a large kitchen knife, and pretends to cut something between his legs; this is the ceremony of "cutting the cords of his feet," to facilitate learning to walk.

Until the "departure from childhood" ceremony, the rite of "passing through the door" is held every year, or every two or three years, and in the case of illness several times a year or even once a month, the frequency varying among families. Several Taoist priests are asked to come in the morning; they build an altar by piling several tables on one another and on them place plates of various foods, candlesticks, images of gods, and so forth. With music and appropriate invocations they invite the deities, especially the "Mother" and the goddesses who are protectors of children, to come and taste the offerings. In the front of the room, said to be "before the heavens," they place a table with plates, etc., and seven piles of rice representing Ursa Major, the Great Bear; they light the lights and perform the customary rite of "worshiping the measure." Toward nightfall a doorway is built in the center of the room. It is made of bamboo covered with red and white paper, and is seven feet high and two and a half to three feet wide. The furniture is so placed in the room that it is possible to move about freely without retracing one's footsteps.

With a bell and a sword decorated with bells in one hand, and a horn in the other, a priest recites incantations. He personifies the "Mother" in the act of chasing evil powers away from the children. The father of the family gathers all the children together, carrying in his arms a child who cannot walk yet or who is ill. Each of the other children holds a lighted candle. The priest, blowing his horn, passes slowly under the door and is followed by the father and the children, one after the other. The other priests beat the sacred drums, and so forth. The priest who leads the procession brandishes his sword or a whip and pretends to strike something which is invisible. Then the door is carried into the four corners of the room in succession, and the procession passes through it in the same fashion, finally returning to the center. The doorway is then demolished, and the pieces are burned in the courtyard or in the street. At each ceremony a small wooden statue is made, representing the child for whose benefit the ceremony is being performed; this statue is kept until the child is sixteen years old and is usually placed next to the image of the "Mother" in the bedroom. If the child dies before he reaches the age of sixteen, the statue is buried with him; if he is very ill, the statue is taken through the door. The child for whom the ceremony is being held, the sick children, and all other children of the household including nephews and nieces and others who happen to be there at the moment must pass through this door.

It is possible, of course, to interpret this entire ceremony as a transference of evil, a rite which is very widespread in the form of a "passage under or across something." Moreover, the rite is partially animistic, as is almost all of Taoism. However, the object under which the children pass is a portal, and when one considers the widespread sanctity of portals in all the Far East (in connection with the previously discussed function of African portals), the rite appears to me to have a direct meaning: the children pass gradually from a dangerous world into one that is favorable or neutral. With the moving of the doorway from the center to the four corners and finally back again to center, the sixfold repetition of the ceremony makes the entire room a safe environment for the children. This interpretation—that a part of the ceremony is a rite of passage—is confirmed by the fact that the rite is repeated with greater solemnity at the time of the children's "maturity" at the age of sixteen. In contrast, the ceremony of "worshiping the measure" (Libra) or those constellations related to life and death is performed for the sick, irrespective of their age.[1]

Leaving aside the celebrations related to school (entering school, honoring Confucius, for progress in studies, etc.), I come to the ceremony of "departure from childhood". "It is very similar to the passage through the door, except that it is more impressive and theatrical."[2] It is believed that at sixteen a boy leaves childhood to enter adolescence and a girl becomes a woman.[3] Once the ceremony has been completed, the "Mother," goddess of children, ceases to have them in her keeping, and the individuals fall under the authority of the gods in general. That is why the ceremony is often called "thanking the Mother."

Doolittle insists that the age of sixteen is actually the beginning of "the age of maturity," although the ceremony may be held earlier if the child is to be married soon, or delayed because of poverty, or for other reasons. The essen-

[1] Doolittle, *Social Life of the Chinese*, pp. 134-36. [2] *Ibid.*, pp. 137-38.
[3] See what is farther on said concerning "social puberty."

tial rite is still a passage through the imitation door. One may suppose either that childhood, as a positive quality (like an illness) is transferred to the door and destroyed with it, or—and I prefer this interpretation—that the door is the boundary between two stages in life, so that in passing under it a person leaves the world of childhood and enters that of adolescence. The destruction of the object used in the rite may be explained by the fact, observed in Australia,[1] South America,[2] and elsewhere, that sacra may be used only a single time; as soon as a ceremonial phase is ended, they must be destroyed (this being the central idea of sacrifice) or put aside, as if emptied of their powers, and for each new phase there must be new sacra, such as new bodily ornamentation, costumes, or verbal rites.[3] Finally, it should be noted that in China every birthday, but especially the ten following the fiftieth, is the occasion for ceremonies which also mark the transition from one period to another.[4]

The following door rites are performed at Blida:

On the seventh day after the child's birth the midwife dresses him and stretches him out in her arms. A round mirror is placed on the swaddled infant's chest; it holds the spindle belonging to the household, a rag full of indigo, and a pinch of salt—objects frequently used in magical operations. The midwife carries the infant and paraphernalia to the door and seven times balances him over the *mdjira*, or drainpipe. She does this at every door, especially at the door of the toilet, which is often in the vestibule, and finally at the door to the street, on the inside. This seventh day is called the day of the child's coming out (*yawm khurūj al-mazyūd*). Does it not seem evident that

---

[1] See *Mythes et légendes d'Australie*, pp. 134–35, n. 3.

[2] Theodor Koch-Grünberg, personal correspondence.

[3] The Ojibway (like many other semicivilized peoples) build special huts of different shapes for each specialized activity and for every new occasion: councils of war, councils of peace, feasts, the healing of a sick person, the seclusion of a shaman, a seer, a pregnant woman, a child to be initiated, etc.; the huts may be used only once and are abandoned afterward. See Josef Kohl, *Kitschi-Gami: Ein Beitrag zur Characteristik der amerikanischen Indianer* (Bremen: Schünemann's Verlag, 1859), I, 60.

[4] See Doolittle, *Social Life of the Chinese*, II, 217–28; Trumbull, *The Threshold Covenant*, p. 176, recalls the custom (English?) of striking a child at each birthday as many times as he has attained years, a rite which might be regarded as a rite of separation from the years that have passed.

this ceremony, performed at the moment when the child is to leave his mother's room, is intended to present him to the spirits of the house, especially the ones who preside over the outlets and exits, so that they may favor him?[1]

I have cited Chinese ceremonies in some detail because they show the order of rites which by degrees carry the individual from birth to adulthood in societies where there is no formal age grading. The period extending from birth to the beginning of adolescence, or to initiation, breaks up into stages whose length and number vary among different peoples. Thus among the southern Bantu, for instance, the period from the first to the second teething includes: (1) rites preceding the appearance of the first tooth; (2) a transitional period between the first and the second set of teeth; (3) at the beginning of this transition the burning of the mat mother and child have used as a bed, secretly performed in the bush by the mother, because the child is supposed to have "mastered his sleep"; (4) the period of instruction, in which a boy is taught that he must no longer sit with the women and is prevented from learning their secret language; he lives only with boys who are of his age or older and even has to leave the hut when his father enters. During the interval between the cutting of the first and second sets of teeth, the child is not informed about sexual phenomena; when the second teeth begin to appear, he is systematically taught about them. Various magical operations are terminated at this time, and only then is it permissible to have him work in the fields.[2] In short, the appearance of the second teeth marks a complete change in the child's life among some southern Bantu tribes and a lesser change among others. He is taken out of the group of women and children, but he will enter the adolescent group only through initiation ceremonies, and that of mature men only through ceremonies of marriage. (For other sets of

[1] J. Desparmet, "La mauresque et les maladies de l'enfance," *Revue des Études ethnographiques et sociologiques* (Paris), 1908, pp. 500–514.

[2] Dudley Kidd, *Savage Childhood: A Study of Kaffir Children* (London: Black, 1906), pp. 81–89.

rituals I refer the reader to the numerous monographs cited throughout this volume.)

In brief, an outline of childhood rites would include the following: the cutting of the umbilical cord, sprinkling and baths, loss of the remainder of the umbilical cord, naming, the first haircut, the first meal with the family, first teeth, first walk, first outing, circumcision, first dress according to the child's sex, etc. I will speak of circumcision in the next chapter; for the moment, a few words about naming and baptism are appropriate.

The rites of naming would merit a monograph to themselves. Though frequently studied,[1] I think they have never been considered in full detail or in their true light. When a child is named, he is both individualized and incorporated into society. He may be brought into the society at large, in which case there is a general celebration involving the whole village; this practice is most prevalent for a male child and is especially so if the boy is a son of the chief. Or he may be incorporated into a restricted group, such as the family in two ascending lines, the paternal family only, or the maternal family only. The variations in detail are countless. Sometimes the child is given a generic name, which indicates only that it is a boy or a girl, or the third or seventh child. Or he may be given the name of one of his ancestors in one line or another. Or he may be allowed to choose his name. Or he may change names as often as he changes age categories in childhood. Often, he first receives a vague name, then a known personal name, then a secret personal name, a family name, a clan name, the name of a secret society, and so forth.[2]

---

[1] See Tylor, *Primitive Culture*, II, 430, 441, 437, etc. On rites of naming, see also Voth, *Oraibi Natal Customs and Ceremonies*, pp. 55, 57; Walter William Skeat and C. O. Blagden, *Pagan Races of the Malay Peninsula* (London: Macmillan, 1906), II, 3 ff.; Doutté, *Merrâkech*, passim.

[2] I would like to point out that an adult's name can also be changed during his lifetime either as a result of special acts (honorable deeds, blunders, etc.; see Elsdon Best, "Maori Nomenclature," *Journal of the Royal Anthropological Institute*, XXXII [1902], 194–96) or systematically (bearing children, passing from one age group or "secret degree" to another, etc.; see an interesting case of the changing of

That the rite of naming the child is a rite of incorporation need not, I think, be demonstrated at length; the documents cited above in themselves prove it. An additional example is found in the description of the former practices in Gabon at the birth of a child:

A public crier announces the birth and claims for the child a name and a place among the living. Someone else, in a distant part of the village, acknowledges the fact and promises on the part of the people that the newborn infant shall be received into the community and have all the rights and immunities pertaining to the rest of the people. The people then assemble in the street, and the newborn infant is brought out and exhibited to public view. A basin of water is provided and the headman of the village or family sprinkles water upon it, giving it a name, and invoking a blessing that he may have health, grow up to manhood or womanhood, have numerous progeny, possess great riches, etc.[1]

It will be noted that in Gabon the rite of naming coexists with a rite which is strikingly analogous to baptism. Baptism has most often been regarded as a lustration, a purging and purifying rite,[2] i.e., a final rite of separation from the previous world, whether it be a secular world or one that is actually impure. This rite must be evaluated with care, however, for it may also signify incorporation when it is performed with consecrated rather than with ordinary water. In that case the person baptized not only loses an attribute but also gains one. This consideration leads us to examine a new set of ceremonies, ordinarily known as initiation rites.

First, however, I should mention that certain rites of

names with each ascending stage in life among the Pawnee: Alice Fletcher, "A Pawnee Ritual Used When Changing a Man's Name," *American Anthropologist*, N.S. I, 82 ff.).

[1] Sir Daniel Wilson, *Western Africa*, quoted by R. H. Nassau, *Fetichism in West Africa: Forty-one Years' Observation and Superstition* (London: Duckworth, 1904), pp. 212–13. A comparison could be made among Lasnet's accounts in *Une mission au Sénégal* (Paris: Chellamel, 1900): pp. 24 (Moors), 50 (Fulah), 64 (Lobi), 76 (Tukulörs), 88 (Mandingos), 127 (Wolofs), 145 (Serers).

[2] See Tylor (*Primitive Culture*, II, 430 ff.), who committed the fallacy noted in the text. For baptism as a rite of initiation, see Farnell, *The Evolution of Religion*, pp. 56, 57, 156–58.

exposure to the sun, the moon, or the earth ought also to be interpreted as rites of passage. It seems to me that Frazer and Dieterich have not understood their true meaning. Among peoples like the Bantu and the American Indians (especially the Pueblos and the Indians of Central America), for whom social and celestial worlds are intimately linked, it is natural that there should be rites incorporating the newborn with the celestial sphere, or at least with its chief elements. From this linkage are derived the rites of presentation to the moon and the sun, of contact with the earth, and so forth.[1] Similarly, even though totemism is defined as a system with an economic purpose, it is also natural that the child should, at one time or another, actually be incorporated with his totem, despite the fact that he is already related to it by birth. Rites of incorporation into a totem group, whether it be anthropo-animal, anthropo-vegetable, or anthropo-planetary, are an exact counterpart of rites of incorporation into the family, to which the newborn child would seem to belong automatically, from the very fact that he is born of a certain mother and undoubtedly of a certain father. Thus we are again brought to a consideration of rites of incorporation into defined groups.

[1] The presentation to the sun is very definitely a rite of incorporation among the Tarahumare (Karl Sofus Lumholtz, *Unknown Mexico*, Vol. I: *Among the Hopi*, p. 273), the Oraibi (Voth, *Oraibi Natal Customs and Ceremonies*), and the Zuñi (M. C. Stevenson, *The Zuni Indians: Their Mythology, Esoteric Fraternities, and Ceremonies* [Twenty-third Annual Report of the Bureau of American Ethnology, 1901–2 (Washington, D.C.: Government Printing Office, 1905)], *s.v.* "Birth," etc.). For cases of presentation to the moon, see Frazer, *Adonis, Attis, Osiris*, pp. 373 ff. Most of the rites described are sympathetic, the idea being that the moon's growth will aid the child's. The moon and the sun are sometimes totems, and in that case, as among certain American Indians, the presentation to the heavenly body is a rite of incorporation with the deity, the newborn child being thereafter considered a child of the sun.

VI INITIATION RITES

Age groups and secret societies have recently been the subject of two monographs, one by Schurtz[1] and the other by Webster.[2] Neither author has sufficiently examined the entrance ceremonies of these groups, however. Webster did devote a chapter to these ceremonies, but he studied them only in isolation and, strangely enough, did not think of comparing their patterns. Moreover, both authors, imbued with the notion that initiation coincides with puberty and that this physiological phenomenon is the point of departure for all such ceremonies, have launched into unacceptable general theories. Schurtz traces everything to an "instinct of sociability" or gregariousness, which fails to provide an explanation either of the variations in the institutions considered or of the nature of the ceremonies which correspond to them. Webster constructs a priori a hypothetical prototype of primitive age groups and secret societies, and he sees deviations and degenerations from it almost everywhere.

In this chapter, I shall first demonstrate that physiological puberty and "social puberty" are essentially different and only rarely converge. Then I shall examine initiation ceremonies of all sorts, including not only those which bring about admission to age groups and secret societies but also those which accompany the ordination of a priest or a magician, the enthroning of a king, the consecration of monks and nuns or of sacred prostitutes, and so forth.

The physical puberty of girls is marked by a swelling of the breasts, an enlargement of the pelvis, the appearance of pubic hair, and above all the first menstrual flow. Therefore it would seem simple to date the transition from childhood to adolescence from the first appearance of these signs. But from a social standpoint this is not the case, for reasons that

[1] H. Schurtz, *Altersklassen und Männerbünde* (Leipzig: G. Reiner, 1902).
[2] Webster, *Primitive Secret Societies*.

65

are primarily physiological. First, sexual enjoyment is not dependent on puberty, but may be experienced earlier or later, depending on the individual; orgasm may even appear several years earlier, so that puberty is important only for the ability to conceive. Second, the first menstrual bleeding does not occur at the same age among the various races, or among individuals within the same race. The variations are so great[1] that one cannot conceive of any institution being founded on an element as undeterminable and as irregular as puberty. Even in Europe the variations do not correspond to legal prescriptions. In Rome, girls are legally marriageable at the age of twelve, but only a twelfth of the Roman girls menstruate at that age; most of them begin to do so only between fourteen and fifteen, while others, very rarely, begin at nine. In Paris it is legal to be married at sixteen years and six months, but the average age at puberty is fourteen years and four months according to Brierre de Boismont and fifteen years and four months according to Aran, the wealthy classes having menses earlier than the working class. *Thus in Rome social puberty precedes physiological puberty, and in Paris it follows physiological puberty.*

Therefore it would be better to stop calling initiation rites "puberty rites." I would by no means deny that some peoples perform rites of physiological puberty which in rare

---

[1] Ploss (*Das Weib in Natur und Völkerkunde*, I, 394–420) collected a considerable quantity of documents on the subject of first menstruation, both normal and abnormal (starting with two months, etc.), among different peoples. The date of first menstruation depends at once on climate, diet, occupation, and heredity. The observers, mostly physicians, have found it very difficult to agree on the average age for the first menstruation in a large population taken as a whole (France, Russia, etc.) or even in a limited area (a large city, for example). It would indeed speak well for the Africans, Oceanic peoples, etc., as statisticians if we were to expect them to discover the average for their own tribes before any methodical study of the influence of climate and diet has been made. Here is a listing for 584 women of Tokyo: at 11 years, 2; 12 years, 2; 13 years, 26; 14 years, 78; 15 years, 224; 16 years, 228; 17 years, 68; 18 years, 44; 19 years, 10; 20 years, 2. Here are the averages for Africa: Wolofs, 11–12 years; Egypt, 10–13 years (Pruner-Bey) or 9–10 years (Rigler); Bogos, 16 years; Swahili, 12–13 years; Nyamwesi, 12–13 years; Berbers of Egypt, 15–16 years; Somali, 16 years; Loango, 14–15 years, rarely 12; Arabs of Algeria, 9–10 years; Fezzan, 10–15 years.

instances coincide with initiation rites. The girls are isolated, sometimes even considered dead and then resurrected.[1] But among other peoples there are no rites at that moment, although there are initiation rites.[2]

One is therefore led to think that most of these rites—whose sexual nature is not to be denied and which are said to make the individual a man or a woman, or fit to be one—fall into the same category as certain rites of cutting the umbilical cord, of childhood, and of adolescence. These are rites of separation from the asexual world, and they are followed by rites of incorporation into the world of sexuality and, in all societies and all social groups, into a group confined to persons of one sex or the other. This statement holds true especially for girls,[3] since the social activity of a woman is much simpler than that of a man.[4]

The question of physical puberty is even more complicated for boys than for girls; its variability is increased by the fact that the first emission of sperm may be preceded by emissions of mucus, that it often passes unnoticed by the subject, and, finally, that in most individuals it occurs only as a result of an external shock whose date depends on circumstances impossible to foresee or direct. Therefore a boy's puberty is established in the opinion of the public by the growth of a beard, pubic hair, etc. But in this respect, too, ethnic and individual variations are considerable.

Physical puberty is, for either sex, a very difficult mo-

---

[1] Factual material was collected by Frazer, in *The Golden Bough*, III, 204–23; see also Hutter, *Wanderungen und Forschungen*, p. 427; Stevenson, *The Zuñi*, pp. 303–4. C. Goddard Du Bois, *The Religion of the Luiseño Indians of Southern California* ("University of California Publications in American Archeology and Ethnology," Vol. VIII, No. 3 [1908]), pp. 93–96.

[2] Albert Ernest Jenks, *The Bontoc Igorrot* ("Philippine Islands Ethnological Survey Publications," No. 1 [Manila: Bureau of Publications, 1905]), p. 66.

[3] Identical findings would result from a comparison of the age of artificial defloration (perforation of the hymen) and that of puberty: the two have no relation to one another except in rare instances among one people. Moreover, the perforation of the hymen is not solely a preparation for coitus, whether nuptial, preceding marriage, or at the time of betrothal. On this rite, see among others Hartland, "Rite at the Temple of Mylitta," pp. 189–202.

[4] [American readers will no doubt take exception to this statement, though there are many societies for which it is valid, including van Gennep's own.]

ment to date, and this difficulty explains why so few ethnographers and explorers have inquired into it. Therefore it is even less excusable that the expression "puberty rites" should have been accepted as designating all the rites, ceremonies, and practices which among different peoples mark the transition from childhood to adolescence. It is appropriate to distinguish between *physical puberty* and *social puberty*, just as we distinguish between *physical kinship* (consanguinity) and *social kinship*, between *physical maturity* and *social maturity* (majority).

It is remarkable that even careful observers, who have at least published the exact details of their observations, did not know that they were dealing with two distinct phenomena and made use of the word "puberty" now in one sense, now in the other. The following are some examples of this confusion. After having described with care the "puberty ceremonies" of girls among the Thomson Indians, which were performed far from the village in a special hut and which included taboos, washings, sympathetic rites, etc., Teit adds: "Girls were often betrothed while mere infants to men sometimes twenty years their senior. They were considered marriageable only after they had finished the ceremonies attendant upon reaching the age of puberty. This was approximately in the seventeenth or eighteenth year but sometimes the ceremonies were continued until the twenty-third year."[1]

The reader will grant that physical puberty cannot be the chief cause of such lengthy ceremonies extending through several stages. Teit says explicitly that for the boys the ceremonies to be performed depended on the occupations (hunter, warrior, etc.) which they proposed to take up, and that they were begun by each adolescent on the day, usually sometime between his twelfth and his sixteenth year, when for the first time he dreamed of an arrow, a

[1] James Alexander Teit, *The Thomson Indians of British Columbia*, ed. Franz Boas ("American Museum of Natural History Memoirs," Vol. II; Jesup North Pacific Expedition Publications [New York: The Museum, 1900]), I, 311–17, 321.

canoe, or a woman.[1] Similarly, nothing in the "puberty ceremonies" among the Lillooet of British Columbia[2] indicates that they pertain to physical puberty. On the contrary, the fact that they extend over a long period for young men who want to become shamans proves that, as among the Chinese,[3] they concern social puberty. I should point out that in our society the age at which young men are allowed to marry does not coincide with the moment of their physiological puberty, and, if one day these two moments, one social and the other physical, come to coincide, they will do so as a result of scientific progress.

While among the Hottentots boys remain in the company of women and children until their eighteenth year,[4] the Elema of the Papuan Gulf perform the first ceremony for a child when he is five years old, the second at ten, and the third apparently only much later, since through it the child becomes a warrior who is free to marry.[5] In short, to the question asked by Frobenius[6]—"Does the moment of novitiate to some extent coincide with sexual maturity?" —I answer a definite no, without even attempting to formulate a precise reply. My view is confirmed by the fact that ceremonies of first menstruation[7] either occur among peoples who have no initiation rites or are emphasized more than later menses only because they concern the *first* appearance[8] of a phenomenon which afterward will always be accompanied by special rites which are due as much to the impurity of the woman herself as to her menstrual blood.

[1] *Ibid.*, pp. 317–18.

[2] James Alexander Teit, *The Lillooet Indians* ("American Museum of Natural History Memoirs," Vol. IV; Jesup North Pacific Expedition Publications [Leiden, 1906]), Vol. II, No. 5, 263–67.

[3] For previous discussion of the Chinese rites, see pp. 79, 85.

[4] Peter Kolb, *The Present State of the Cape of Good Hope*, trans. from the German by Medler (London: W. Innys, 1731), I, 121, quoted by Webster, *Primitive Secret Societies*, p. 24.

[5] J. Holmes, "Initiation Ceremonies of the Natives of the Papuan Gulf," *Journal of the Royal Anthropological Institute*, XXXII, (1902), 418–25.

[6] Leo Frobenius, "Die Masken und Geheimbünde Afrikas," *Nova acta Leopoldina*, etc. (Halle, 1898), p. 217.

[7] See among others, *The Golden Bough*, I, 326.   [8] See chap. ix.

The distinction between physical puberty and social puberty is most clearly apparent in certain ceremonies of the Todas, who are polyandrous and are betrothed from the age of three. Sometime before physiological puberty, a man who belongs to a clan different from the girl's comes to her village during the day; he lies down beside her and stretches out his coat so that it covers both of them. After they stay that way for a few minutes, the man leaves. Two weeks later, a strong and well-built man belonging to any section or clan comes to spend a night with the girl and deflower her. "This must take place *before puberty*, and it seemed that there were few things regarded as more disgraceful than that this ceremony should be delayed till after this period . . . it was even said that men might refuse to marry her."[1] The ceremonies of marriage do not begin until the age of fifteen or sixteen, or several years after puberty.

Variations in the age at which circumcision is practiced should themselves show that this is an act of social and not of physiological significance.[2] Among many peoples the operation is performed at fairly great intervals—for instance, every two, three, four, or five years—so that children of different degrees of sexual development are circumcised at the same time. Moreover, within a single region inhabited by populations of the same somatic type (race), remarkable variations will be found. Thus, in regions of Morocco explored by Doutté[3] one finds that the time of circumcision is, in Dukālla, from seven or eight days after birth up to twelve or thirteen years; among the Rahūna, between two and five years; in Fez, between two and ten years; at Tangiers, at eight years; among the Djabāla,[4] from five to ten years; around Mogador, from two to four years; in Algeria, at seven or eight years; and among

[1] Rivers, *The Todas*, p. 503.

[2] See to what strange conclusions Webster is led (*Primitive Secret Societies*, chap. ii, iii, pp. 36, 200–201, 205–6).

[3] Doutté, *Merrâkech*, pp. 262–63, 351–53, etc.

[4] [As used at present, the term "Djabāla" applies to an area which includes both the village of Dukālla and the Rahūna tribe cited.]

orthodox Moslems, the seventh day after birth or as soon as possible thereafter.[1] A similar picture may be drawn with the help of materials assembled by Andree[2] and by Dr. Lasnet[3] in Senegal. Thus the same rite sometimes marks the beginning of childhood, sometimes of adolescence, but it has nothing to do with physical puberty.

Few practices have been so much discussed at random. Of all the works known to me on the subject of circumcision, Andree's shows the greatest awareness of the complexity of the problem. However, he did not point out the important fact that circumcision cannot be understood if it is examined in isolation; it should be left within the category of all practices of the same order which by cutting off, splitting, or mutilating any part of the body modify the personality of the individual in a manner visible to all. Doutté has rightly compared circumcision with the first haircut and the ceremonies of the first teething,[4] and Lasch[5] and Westermarck[6] have compared it with other bodily mutilations; but the first was wrong in seeing these as rites of purification, the other two in interpreting the whole series of mutilations as practices meant to attract the female sex. Cutting off the foreskin is exactly equivalent to pulling out a tooth (in Australia, etc.), to cutting off the little finger above the last

[1] That the excision of the clitoris is also independent of physical puberty and characterizes social puberty (here the right to marry) is apparent from the following list, which I have drawn up according to Ploss, *Das Weib in Natur und Völkerkunde*, I, 248–49: Arabia, several weeks after birth; Somalis, 3–4 years; southern Egypt, 9-10 years; Nubia, early childhood; Abyssinia, about 8 years, or 80 days after birth; delta of the Niger, during childhood, no fixed time; Malinkes, Bambara, 12–15 years; Malays, etc., about the time of the second dentition; Javanese, 6–7 years; Makassarese, 3–7 years; Gorontalos, 9, 12, or 15 years, etc.

[2] Richard Andree, "Beschneidung," in *Ethnographische Parallelen*, 2d ser. (Leipzig, 1899), pp. 166–212.

[3] In Lasnet, *Une mission au Sénégal*, p. 14 (Moors, 7 years), p. 108 (Khasonke, in childhood and later up to 15 years, corresponding to a greater wealth of the family); the usual age (Fulah, p. 64; Malinke, p. 88; Serers, p. 145; etc.) is from ten to fifteen years, but circumcisions are performed at fairly long intervals, depending on the number of children.

[4] Doutté, *Merrâkech*, I, 353.

[5] R. Lasch, "Die Verstümmelung der Zähne in Amerika und Bemerkungen der Zahn Deformierung im allgemeinen," *Mitteilungen der anthropologischen Gesellschaft in Wien*, XXXI (1901), 21.

[6] Westermarck, *The Origin and Development of Moral Ideas*, I, 205.

joint (in South Africa), to cutting off the ear lobe or perforating the ear lobe or the septum, or to tattooing, scarifying, or cutting the hair in a particular fashion. The mutilated individual is removed from the common mass of
humanity by a rite of separation (this is the idea behind
cutting, piercing, etc.) which automatically incorporates
him into a defined group; since the operation leaves in-
eradicable traces, the incorporation is permanent. The
Jewish circumcision is in no way extraordinary: it is clearly
a "sign of union" with a particular deity and a mark of
membership in a single community of the faithful.[1]

Finally, if one also considers excision of the clitoris,[2] perforation of the hymen, section of the perineum, and subincision, it becomes apparent that the human body has
been treated like a simple piece of wood which each has cut
and trimmed to suit him: that which projected has been
cut off, partitions have been broken through, flat surfaces
have been carved—sometimes, as among the Australians,
with great imagination. Circumcision is among the simplest
and least serious of all these practices; and for the sake of
sensible interpretation it is really regrettable that the Jews
should have practiced it, for as a result Bible commentators
have given it a place apart which it in no way deserves. If

[1] James G. Frazer's theory ("The Origin of Circumcision," *Independent Review*,
IV [October, 1904–January, 1905], 204–18), that a part of the individual is sacrificed
to save the remainder, takes only a few facts into consideration; Crawley's (*The
Mystic Rose*, pp. 396, 397), that circumcision and perforation of the hymen aim "to
counteract the hylo-idealistic danger resulting from an apparent enclosure," is
almost fantasy; A. J. Reinach's ("La lutte de Jacob et de Moïse avec Jahvé et
l'origine de la circoncision," *Revue des Études ethnologiques et sociologiques*, 1908,
pp. 360–62), that circumcision is a kind of *blood covenant*, introduces an unnecessary
factor—that of blood (for it would have to be proved that the blood from the wound,
of which there is precious little, was collected and made the object of additional
rites); furthermore, even if his explanation is valid for the Jews, it does not explain
either circumcision or excision found among the semi-civilized peoples. As a last
resort, Andree also turned to an explanation on the basis of the sacredness of the
blood spilled, "Beschneidung," pp. 206–7).

[2] The length of the clitoris varies with individuals and races. In certain cases, the
object of the excision may be to remove the appendage by which the female
resembles the male (a view which is correct from an anatomical point of view), and
the operation is nothing more than a rite of sexual differentiation on the same order
as the first (ritual) assigning of dress, instruments, or tools proper to each sex.

the Jews had linked themselves with Yahweh by perforating the septum, how much fewer would have been the errors in ethnographic literature?

It will be apparent that I do not see any relation between circumcision and procreation, for several reasons: (1) because the age at which it is practiced varies from the seventh day to the twentieth year (or later in the case of adoption, of conversion to Judaism or Islam, etc.); (2) because it is practiced, together with other mutilations of the sex organs, by peoples who are ignorant of the physiological basis of procreation;[1] and (3) because it tends to hinder coitus, since desire is reduced by a lesser sensitivity of the *glans penis*. Similarly, excision of the clitoris (that is removal of an erogenous center), section of the perineum, and subincision of the penis also diminish sexual excitability. Actually, semicivilized peoples did not look that far; they cut those organs which, like the nose or the ear, attract the eye because they project and which can, because of their histological constitution, undergo all sorts of treatment without harming an individual's life or activity.[2]

[1] See van Gennep, *Mythes et légendes d'Australie*, chap. v, and "Questions australiennes," *Man*, Vols. VII (1907), VIII (1908).

[2] The detached foreskin is either destroyed or saved, etc. The variation of customs in this regard is without limit, as has been said with reference to the umbilical cord, hair, etc. (see above, p. 51). It should be noted that the length of the foreskin varies with races; it is relatively short among the light-skinned people of Europe and disproportionately long among the Negroes and Arabs. Extensive inquiries on this point would be of great use. The old theory of the sexual significance of circumcision is still held by Père Marie-Joseph Lagrange (see *Études sur les religions sémitiques* [Paris: Lecoffre, J. Gabalda, 1903], pp. 242 ff.): "It is as if through a bloody sacrifice the sexual life to which the young man is henceforth admitted is consecrated," and by Peter Wilhelm Schmidt (in *L'origine de l'idée de Dieu*, chap. iv, trans. J. J. Pietes, *Anthropos* [Vienna, 1908], pp. 602–3 n.): "It seems more and more evident among the semicivilized peoples that circumcision was supposed, according to their simple and incorrect ideas, to facilitate the reproductive act, and it is usually performed during mysterious puberty feasts when manhood is reached." Fewer words could not express all the theoretical errors made by these two scholars. As for Preuss (in "Der Ursprung der Religion und Kunst," p. 362), he thinks that circumcision would help "the generative breath" through which the father transmits his soul to the child; likewise, Schurtz believes that the purpose of circumcision is to increase fertility (*Altersklassen und Männerbünde*, pp. 96–97). This would all be very well if semicivilized people knew as much as our physicians and more than our peasants about what regulates the mechanisms of conception. To those who are interested in

73

Whether each type of mutilation was invented only once and transmitted from people to people by borrowing, or whether each was invented several times independently, is a question without interest to the purposes of this work. I only want to point out that, since each type of mutilation was a procedure of collective differentiation, there could be no borrowing between adjacent tribes; it could occur only when a particular form was still unknown and would serve to further differentiate a given group from their neighbors.

Mutilations are a means of permanent differentiation; there are also temporary differentiations such as the wearing of a special dress or mask, or body painting (chiefly with colored clay). The temporary ones play a considerable role in rites of passage, since they are repeated at every change in an individual's life.

After this introduction I can now make a detailed examination of several sequences; shall begin with initiation into totem groups. Thanks primarily to Spencer and Gillen,[1] Roth,[2] Howitt,[3] and Matthews,[4] the ceremonies of initiation into totem groups are known down to the most minute details for several Australian tribes. These ceremonies last from the tenth to the thirtieth year. The first act is a separation from the previous environment, the world of women and children. The novice is secluded in the bush, in a special place, in a special hut, etc., just as a pregnant woman is; and the seclusion is accompanied by all sorts of taboos, primarily of a dietary nature. Sometimes the novice's link with his mother endures for some time, but a moment always

this subject, I highly recommend Havelock Ellis, *Studies in the Psychology of Sex* (London: Society of Psychological Research, 1904); Ploss, *Das Weib in Natur und Völkerkunde*; and in general other studies on physiological and psychological sexual matters.

[1] Spencer and Gillen, *Native Tribes of Central Australia*, pp. 212–386; *The Northern Tribes of Central Australia*, pp. 328–79.

[2] W. E. Roth, *Ethnological Studies among the West-central Queensland Aborigines* (Brisbane: E. Gregory, 1897); *North Queensland Ethnography Bulletin* (Brisbane), 1901 ff.

[3] Howitt, *The Native Tribes of South-east Australia*, pp. 509–677.

[4] R. H. Matthews, numerous articles in anthropological reviews of Paris, Vienna London, Washington, and the learned societies of Australia.

comes when, apparently by a violent action, he is finally separated from his mother, who often weeps for him. As Howitt says of the Kurnai:

The intention of all that is done at this ceremony is to make a momentous change in the boy's life; the past is to be cut off from him by a gulf which he can never re-pass. His connection with his mother as her child is broken off, and he becomes henceforth attached to the men. All the sports and games of his boyhood are to be abandoned with the severance of the old domestic ties between himself and his mother and sisters. He is now to be a man, instructed in and sensible of the duties which devolve upon him as a member of the Murring community.[1]

What Howitt says about the ceremonies of the Kurnai is also true for the other tribes of south, southeast, and central Australia.

In some tribes the novice is considered dead, and he remains dead for the duration of his novitiate. It lasts for a fairly long time and consists of a physical and mental weakening which is undoubtedly intended to make him lose all recollection of his childhood existence. Then follows the positive part: instruction in tribal law and a gradual education as the novice witnesses totem ceremonies, recitations of myths, etc. The final act is a religious ceremony (where there is a belief in Daramulun, etc.) and, above all, a special mutilation which varies with the tribe (a tooth is removed, the penis is incised, etc.) and which makes the novice forever identical with the adult members. Sometimes the initiation takes place all at once, sometimes in stages. Where the novice is considered dead, he is resurrected and taught how to live, but differently than in childhood. Whatever the variations of detail, a series which conforms to the general pattern of rites of passage can always be discerned.[2]

---

[1] Howitt, *The Native Tribes of South-east Australia*, p. 532.

[2] Generally, an exaggerated importance has been placed on what happens to the severed foreskin. As I have said, this portion of the body comprised a part of the person from whom it was removed, but no more so than hair that had been cut off, nail parings, saliva, urine, or teeth that had been extracted, all as a part of initia-

Magico-religious "fraternities" are essentially based on a clan organization—that is, on social kinship—but they are a thing apart. Although in British Columbia the totem clan still remains identical with the fraternity, it exists side by side with the fraternity on the Great Plains and has disappeared among the Pueblo Indians, where the fraternity is formed on a territorial basis (e.g., the Tusayan, the Hopi, etc.).[1] For the initiation ceremonies of the Kwakiutl, I refer the reader to Boas' memoir.[2] Among the Australians the right to belong to a totem group is hereditarily transmitted; among the Kwakiutl it may be acquired by marriage as well; but, in any event, an individual can enter totem groups only through ceremonies of passage which separate him from his previous environment and incorporate him into his new restricted environment. Among the Australians a child is separated from his mother, from women, and from children. Among the Kwakiutl the previous world is personified by a "spirit" which must be exorcised—a point of view which is identical to that of Christians who exorcise Satan at the time of baptism. The idea of death and resurrection is also present. Finally, for the Kwakiutl, incorporation into the group consists of acquisition of the "spirit" who is the pro-

tion. Among the Australian tribes who practice this rite, the tooth is picked up and carefully saved (*ibid.*, pp. 542, 562, 565, 569 ff.; Spencer and Gillen, *The Northern Tribes of Central Australia*, p. 594), or pulverized, mixed with meat, and swallowed by the mother of the girl to be initiated or the mother-in-law of the boy, or it is thrown into a small pond in order to drive the rain away, or buried (*ibid.*, pp. 593, 594). The tooth is always a sacred object to some degree (*ibid.*, pp. 594–95); however, among the Kaitish, the tooth is left where it has fallen, and it is not believed that it can be used as part of magical operating (*ibid.*, p. 589). If then it is only a question of its part in rites, I cannot see how the foreskin would be the seat of vital power more than the hair, teeth, fingernails, urine, blood defecation, etc.; it surely cannot be that of reproductive power or some kind of a live or independent embryo.

[1] [Van Gennep is misinformed on this point. The Pueblo clans still exist and are intertwined with the system of fraternities, though not identical with them (see Fred Eggan, *Social Organization of the Western Pueblos* [Chicago: University of Chicago Press, 1950]).]

[2] Franz Boas, "The Social Organization and the Secret Societies of the Kwakiutl Indians," *U.S. National Museum Reports*, 1895 (Washington, D.C., 1897), pp. 315–733; report analyzed in detail by Schurtz (except for rites) and by Hutton Webster; see also *Handbook of the American Indians*, ed. Frederick Hodge (Bulletin of the Bureau of American Ethnology No. 30 [Washington, D.C., 1907]), Vol. I, *s.v.* "Kwakiutl."

tector of the whole clan and is the equivalent of the Australian totem.

The animistic element is even more marked among the Omaha and Ojibway, where the acquired protector is more individualized than among the Kwakiutl and loses his generic character. Kohl[1] has described in detail the Ojibway ceremonies of entrance into the "order of the Mide," whose sequence is as follows: a sacred hut is built;[2] the child is attached to a board and during the entire ceremony behaves as if he had lost all personality; the participants are dressed, painted, etc.; there is a general procession to the interior of the hut; the chiefs-magicians-priests kill all the participants and resurrect them one after the other; the procession, the massacre, and the resurrection take place after every important scene of the ceremony; the father, accompanied by men and women sponsors, presents his child to the chiefs and then dances with those who accompany him. This continues until noon. In the afternoon the sacra are laid out in the center of the hut. They consist of boughs covered with a cloth, and a procession moves around them once, twice, five times, until the cloth is covered with a pile of colored shells that each participant drops from his mouth. Then the procession begins again, and each person in passing picks up a shell, which, having become sacred, can serve as powerful "medicine." Each in turn beats the sacred drum and sings a sort of prayer, and the men all smoke (a ritual act). Toward evening, the chiefs and priests receive gifts from the father, to whom they give in exchange "medicines," amulets, etc.; the grandfather makes a speech calling for "the divine benediction of Gitchi Manito"; a meal of maize cooked in water is eaten in common, and the children partake of it. During the course of the ceremony, the child receives a name.

Among the Zuñi of New Mexico[3] each male child must be

---

[1] Kohl, *Kitschi-Gami*, I, 59–76.   [2] *Ibid.*, II, 71.

[3] Stevenson, *The Zuñi*, pp. 65, 490–511, 522–27, 532–49, 550–64, 570–72, 578 ff.; then 413, 415, 421, 426, etc.; also 103–94. For initiation of children in early childhood, see pp. 94–101.

received in the Ko'tikili (or Katcina society)[1] and associated with one of the *kiwitsiwe* (the sacred ceremonial house popularly termed "kiva"), which should be that of the husband, eldest son, or eldest brother of the midwife who brought the child into the world. The same man serves as the child's sponsor at initiation, which may be either involuntary (at an early age) or voluntary (at about twelve or thirteen years). In addition, every individual, man or woman, belongs to several magico-medical or rain "fraternities," for each of which there is a different initiation rite.

The following is an outline of rites for entering the Ko'tikili through voluntary initiation: The sponsor introduces the novice into the kiva. Two women place on the novice's back four rugs folded into four parts. The sponsor wraps the novice's head in a cloth, so that he cannot see anything. The novice is struck on the back with yucca branches four times by each of the Sayathlia gods (men wearing masks). Each woman is struck once on the back with a yucca branch by each Sayathlia, and the four rugs are removed. The young man is again struck four times by each god. The sponsor takes the cloth off the novice's head and attaches to his hair an eagle's feather, which is a sacred ornament. The four gods remove their masks, and the novice recognizes them as men. Four novices are brought before the four Sayathlia, and each receives from them a mask and a yucca branch. With this branch the novices strike each Sayathlia on his right and left arms and right and left ankles. The novices give each Sayathlia back his mask. The latter put their masks back on and strike each sponsor on the arms and ankles, and the initiation is terminated.

It will be noted that in this ceremony whipping is clearly first a rite of separation, then a rite of incorporation.[2] The

---

[1] [This group—also referred to as the Kotikane—has a membership of all adult males. The impersonators of the gods are drawn from among them (see Ruth Bunzel, "Introduction to Zuñi Ceremonialism," *Forty-fourth Annual Report of the Bureau of American Ethnology* [Washington, D.C., 1932], pp. 516–17).]

[2] On whipping as a rite of initiation, see interesting facts in Lafitau, *Mœurs des sauvages amériquains,* I, 273.

same use of whipping is to be found in the initiation rites of the Navaho,[1] which are almost identical to those described above; the only differences lie in the number of divine actors, number of blows received, etc. Navaho novices are also sprinkled with corn meal; women, in their initiation, are in addition touched with special sacra (an ear of corn with four grains very close together, attached to four branches of yucca). The soles of the feet, the palms and forearms, the top of the breast and the collarbones, the shoulder blades, and the two peaks of the head are in succession touched with the sacra and sprinkled with corn meal. The similarity of these rites to those of Christian baptism will be noted; they are rites of incorporation into the community. It should be added that there is no set age for initiation and that the same series of rites has to be repeated four times to enable an individual to participate in all ceremonies without exception and to wear the sacred masks. At the close of the ceremony the novice puts on the mask, sprinkles the mask with sacred powder, and inhales sacred smoke. In the beginning, a receptacle is overturned to serve as a drum; at the end it is turned upright, and the ceremony is completed.

Before examining other sets of rites I should like to call attention to one fact: in North America, as in Australia, the sacra are unveiled to the novices; they are revealed respectively as masks and bull-roarers.[2] The exposing of these bogymen of their childhood is the central event of the ritual. Furthermore, it is the privilege of the initiated to manipulate the sacra according to precise rules without danger from the supernatural. These elements also constitute the culminating points of initiation into Asian and Greek mysteries.

A very interesting ritual is the repeated baptism undergone by the Sabians,[3] whose religion was supposedly founded

[1] Washington Matthews, *The Night Chant:* A Navaho Ceremony (Memoir of the American Museum of Natural History, Vol. VI [New York, 1902]), pp. 116–20.

[2] Regarding divine bogymen, see my *Mythes et légendes d'Australie,* chap. vii.

[3] [The Sabians are also known as Mandaeans. It has been suggested that their claim upon John the Baptist was due in part to missionary influence, in part to expediency (see W. Brandt in *Hastings Encyclopedia of Religion and Ethics* for discussion and further references).]

by John the Baptist and is a mixture of Mazdaism, Judaism, Christianity, Islam, etc. There are three categories of baptism: that of the child (at one year), that which purifies or cleanses of various pollutions, and the collective baptism, lasting for the five days of the annual celebration of Pancho. One is Sabian by birth; no stranger can be admitted to the religion of the Subba, and there is therefore no rite of separation. This fact places the Sabian group in a special category.[1]

The "secret societies" of Oceania (excepting Australia) and Africa do not have for their purpose the control of nature, as do totem clans and fraternities. Though they appear to be magico-religious in nature, their object is more political and economic in the worldly sense. Nevertheless, the general tenor and often even the details of their initiation rites are similar to those just discussed. The parallelism is especially striking for the rites of the Congo, described in detail by De Jonghe.[2] Unfortunately, he saw them as "puberty rites," although the age of novices varied from seven to twenty years, with the usual age falling between ten and fifteen.[3]

The precise age of physiological puberty for the Negroes of the Congo is not known. All members of the lower Congo tribes are not obligated to join *nkímba* or *nyembo*, so that these are really special restricted groups—which I shall continue to call "secret," although this term is not strictly accurate[4]—and puberty, procreation, and the right to marry are not involved in their initiation ceremonies. In the Congo, as on the Gulf of Guinea, secret society memberships cut

---

[1] For details, see Nicolas Siouffi, *Études sur la religion des Soubbas ou Sabéens: Leurs dogmes, leurs mœurs* (Paris: Imprimerie Nationale, 1880), pp. 76–82.

[2] Edouard de Jonghe, *Les sociétés secrètes au Bas-Congo*, reprinted from *Revue des questions historiques* (Brussels), October, 1907. Frobenius' "Die Masken und Geheimbünde Afrikas" should be consulted only with the greatest caution; De Jonghe's data should be supplemented by Nassau, *Fetichism in West Africa*, pp. 250 ff., 263, and by Pechüel-Loesche, *Volkskunde von Loango*, p. 452.

[3] See De Jonghe, *Les sociétés secrètes au Bas-Congo*, pp. 21–23.

[4] All the ordinary members of the tribe know full well who does or does not belong to the society, while in Europe, for example, we do not know, at least in theory, who is or is not a freemason.

across tribes (geographic units). Only the most intelligent sons of free men or of rich slaves are admitted.

The ceremonies last two months to six years, their length varying with the tribe and with the observers. They include all sorts of negative rites (taboos) and positive rites. The order of rites is as follows: the novice is separated from his previous environment, in relation to which he is dead, in order to be incorporated into his new one. He is taken into the forest,[1] where he is subjected to seclusion, lustration, flagellation, and intoxication with palm wine, resulting in anesthesia.[2] Then come the transition rites, including bodily mutilations (circumcision, sometimes practised at an early age and in no relation to the secret society) and painting of the body (in white,[3] in red); since the novices are considered dead during their trial period, they go about naked and may neither leave their retreat nor show themselves to men; the *ngànga* (a priest-magician) instructs them; they speak a special language and eat special food (dietary taboos).

The trial period is followed by rites of reintegration into the previous environment, an element which need not exist for initiates into a totem clan or a fraternity. The initiates pretend not to know how to walk or eat and, in general, act as if they were newly born (resurrected) and must relearn all the gestures of ordinary life. Before they enter the relearning process, which takes several months, the initiates bathe in a stream, and the sacred hut is burned.

---

[1] Since the first part of most of the ceremonials studied in this book was a more or less confined and long seclusion, it seems useless to discuss the strange interpretations of De Jonghe, *ibid.*, p. 30, and of Frobenius, "Die Masken und Geheimbünde Afrikas," *passim.*

[2] The initiate's anesthesia is an important factor in the rite of initiation. In America, it is accomplished by swallowing tobacco or peyote; elsewhere by fumigations, flagellations, poor treatment, corporal punishment, etc. The purpose is to make the novice "die," to make him forget his former personality and his former world.

[3] On this subject, see Frazer, *The Golden Bough*, III, 430, and a note by Webster (*Primitive Secret Societies*, p. 44), who points out that white is often considered the color assumed by the dead, so it would seem that this custom too indicates that the novice is "dead."

In short, there is a double series: rites of separation from the usual environment, rites of incorporation into the sacred environment; a transitional period; rites of separation from the local sacred environment, rites of incorporation into the usual environment. But as a result of this passage through the sacred world, the initiate retains a special magico-religious quality. The initiation ceremonies of the Yaunde of the southern Cameroons[1] and of the peoples of the Gulf of Guinea in general (the secret societies of Poro, Ékpò, Orò, Mumbo-Jumbo, etc.) also conform to this pattern.

For data on secret societies of Melanesia I first refer the reader to the excellent book by Codrington,[2] who describes the initiation ceremonies of Fiji, the Banks Islands, and the New Hebrides. The author is not certain whether or not there is a relationship between these associations and totemism.[3] Recently Parkinson[4] has provided new data on the secret societies of the Bismarck Archipelago and the Solomon Islands known as Duk-duk. The following is the order of their rites, which vary only slightly, even in their details: The novice is taken to the sacred place. There he is beaten with more or less heavy sticks (depending on his age) by the *tubuan*, a sort of divine bogyman. The novices's screams are answered from afar by the lamentations of his mother and other relatives. The sponsor distributes gifts to those present and gives the novice something to eat. The *tubuan* undresses completely, so that the novice recognizes that he is a man. The *tubuan's* clothing stands alone because it is armored, proving that it is imbued with power (the Melanesian mana). The participants dance and teach their dance and the secrets of the society to the novices. All the

[1] For details, see Frobenius, "Die Masken und Geheimbünde Afrikas," pp. 67–74, taken from Zenker, *Mitteilungen aus den deutschen Schutzgebieten*, Vol. VIII (1895).

[2] R. H. Codrington, *The Melanesians* (London: Frowde, 1891), pp. 69–100.

[3] On the subject of Melanesian totemism, see discussion by Andrew Lang and J. J. Atkinson, *Social Origins: Primal Law* (London: Longmans, Green, 1903), pp. 176–207.

[4] R. Parkinson, *Dreissig Jahre in der Südsee: Land und Leute, Sitten und Gebräuche im Bismarck Archipel und auf den deutschen Salmoninseln* (Stuttgart: Strecker & Schröder, 1907), pp. 567–612, 582–86.

participants share a meal. Novices about twelve years old receive ceremonial costumes, but small children have to wait several years for them. The gift of the costume, which concludes the initiation, is made on another day and according to a special ceremony. Again there emerges a pattern of rites of separation, transition, and incorporation.[1]

The same pattern is apparent in Fijian ceremonies, which include a rite requiring the novice to pass between two supposed corpses, painted black from head to foot, whose entrails (actually those of pigs that have been sacrificed) are hanging out.[2]

The Arioi—a political, warrior, and plundering association of Tahiti and other parts of Polynesia—included seven classes, grades, or degrees, whose members could be distinguished by taboos which grew increasingly complicated and numerous as one rose in the hierarchy.[3] Members of the association were recruited from all classes of society. Whoever wanted to join presented himself, dressed and decorated in an unusual fashion, and behaved as if mentally deranged; if the Arioi thought him useful, they adopted him as a servant. This first act, through which a person showed that he differed from the common run, is to my mind a voluntary rite of separation. After some time the novice was incorporated: his name was changed; he was required to kill his children; he had to learn a particular posture necessary for the singing of a certain sacred chant; and he seized the dress of the chief's wife and thus entered into the seventh class.

The passage to the next grade was made as follows: All the Arioi met in ceremonial costume. An invocation was

[1] Boys of the Gazelle Peninsula join a children's society called "Marawol" or "Ingiet" by having their fathers or uncles make a gift of local money to the secret society; but their novitiate, which consists of learning special and extremely complicated dances, lasts a long time. On the basis of Parkinson's data (*ibid.*, pp. 598 ff.), this society appears to me to belong to the same category as certain magical-medicinal fraternities of the Zuñi.

[2] A detailed description, which completes those given by Fison and by Joske, may be found in Basil Thomson's *The Fijians: A Study of the Decay of Custom* (London, 1908), pp. 148–57.

[3] William Ellis, *Polynesian Researches* (8th ed.; London: Fisher, 1829), I, 319–24.

83

made to the sacred pig and to the national temples, and the names of candidates were listed, together with the degreee to which they aspired. There was a processional entrancs into the temple, and an offering to the god was made by the candidate; it consisted of a sacred pig, which was either killed and eaten in common or let loose. A great feast was held, accompanied by lifting of the sexual and dietary taboos to which each grade ordinarily had to adhere; from Ellis' account it would appear that there was not only heterosexual debauchery but also sodomy.[1] There were music, dancing, and dramatic presentations. The candidate was tattooed according to his new grade.

Melanesian ceremonies[2] marking entrance into a grade and passage from one to another are simpler than those of the Arioi. The central elements consist of a ceremonial exchange of coins (on Mota in the Banks Islands) or mats (on Oba), gifts of pigs to members of the association (the *suqe*, *huqe*, etc.), and ceremonial feasts called *kole*, which are reminiscent of the potlatch, of British Columbia. Although the significance of the *suqe* is primarily social and economic, the magico-religious element is apparent in the fact that the passage from one degree to another (on the Banks Islands there are eighteen degrees) is based on an individual's wealth, which in turn is dependent on his mana. Consequently, the higher an individual's rank in the *suqe*, the more he is considered to be imbued with mana, and each degree in the *suqe* has a given quantity of mana. The concepts of manito, orenda, and nagual play similar roles in American Indian fraternities.[3]

With regard to the initiation into age groups, I shall here examine in detail only the ceremonies of the Masai. The fact that among several Australian tribes the rites are

[1] William Ellis, *Polynesian Researches*, p. 325.

[2] Codrington, *The Melanesians*, pp. 101–15. Also see pp. 110–12 for a very interesting passage on the magico-religious importance of communal ceremonial meals, and p. 103 on the subject of mana.

[3] [Students of the American Indian will realize that all these concepts are not entirely parallel.]

spread over a fairly long time caused Schurtz[1] and Webster[2] to confuse the passage to successive age groups with rites of initiation into a totem group.

Among the Masai "puberty occurs about the age of twelve,"[3] and the circumcision of boys occurs "as soon as they are sufficiently strong, that is, between the ages of twelve and sixteen." It is sometimes performed sooner if the parents are rich, but if they are poor the ceremony is put off till they are able to pay the cost—proof that here, too, social puberty differs from physical puberty. The circumcision takes place every four or five years, and all those who are circumcised at the same time form an age group bearing a special name chosen by the chief. Among the Masai of Kenya a boy cannot undergo circumcision, or a girl clitoral excision, unless the father has performed a ceremony called "passing over the fence," which signifies his acceptance of the status of an "old man," to be called from then on "Father-of- (his child)."[4]

The order of their circumcision ceremonies is as follows: all the candidates assemble, without weapons. They smear themselves with white clay and wander from kraal to kraal for two or three months. Their heads are shaved, and an ox or a sheep is killed. The morning after the slaughter each candidate cuts down a tree (a species of asparagus) which the girls plant in front of his hut. The following morning the boys go out into the cold air and wash with cold water (to toughen themselves, according to Merker). The operator cuts the foreskin; an ox hide containing the blood which has been shed is placed on each boy's bed. The boys remain shut up for four days. Then they come out and tease the girls and often dress as women; they paint their faces with white clay. They adorn their heads with small birds and

[1] Schurtz, *Altersklassen und Männerbünde*, pp. 141–51; in his discussion has also introduced another category, matrimonial groups and phratries.

[2] Webster, *Primitive Secret Societies*, pp. 84–85.

[3] Merker, *Die Masai*, p. 55; no doubt physical puberty is in question, but he does not state whether it is that of the boys or the girls; see also pp. 60–61.

[4] A. Hollis, *The Masai: Their Language and Folklore* (London: Frowde, 1905), pp. 294–95, also pp. 296–99.

ostrich feathers. When they are healed, their heads are shaved; when their hair grows back sufficiently to be combed, they are called *múrràni*, or warriors.

In the girls' ceremony, an ox or a sheep is killed, the excision is performed in the house; the girls adorn their heads with leaves of the doom palm or with grasses; when they are healed, they are married off. Among the Masai of Tanganyika, the rites for the boys is the same as that cited above, except that after the operation there is a great feast in which the fathers of those circumcised and all the men of the neighborhood participate; the young warriors (bachelors) dance and amuse themselves with the girls, their mistresses; the seclusion of those operated upon lasts seven days; and on the day they first come out, they kill a white goat, divide the flesh among themselves, and throw the bones in the fire. The rites for the girls differ in the following respects: several are excised at a time; their heads are shaved; they remain at home until scar tissue forms on the wound; they adorn their heads with grasses, among which they place an ostrich feather, and smear their faces with white clay; all the women of the kraal eat a communal meal; and the marriage takes place as soon as the fiancé is able to pay what he owes on the dowry.

Though the ceremonies in question are independent of puberty, they are of a sexual nature, since they incorporate the boys and girls into the adult society of the sexes. It will be noted, moreover, that although the purpose of the girls' operation is marriage, it is marriage as a social institution, not as a sexual union. Before the clitoral excision, beginning at an age not indicated by Merker, little girls live in the kraal of the young warriors (first age group), and each has one or more lovers, under the absolute condition that she must not become pregnant.[1]

For the girls, the next age group is that of married women, and the last age group is marked by gray hair and the

---

[1] Merker, *Die Masai*, pp. 60–66; pp. 83, 66–67 for details on marriage, which for the Masai involves a change in one's way of life much more complete than among us.

menopause. The young lads have first been boys (*ayíoni*), then candidates (*sípolio*); for two years, as warriors, they are novices or apprentices (*barnoti*), and after that they become full-fledged warriors (*múrráni*). They remain in this group until they are twenty-eight to thirty years old, when they marry and become adults (*moruo*). Here, as among many other peoples, marriage ceremonies are rites of passage from one age group to another.

I also want to mention the rites of the Yao, because they are at once rites of age groups and rites of successive stages and transitions similar to those found, for example, among the Toda of India. The *unyago* of the girls is divided into four stages: (1) *Ciputu*, from the age of seven, eight, or nine until the first menses—marked by seclusion, sexual instruction, systematic deformation of the *labia minora* to a length of seven centimeters or more, erotic dances, etc. (2) *Matengusi*, celebration of the first menstruation. The girl is secluded and taught the taboos pertaining to the menstrual period. Although during the *ciputu* the girl gets married, she leaves her husband at the first menses. (3) *Citumbu* rites of the first pregnancy; during the fifth month, the woman's head is shaved; she is given instruction pertaining to maternity and is taught the taboos for pregnant women. (4) *Wamwana*, first childbirth; the husband does not obtain the right to resume sexual relations except by asking the village chief, after the child is able to sit or when he is six or seven months old. The solidarity of the sexes is very clearly expressed in all these ceremonies.[1] One can see how "initiation rites" become extended among the Yao.

Among some American Indians (Arapaho, etc.)[2] the passage from one age group to another involves a ritual whose nature is more or less magico-religious, but among most peoples who have age groups, advancement is determined

[1] K. Weule, *Wissenschaftliche Ergebnisse meiner ethnographischen Forschungsreise in den Südosten Ostafrikas* ("Mitteilungen der deutschen Schutzgebieten," Ergänzungsheft [Berlin, 1908]), No. 1, Part 4, pp. 31–34.

[2] Alfred Louis Kroeber, *The Arapaho* (Bulletin of the American Museum of Natural History [New York, 1902–17]), XVIII, Parts I, II, IV, 156–58.

by prowess in war or raiding, or by all sorts of presents and feast giving, and age is never very rigidly taken into account.

I now move on to the rites of entering Christianity, Islam, and the ancient mysteries, although the last belong to the same category as the magico-religious fraternities of the Pueblo Indians. But Christianity borrowed so extensively from the Egyptian, Syrian, Asiatic, and Greek mysteries that it is difficult to understand the one without taking the others into account. The economic end—sometimes specifically agricultural, sometimes generally economic (a multiplication of all the means of subsistence and life, of animals, vegetables, the fertility of the earth, irrigation, etc., the regular course of the divine stars which condition life in general)—of the ancient mysteries (Osiris, Isis, Adonis, the Syrian goddess, Attis, Dionysus, and even Orphism, etc.) has been established by the researches of Mannhardt,[1] Frazer,[2] Reinach,[3] Harrison,[4] Goblet d'Alviella,[5] Cumont,[6] and several others. But the rites which constitute these ceremonies have been closely studied only as sympathetic rites of multiplication or fertility and as a means of coercing cosmic and terrestrial processes.

The pattern of these rites, on the other hand, has hardly been examined,[7] although the study of certain modern rituals which are known in the greatest detail (for Australia and the Pueblo Indians), as well as an examination of ancient books of ritual (of Egypt and India), shows that the main outline, and sometimes the smallest details, the order in which rites follow each other and must be executed

---

[1] Mannhardt, *Antike Wald und Feldkulte.*

[2] Frazer, *The Golden Bough; Adonis, Attis, Osiris.*

[3] Reinach, *Cultes, mythes, et religions,* 3 vols. [Vols. IV and V appeared 1912 and 1923, respectively.] See especially I, 85–122.

[4] Harrison, *Prolegomena to the Study of Greek Religion.*

[5] Eugène Goblet d'Alviella, "De quelques problèmes relatifs aux mystères d'Éleusis," *Revue de l'histoire des religions,* Vol. XLVI (1902), Nos. 2, 3; Vol. XLVII (1903), Nos. 1, 2.

[6] Franz Cumont, *Les religions orientales dans le paganisme romain* (Paris: E. Leroux, 1906).

[7] Harrison (*Prolegomena to the Study of Greek Religion,* p. 155) even writes: "the exact order of the different rites of initiation is certainly of little importance."

is a magico-religious element in itself of fundamental significance. The primary purpose of this book is precisely to react against the "folkloristic" or "anthropological" procedure, which consists of extracting various rites—whether positive or negative—from a set of ceremonies and considering them in isolation, thus removing them from a context which gives them meaning and reveals their position in a dynamic whole.

"Mysteries," as defined by Harrison, are "a rite at which are exhibited certain *sacra* which may not be seen by the worshipper if he has not undergone a certain purification."[1] As I use the term, "mysteries" comprise the ceremonial whole which transfers the neophyte from the profane to the sacred world and places him in direct and permanent communication with the latter. The display of sacra at Eleusis, as also in Australia (churinga, sacred bull-roarer) or in America (masks, sacred ears of corn, katcinas, etc.), is the culminating rite but does not by itself constitute the "mysteries."

The following is the order of initiation rites at Eleusis:[2] (1) The candidates were brought together, and the hierophant (chief priest) excluded by an interdict (a taboo) all those whose hands were impure and who spoke in an unintelligible fashion[3] (this choice recurs in African secret societies, where a magician-priest is charged with making

[1] *Ibid.*, p. 151.

[2] For the Eleusinian mysteries, I have used Jane Harrison's book, already cited, and Paul François Foucart, *Recherches sur l'origine et la nature des mystères d'Éleusis*, Vol. I: *Le cult de Dionysos en Attique*, Vol. II: *Les grands mystères d'Éleusis* ("Mémoires de l'academie de l'inscriptions et belles lettres," XXXV [1895], XXXVII [1900]) (Paris: C. Klinckseick); Goblet d'Alviella, "De quelques problèmes relatifs aux mystères d'Éleusis"; since they have nothing to do with initiation proper, I shall omit the ceremonies of the thirteenth Boedromion (departure of the ephebi for Eleusis) and the fourteenth (transporting the sacra to Athens). We know that knowledge of the rites, the procedure of the ceremonials, the protection of the sacra, etc., was restricted to certain families (Eumolpides, etc.); it is the same even in Australia and among the Pueblos, etc.; there are certain designated groups (totem or otherwise) who "possess the mysteries." On the subject of teachers (mystagogues), see Foucart, *L'origine et la nature des mystères d'Éleusis*, II, 93–95.

[3] Foucart, *L'origine et la nature des mystères d'Éleusis*, I, 31–33; II, 110–11; Goblet d'Alviella, "De quelques problèmes relatifs aux mystères d'Éleusis," pp. 354–55.

it). (2) These neophytes were brought into the Eleusinion, and, entering the enclosure, they blessed themselves at the vase of sacred water placed near the door (cf. our holy water fonts). (3) With the cry "halade mystai" (to the sea, mystics), the neophytes were taken (perhaps running) to the seashore; that procession was known as *elasis*, "removal" or "banishment." (According to Harrison, this meaning may recur in the Greek word *pompe*.)[1] This rite has until now been interpreted as a casting out of evil forces, demons, or evil, but I see it as a rite of separation from the secularity of the neophyte's previous life. (4) The neophyte bathed in the sea, a rite of purification through which the profane and impure qualities were washed off—reinforcing the preliminary rite above. Each neophyte carried a pig, who bathed at the same time with him—a rite reminiscent of many Melanesian ones.[2] (5) The return to the Eleusinion and a sacrifice closed the first act.

The neophytes who had taken part in the ceremonies of the fifteenth and sixteenth of Boedromion (about the end of September) and who had received instruction in the lesser mysteries did not appear in public after the race to the sea and the sacrifice, but waited in the retreat (subject to dietary taboos, etc.) for the departure to Eleusis, twenty kilometers away. They transported the image of Iacchus and the sacra to the Eleusinion, making numerous stops on the way: in the quarter of the sacred fig tree, at the palace of Crocon (saffron), at the estate of Raria (the sacred area), at the wells of Callichoros, at the stone of Demeter, etc. The stops all pertained to agriculture.[3] (7) The procession entered the enclosure, whose high walls, like those at Athens, were meant to conceal from the profane what was going on in the sacred world; the entrance prohibition applied to the

---

[1] Harrison, *Prolegomena to the Study of Greek Religion*, p. 152, and Reinach, *Cultes, mythes, et religions*, II, 347–62.

[2] See works cited by W. Ellis, Codrington, etc.; and for Demeter as a pig, Goblet d'Alviella, "De quelques problèmes relatifs aux mystères d'Éleusis," pp. 189–90.

[3] On the subject of these two first stops, see Reinach, *Cultes, mythes, et religions*, III, 102–4.

whole *temenos*, and the penalty, at least on days of the mysteries, was death. Information is lacking on the details of the ceremonies that followed. It is known that the initiation included:[1] (*a*) a voyage through a hall divided into dark compartments which each represented a region of hell, the climbing of a staircase, the arrival in brightly illuminated regions, and entrance into the megaron, where sacra[2] were displayed; and (*b*) a representation of the rising of Kore, containing elements unknown to the profane and not understood in the legend that was popularly known. This part corresponds exactly to the representations of the acts of the alcheringa ancestors in Australian ceremonies. The first part also is almost universal: the novices, dead to the profane world, run through Hades and are reborn, but into the sacred world.[3] (8) No precise information is available on the rites, chants, dances, and processions which followed.[4]

The main outline of the rites of initiation to the mysteries of Eleusis corresponds to that of ceremonies in the same category that have already been examined. This same order, including a dramatization of the novice's death and rebirth, also recurs in the initiation into Orphism and the religious associations of Thrace, as well as in the cult of Dionysus, Mithras (initiation by stages),[5] Attis, Adonis, Isis, etc. The initiation to the "fraternity of Isis" is fairly well known, and the "passage through the elements" of which Apuleius speaks expresses even better than the

[1] See Foucart, *L'origine et la nature des mystères d'Éleusis*, I, 43–74; II, 137–39.

[2] On these sacra and their nature, see Harrison, *Prolegomena to the Study of Greek Religion*, pp. 158–61.

[3] This is why Plutarch said that to become initiated is to die; initiation into the mysteries of Orpheus, on the other hand, is considered a sacred marriage or a sacred birth.

[4] It goes without saying that I cannot accept Foucart's theories on the Egyptian origin of the Eleusinian mysteries, either in their entirety or separately. The necessity to express by actions the idea of passage from one state to another causes the similarities that Foucart saw as borrowings. How should one explain the exact similarities of the Greek, Egyptian, or Asiatic rites with those of Australia and of the Bantus, the natives of Guinea, and the Indians of North America?

[5] On the initiation to the seven grades and the passing of the neophyte's soul across the seven planetary spheres in succession, see references given and the discussion by Cumont, *Les religions orientales*, pp. 299–300, 310.

voyage through Hades[1] the idea of the neophyte's death, since it was even believed—or so it would seem—that he was decomposed and later reconstituted into a new individual.

The same idea may also be found in the initiation rites of the cult of Attis. First it should be noted that Attis, Adonis, and the deities of vegetation in general die in the autumn and are reborn in the spring, and that the ceremonies of their religions include a dramatic re-enactment of that death, with funerary taboos (mourning, etc.) and lamentations, a transitional period with a cessation of ordinary life, and the resurrection, or, more precisely, the rebirth. The order of these rites has been established to the least detail by Mannhardt, Frazer,[2] and their disciples, but they failed to see them as groupings of rites of passage which are at once cosmic, religious, and economic, and which constitute only a small part of a far vaster category which it is the purpose of this book to outline. Death, the transition, and resurrection also constitute an element in ceremonies of pregnancy, childbirth, initiation into associations with no agricultural purpose, betrothal, marriage, and funerals.[3]

Since Attis dies and is reborn, it is thought that the rites of initiation also cause her future worshiper to die and be reborn: (1) through fasting he removes the profane impurity from his body; (2) he eats and drinks from the sacra (a drum and cymbal); (3) he goes down into a pit, and the blood of a sacrificed bull poured over him covers his entire body;[4] then he comes out of the pit, bloody from head to foot; (4) during

[1] On the subject of voyages to the land of the dead, see Philippe de Félice, *L'autre monde: Mythes et légendes, le purgatoire de saint Patrice* (Paris: Champion, 1906). He did not perceive, however, that these myths and legends are in some cases only the oral residue of rites of initiation; one should never forget that in the ceremonies of initiation in particular, the elders, instructors, or ceremonial chiefs recite what the other members of the *group* perform. See, among others, my *Mythes et légendes d'Australie*, chap. ix. For the general theory, see chap. vii of this work.

[2] Frazer, *Adonis, Attis, Osiris*, pp. 229–30.   [3] See chap. ix.

[4] I have not sufficient space to discuss the "taurobolium," or rite of bathing in the blood of a bull, but it seems to me that none of the interpretations offered so far can be accepted in the light of comparisons with semicivilized rites and what is said here of the rites of passage.

several days he is fed only milk, like a newborn child. The rite of blood is commonly considered a baptism in the Christian sense—that is, a remission of sins. This interpretation is based on the word of informants who, after all, were recent (Clement of Alexandria, Firmicus Maternus, etc.), and it seems to me that the rite originally had a direct and physical meaning: the neophyte came out of the pit covered with blood like the newborn child emerging from its mother's body.

Under the influence of Asian as much as Greek and Egyptian religions, the community of Christians, which was at first undifferentiated, gradually became divided into classes which corresponded to the degrees of the mysteries;[1] the rites of entrance became more and more complicated and were systematized in the *ordo baptismi* (at the beginning of the eleventh century) and in the missal of Pope Gelasius II. Thanks to the rapid diffusion of Christianity, the time soon came when there were only children left to baptize, but for a long time a number of traits were preserved in the ritual which are suitable only for the baptism of adults. They are the ones I shall examine here.

The first degree was that of the catechumen; entrance to this degree involved (1) exsufflation with a formula of exorcism, (2) the sign of the cross on the forehead, (3) the administration of salt which had been exorcised. These rites are no longer direct, as among some semicivilized peoples, but already animistic,[2] like those of certain Africans and American Indians. The first rite is one of separation; the second one separates and at the same time incorporates, and it is equivalent to the marking (σφραγή) of the Greek mysteries and of primitive Christianity;[3] the third rite is a

[1] See the works cited by Goblet d'Alviella, S. Reinach, and Cumont; then E. Hatch, *Greek Ideas and Usages: Their Influence upon the Christian Church* (Hibbert Lectures, 1888 [London: Williams, 1890]), and Louis Duchesne, *Les origines du culte chrétien: Étude sur la liturgie latin avant Charlemagne* (Paris: E. Thorin, 1889. 3rd ed.; Paris: A. Fontemoing, 1902).

[2] On the origin of these animistic rites, see Hatch, *Greek Ideas and Usages*, p. 20, n. 1; Reinach, *Cultes, mythes, et religions*, II, 359–61 (the *abrenuntiatio*).

[3] See Hatch, *Greek Ideas and Usages*, p. 295 and notes.

rite of incorporation, especially in the prayer which accompanies it.[1]

Then came the transitional period: the catechumen, just like those initiated into the lesser mysteries, was permitted to attend religious assemblies and had a special place in the church, but he was required to withdraw before the beginning of the true mysteries (the Mass). He was periodically submitted to exorcism and thus separated more and more from the non-Christian world; he was gradually instructed; his "ears were opened." After a last exorcism came the *effeta*: the priest moistened his finger with saliva and touched the top of each catechumen's upper lip; the candidates undressed, and their backs and chests were anointed with consecrated oil;[2] they renounced Satan, swore to ally themselves with Christ, and recited the Credo. Thus ended the transitional period, which included at the same time rites of separation and rites preparatory to incorporation; the length of this period was not limited, and it could last until the eve of death.

It was followed by rites of the incorporation proper. Water was blessed,[3] and the catechumen was sprinkled with it and hence became *regeneratus*, or *conceived again*, according to the very terms of the prayer pronounced during the rite which followed.[4] Those baptized removed their clothing and dressed in white, assisted by their godfathers and godmothers.[5] They gathered in front of the bishop, who

---

[1] Duchesne, *Les origines du culte chrétien*, pp. 296–97.

[2] Cf. the Pueblo rite cited above (p. 78) and the sequence of extreme unction, which is a rite of passage from the world of the living Christians to that of the dead Christians.

[3] See Duchesne, *Les origines du culte chrétien*, pp. 311, 321, and Dieterich, *Mutter Erde*, pp. 114–15. To the direct sexual interpretation of this rite must be added the idea that the catechumen, like the Brahman infant, must be conceived again. It should be noted that in the old Christian churches the baptistry is always found outside the church proper, so that until the Middle Ages the catechumens, penitents, newborn, and recently baptized were obliged to remain in a liminal section. Likewise, the temples of all peoples have a court, vestibule, and anteroom, which prevent the sudden passage from the profane to the sacred.

[4] The verb *regenerare* should be taken in its literal sense.

[5] The question asked of the godmother and godfather and their replies reveal most clearly the foremost purpose of the ritual; here it would be well to compare

"marked" them with the sign of the cross—obviously a rite of appropriation by the deity[1] and of incorporation into the community of the faithful. Only after it was performed were the neophytes admitted to communion. They were then given a beverage which had been consecrated a few moments earlier and which was made of honey, water, and milk. Usener traced this drink—erroneously, according to Duchesne—to the mysteries of Dionysus, but I want to make the point that it was also the beverage given to newborn babies, undoubtedly before the appearance of the mother's milk. The "rebirth" was marked at the end by a procession of those baptized, carrying lighted candles. The Great Light is reminiscent of those of the Greek mysteries and in any case indicated that the "dead" had been born into the "true light."

These, then, are the steps in the Catholic ritual of Rome, but the same ideas and the same sequence recur in the Gallican ceremonies.[2] It must not be forgotten, however, that all this systematization of the baptism ritual is fairly recent and that during the first centuries the rites were fewer in number and less complicated. There was a strong influence of Gnosticism, which also had degrees and successive rites of initiation which fit the pattern of rites of passage.[3] Early Christian baptism included a fast and an

---

the Orthodox ritual with the modern practices of the Slavs. The limitations of space do not permit a discussion of special relationships created by sponsorship in the rites of initiation, among semicivilized peoples as well as Christians.

[1] On the passage from the human condition to a divine condition, see Farnell, *The Evolution of Religion*, p. 49; Reinach, *Cultes, mythes, et religions*, I, 127.

[2] [The Gallican system of ritual, prevalent from the earliest times in "Gaul" and certain parts of Europe north of the Alps, differs on a few points of liturgy from the ritual performed in the Diocese of Rome and hence in all churches called Roman Catholic. However, the churches adhering to the Gallican system are in the Patriarchate of Rome—though papal decrees and treaties have sometimes granted them a degree of autonomy—and continuous contact and consultation have brought increasing conformity to the Roman rite. The origin of the distinctive features of the Gallican ritual is uncertain. Some assert that they are due to the retention of features in the original Roman ritual, subsequently modified; others believe that they derive from Antioch (see *The Catholic Encyclopedia* [New York: Universal Knowledge Foundation, 1913]).]

[3] See among others Goblet d'Alviella, "De quelques problèmes relatifs aux mystères d'Éleusis," pp. 145–46.

immersion into consecrated water or a sprinkling with it. Furthermore, in various places and times all sorts of ritual details (of purification, exorcism, etc.) have been added under the influence of local beliefs and practices.

It would be easy to show that the ritual of the Mass also constitutes a sequence of rites of separation, transition, and incorporation. The only theoretical distinction between initiation and the Mass is that the latter is an initiation which is periodically renewed, like the Hindu sacrifice of soma and, in general, sacrifices whose purpose is to insure the normal course of cosmic and human events.

It is known that admission to Islam is achieved through circumcision and the recitation of the *Fātiḥa*. Nevertheless, a detailed study of many accounts of remarkable conversions and of variations in the circumcision ritual among various Moslem peoples would show that wherever there is a tendency to ritual development—for example, in Asia Minor, the Caucasus, central Asia, and India—the tripartite pattern outlined here would be equally distinguishable.

The same sequence may also be found in the passage from one religion to another, the rite of separation being constituted by the renunciation.[1] In the case of a return to the original religion, for instance in the Christian ritual of penance, the penitent was considered a Christian who for some reason had lost his initiation and was striving to recover it. Religious instruction and examination was replaced by "ascetic exercises"—the penitent was not to marry and had to dissolve a marriage already concluded, to resign his position, to maintain dietary and sumptuary austerity. In short, his "separation" from the profane world was much greater than that of the catechumen; the penance was terminated by a laying on of hands by the bishop and a public confession by the penitent, who was then required to go into mourning or withdraw to a monas-

---

[1] On the ritual of renunciation of Islam, see Edouard Louis Montet, in *Revue de l'histoire des religions*, LIII (1906), 145–63, and Ebersold, *Revue de l'histoire des religions*, LIV (1907), 230–31.

tery. The ceremony of reincorporation into the community of the faithful included an admonition, a prayer of "reconciliation," and, in Spain, the ceremony of *indulgencia*.[1]

Now let me turn to rites of initiation into religious brotherhoods. Since documents on ceremonies governing entrance into Buddhist brotherhoods are readily available,[2] I shall cite those pertaining to the sect of Sikhs.[3] Through prayer, some sugared water is consecrated and stirred with a small dagger. Some of it is then poured on the head and eyes of the neophyte, who also drinks the remainder. He then eats a special sort of pie with his consecrators. The neophyte, who is thus regenerated, is required to answer in reply to questions, no matter what his true nationality might be, that he was born in Patna and lives in Aliwal, birthplace and home of Guru Govind Singh, and that he is the son of Govind Singh, the last of the ten gurus of the Sikhs. In the ceremonies of initiation into the Chamar sect of Śivanārāyanī[4] there is an initiation lasting several days. At the end of this period, if the neophyte passes the tests for membership, he is asked to appear with a present for the headman, also called a guru. He washes the guru's big toe and distributes cakes to the members of the brotherhood. There are also such other acts as the burning of camphor.[5]

Initiation into Moslem brotherhoods is called *wird* in Morocco, and its principal rite of incorporation consists of

[1] Duchesne, *Les origines du culte chrétien*, 3d ed., pp. 434–45.

[2] See among others Hermann Oldenberg, *Le Bouddah: Sa vie, sa doctrine, sa communauté* (2d ed.; Paris: F. Alcan, 1902), trans. A. Foucher from 2d ed. of *Buddha: Sein Leben, sine Lehre, seine Gemeinde* (Berlin: W. Hertz, 1899); on the rites of initiation into the Chinese Buddhist sect called Lung-hua, see Jan M. de Groot, *Sectarianism and Religious Persecution in China* (Amsterdam: Johannes Muller, 1903), I, 204–20.

[3] J. C. Oman, *Cults, Customs, Superstitions of India* (London: Unwin, 1908), p. 95.

[4] [The Śivanārāyanī is a Chamar sect, monotheistic and open to all castes. Its legendary founder is said to have been a Brahman but to have lost his status through accidental pollution; because of his Brahman origin he had occasion to point out that he was as good as any who later looked down on him (see W. Crooke, "Typical Castes and Tribes").]

[5] Crooke, "Typical Castes and Tribes," pp. 173–74. "Guru" is a general term applied to a priest, a teacher of religion, or a director of conscience and morals; it should be noted that there is no organized hierarchy of clergy in India.

going down to a watering place and quenching one's thirst, drinking a liquid or receiving it in the mouth. To join the order of the Isawa, the neophyte opens his mouth wide, and the leader of the ceremony spits three times into his throat; other rites accompany this central one.[1] According to Lane, the '*ahd*, or rite of initiation, is about the same for the various brotherhoods in Cairo; the novice sits on the ground facing the sheik, and they take each other's right hands, lifting the thumbs and pressing them against each other, while the sheik's sleeve covers the hands; the novice repeats certain sacred formulas after the sheik a given number of times. Then the initiate kisses the sheik's hand. These rites are identical with those of the marriage contract, except that in the latter the hands of the man and the representative of his betrothed are hidden under a handkerchief, the terminology is legal, and the man kisses the hands of those present only if he is of lower social standing.[2]

In Roman Catholic ceremonies of affiliation to a religious order, there is always a portion which is in conformity with Roman, Gallican, or other prescribed ritual, and another portion which varies according to the religious order. Thus entry into the order of the Carmelites includes funeral rites followed by rites of resurrection.

Sacred virgins and prostitutes, to assume their new positions, must also submit to ceremonies constructed on the pattern of rites of passage. First, here is the order of rites of consecration for Catholic virgins, according to the Roman Pontifical:[3] The virgins are brought in dressed in the novice's

[1] See Edouard Louis Montet, "Les confréries religieuses de l'Islam marocain," *Revue de l'histoire des religions*, XLV (1902), 11; see also Doutté, *Merrâkech*, p. 103, n. 3. Regarding saliva as a rite of incorporation, see Hartland, *The Legend of Perseus*, II, 258–76; but spitting on someone is sometimes a rite of separation (see Nassau, *Fetichism in West Africa*, p. 213) and of expulsion from the group (for gypsies, see E. O. Winstedt, "Gypsy Initiation and Expulsions" (Notes and Queries, No. 14), *Journal of the Gypsy-lore Society*, N'S. II (1908), No. 2, 185–90.

[2] E. W. Lane, *Manners and Customs of the Modern Egyptians*, 1833–1835 (London: Nelson, 1895), pp. 252–53, 174–75.

[3] Abbé Jacques Paul Migne, *Encyclopédie théologique* (Paris: Ateliers Catholiques de Petit-Montrouge, 1845), Vol. XVII; Abbé Victor Daniel Boissonnet, *Dictionnaire alphabético-méthodique des cérémonies et des rites sacrés* (Vols. XV–XVII of the *Encyclopédie théologique*), Vol. III (1847), cols. 539–63.

habit "without veils, robes, or hoods." They light their candles and kneel, two by two. Three times the bishop says to them, "Come," and they approach him in three stages. They stand up in a circle, and each one comes and promises him to consecrate herself to virginity. He asks them if they are willing "to be blessed, consecrated, and united as spouses to Our Lord Jesus Christ," and they reply, "We wish it." The bishop chants the *Veni Creator spiritus* and blesses the future habits of the virgins. They take off their usual habits and put on the others. He blesses the veils,[1] then the rings, then the coronets. The virgins chant: "I have renounced the worldly kingdom and all the attractions of the world—my heart is no longer free, for I am in the service of the King, Him whom I have seen." The bishop prays and then recites the *Vere dignum*; he replaces his miter and says, "Come, beloved soul, you are close to my throne; the King has sought your union." They come forward, two by two, kneel, and "the bishop places the veil on the head of each one, lets it fall over the shoulders and the breast and moves it forward over the head to the eyes, saying: "Receive the sacred veil as proof that you have renounced the world and that . . . you have become . . . the spouse of Jesus Christ." When all are veiled, he reminds them, "Come to celebrate your wedding, etc.," and he places the ring on the third finger of the right hand, saying, "I unite you, etc." The same ceremony is performed with the coronet. There are liturgical chants, prayers, the alleluia, communion, benediction, and—in convents where the nuns observe canonical hours and have the right to read the office in the church—a ritual presentation of the breviary. Finally, the consecrated virgins are placed under the charge of the abbess. The ideas expressed include a separation from the profane world through the changing of habit and veiling, and an incorporation into the holy world

---

[1] There are no ancient accounts of these rites; in any case, this veiling has no connection with the veil which replaced the Roman sheepskin placed over man and wife in early Christian marriage.

by a marriage with Jesus Christ, the ring and the coronet also being ritual objects of secular marriage. It will be observed that the rites of separation here end the transitional period (the novitiate), which is characterized by a semi-seclusion, that a complete seclusion follows the consecration, and that both novitiate and consecration are accompanied by a physical separation (convent, railing, etc.) from the profane world.

Since little is known about the consecration rituals of the sacred prostitutes of antiquity,[1] I shall cite several Hindu rites for illustrative purposes.[2] In the Kaikōlan musician caste of Coimbatore, at least one daughter in each family must be attached to the temple as dancer, musician, and prostitute. The first series of ceremonies she undergoes is the equivalent of the betrothal; the second series, of marriage. The tali (equivalent of our wedding ring) is tied around her neck by a Brahman, as for a betrothal and marriage. Then the maternal uncle attaches a gold band around her forehead and places her on a board in front of the people. At the time of the first coitus, a sword is at first placed between the two people for several minutes—a nuptial rite which is very common in India. In short, the ceremonies of consecration to the deity differ only in small details from ordinary wedding ceremonies, and the same is true among the Kaikōlan weavers. In the ceremonies consecrating *basavi* (sacred prostitutes) of the Bellary district, a sword representing the absent fiancé is placed alongside the seated novice, who holds it in her right hand; after various rites she rises and goes to place the sword in the god's sanctuary. If she is a sacred dancer, the fiancé is represented by a drum, and she bows before it. The *basavi* are bound to the deity by the tali and tatooed with a chakra (a disk hollow in the center) and a shell (*Turbinella rapa*).

[1] Here I am not going to take up temporary sacred prostitution (Mylitta, Heliopolis, Anaitis); see Hartland, "Rite at the Temple of Mylitta," pp. 189–202.

[2] E. Thurston, *Ethnographic Notes in Southern India* (Madras: Government Press, 1906), pp. 29–30.

In a discussion of initiation rites, classes, castes, and professions should also be considered. Even where membership in a given caste or social class is hereditary, as in certain totem and magico-religious groups, the child is rarely considered a fully "complete" member from birth. At an age which varies among different peoples, he must be incorporated into his group through ceremonies which differ from those which have been thus far discussed in that the magico-religious element is weaker; in contrast, the politico-legal and generally social elements are more important. Among the Lekugnen, a Salish tribe of British Columbia,[1] there are four classes—chiefs (hereditary), nobles (hereditary), commoners, and slaves—which are endogamous and which abide by a rigid protocol for daily living (table seating, etc.).

Membership in a given class is indicated by a person's name, and there is therefore a naming ceremony which always comes later than the ceremonies of puberty. The father organizes a great feast, and, when all those invited have gathered, he leads his son, together with sponsors, onto the roof of the house (whose interior is hollowed out of the ground) and sings and dances one of the family songs and dances. Gifts are then distributed in the name of the ancestors. The father asks forty nobles to act as witnesses. Two elder chiefs come forward, with the young man standing between them, and the oldest one announces in a loud voice the name and titles of that ancestor for whom the father wishes his son to be named. These are usually the grandfather's. The consent of those present is expressed by hand clapping and shouts. Gifts are again distributed to the participants and, if the father is rich, also to the commoners who have come out of curiosity. The common meal follows, and afterward the young man is known only by the name and title acquired at that time. Here, in a semicivilized form, are ceremonies which have been greatly elaborated elsewhere—for instance, in Europe of the Middle Ages (cf.

[1] Hill-Tout, "Ethnology of the Southeastern Tribes of Vancouver Island," pp. 308–10.

their resemblance to the arms vigil of knights and to the novitiate) and in Japan. The exterior emblem is the coat of arms, which corresponds to the representation of the totem for the totem groups and to such signs as scarifications and tatoos for age groups and secret societies. The affixing of the coat of arms, like that of the totemic emblem, is clearly a rite of incorporation, as is the "marking" of the mysteries. Only in form do the rites vary according to peoples and kinds of restricted groups.[1]

Membership in a caste is, by definition, hereditary, but a caste also is occupationally specialized, and each person has his assigned place in a precise hierarchy.[2] Incorporation into a caste therefore occurs only under specified conditions. (1) A child is incorporated through ceremonies which fall into the category of childhood rites discussed in chapter v. Of course, the ritual use of tools pertaining to a given occupation assumes an important place here; it is not a sympathetic rite, as it is among peoples without castes, but a true rite of incorporation which places an individual in a restricted collectivity. (2) Although one cannot move upward from a lower caste to a higher one, a person can move in the reverse direction. It follows that, in such instances, the rites of incorporation either are simplified or show a pivoting, because it is the lower caste which is honored, not the new arrivals. In addition, there are castes in some regions of India which are primarily tribes, and among them the rites of incorporation seem to ignore the scale of valuation which is the basis of caste; they retain only the features of ceremonies performed elsewhere than India for the incorporation of a stranger into a clan or tribe.[3] (3) Rites of

[1] This idea will be further developed in my "Débuts du blason," which is in preparation; meanwhile, see my "Héraldisation de la marque de propriété," *Revue héraldique* (Paris), 1906.

[2] On the theories of castes, consult C. Bouglé, *Essais sur le régime des castes* (Paris: F. Alcan, 1908).

[3] For cases of this kind (communal meals, special alimentary rites of incorporation) see H. H. Risley, *The Tribes and Castes of Bengal* (Calcutta: Bengal Secretariat Press, 1891), II, 40–49, etc. It should be noted that incorporation into a caste may be accomplished also through marriage. Among the tribes of the Nilgiri Hills, the

separation play an important part here, even though their conscious and voluntary element may be absent. Each caste is separated from all others by taboos; touching a person of a lower caste, eating with him, lying down on his bed, or entering his house can cause a person to be automatically removed from his own caste, though he is not incorporated into the caste of the person he has touched. In such a case it often happens, for instance in Bengal,[1] that the outcast becomes a Moslem, since theoretically and in practice, in certain parts of India, Islam does not accept the hierarchy of castes. Persons of all castes may also enter the Buddhist brotherhoods or "sects" such as the Arya Samaj[2] and the Śivanārāyaṇī, which are compromises, in varying degrees, among Hinduism, Brahmanism, Buddhism, and Islam.

The entrance into European occupations in the past included special ceremonies, at least some of which were of a religious nature—especially when the guilds coincided with special kinds of religious brotherhoods. Even when, in former times, apprenticeship did not involve a separation from a previous environment, it terminated with rites of incorporation (a common meal, etc.). It is known that recruitment into guilds was strictly regulated. One should not think, however, that in our time all the barriers within the same professions or trades, or between the various professions or trades, have disappeared. Undoubtedly, nothing ritualistic remains in the obstacles to movement, but a few words should nevertheless be said about them, because the new form corresponds to tendencies also expressed in rites of passage, though on a different basis. Thus the helper

girl changes caste through marriage; the change is enacted in a ceremony called "cutting off from the tribe." The women of the tribe prepare a meal to which they invite the future wife and thereby "cut her off" from her first caste and admit her into theirs.

[1] See Arnold van Gennep, "Pourquoi on se fait musulman au Bengale," under "Notes et analyses" *Revue des idées*, December 15, 1908, pp. 549–51.

[2] [Arya Samaj is a sect, founded about 1860, which considers the Vedas the only inspired scriptures and teaches that God, spirit, and matter are the three eternal substances. Its members have advocated the reform of the caste system and the abolition of child marriage.]

(blacksmith's helper as well as carpenter's helper) tends to remain a helper all his life, no matter what his personal aptitudes may be; he is unable to pass into full occupational status (blacksmith, carpenter) except under special circumstances (sometimes by marriage).

An acute form of this tendency has often manifested itself in the United States, for example in the struggle between the mason's helpers and the masons, when the masons forbade their helpers to use their tools[1] (trowels, etc.[2]). As Cornelissen has shown, the distinction between the grades is based not on personal aptitudes (strength, skill, etc.) but on a kind of traditional pressure which allows a person to advance only within the occupational area where he begins;[3] if one starts as an apprentice mason's helper or apprentice mason, he remains in this category for the rest of his life. But within the group of helpers or journeymen it is fairly easy to pass from one vast category to another—from mason's helper to stonecutter's helper, from carpenter to joiner to cabinetmaker. Furthermore, when all salary levels are examined and all factors taken into account, it becomes apparent that salaries range between a minimum and a maximum, and that here too there exists a transitional area which a person must cross before achieving a full satisfaction of his needs in a given country, at a given time, and in a given occupation.

The class of Brahmans, the "twice-born," exemplifies the transition between the caste and a magico-sacerdotal pro-

---

[1] United States Bureau of Labor, *Bulletin*, XIII (1906), No. 67, 746–47.

[2] [The 1906 *Bulletin of the United States Labor Bureau* reported that many unions in the construction trades had restricted the use of certain tools and the performance of certain tasks to persons who had been properly trained and who had complied with apprenticeship regulations. The purpose of these restrictions, according to the report, was to preserve the high standards of the craft and to prevent employers from hiring helpers—at lower wages—to perform journeymen's tasks. This did reduce the number of helpers that could be hired, but it seems to have little relation to van Gennep's picture of occupational mobility in the United States. His generalization on this point, as well as his description of salary levels, must be read in the context of his time rather than the present.]

[3] Christian Cornélissen, *Théorie du salaire et du travail salarié* (Paris: Giordet Brière, 1908), pp. 173–201. See also p. 658.

fession. The term "twice-born" clearly indicates the true role of rites of passage: the Brahman, who belongs to his caste by birth and is incorporated into it by childhood rites, later undergoes initiation ceremonies enacting death in a previous world and birth in the new one, and giving him the power to devote himself to the magico-religious activity which is to be his occupational specialty. Since the Brahman is a born priest, one cannot really speak of his ordination, in the Catholic sense; but, whatever Bouglé may think on this matter,[1] the novitiate and the initiation are necessary, especially because of the importance of formulas and their "correct recitation" in Hindu ritual. One is born a Brahman, but one must learn to act like a Brahman. In other words, within the sacred world which the Brahman inhabits from birth there are three compartments: a preliminal one lasting until the *upanayana* (beginning of a relationship with a teacher), a liminal one (novitiate), and a postliminal one (priesthood). The succession of periods through which a Brahman passes is identical to that experienced by the son of a semicivilized king, since the entire development of both takes place within the sacred world, while that of a non-Brahman or an average African is confined, except for special periods (initiation, sacrifice, etc.), to the realm of the profane.

The Brahman ceremonies include, first, a tonsure, a bath, a change of clothing, possession of the child's heart by the teacher who takes the responsibility for its guidance, a change of name, a handclasp—culminating in the child's ritual death.[2] Once the child has become a novice (brahmachari), he is subject to all sorts of taboos; he studies the sacred literature, learns formulas and gestures. His union with the teacher is identified with a marriage; the teacher "conceives" at the moment when he places his hand on the child's shoulder, and on the third day, when the Gayatri is

[1] See Émile-Louis Burnouf, *Essai sur le Véda* (Paris: Dezobry F. Tandou & Co., 1863), pp. 283–85, and Bouglé, *Le régime des castes*, pp. 73–76, 77. My interpretations reconcile the viewpoints of Burnouf and Oldenberg.

[2] See Oldenberg, *La religion du Véda*, pp. 399–402.

recited,[1] the child is reborn. According to other texts, the Brahman is born "at the moment when the sacrifice turns toward him." Thus, contrary to what has been observed in initiation ceremonies of Australia, the Congo, and elsewhere, the novice's death does not last through the entire time of the novitiate. The duration of the Brahman's novitiate is not specified in the texts. After it comes the ceremony of "return" (*samāvartana*); the novice takes off the signs of the novitiate (belt, stick, antelope skin) and throws them into the water; then he bathes and puts on new clothes.[2] He is reincorporated into the sacred society through a separation from the transitional period, which is also sacred.

I shall not stress the novitiate and ordination ceremonies of Roman Catholic and Orthodox Catholic priests. The same series of rites of separation, transition, and incorporation will be recognized among them, but they are systematized in their own ways.[3] The "tonsure" is the principal rite. Since it is a permanent symbol, like the veil, it is at the same time a rite of separation and incorporation. After the priest is ordained, he must read his first Mass, and this ritual act also sometimes takes the form of a marriage. Often it is combined with local nuptial rites, as it is in certain districts of Tirol.[4] The church is impersonated by a girl, eight to twelve years old, who is a sister or close relative of the priest. An attempt is made to "steal" her, as in the case of a regular fiancée; that is, she is taken to an inn other than the one at which the wedding breakfast is held after the first Mass; shots are fired, firecrackers are set off, and wedding songs are sung, including some of an erotic

[1] [The Gayatri, is a prayer, taught to the brahmachari by the teacher during the ceremonies (see Margaret Stevenson, *The Rites of the Twice Born* [London and New York: Oxford University Press, 1920], pp. 34–35).]

[2] *Ibid.*, p. 350. For further details, see Henry, *La magie dans l'Inde antique*, pp. 84–85 ff.

[3] Among others, see Boissonnet, *Dictionnaire*, cols. 985–1032, 1032–43: "general ordinations," which correspond to circumcision, marriages, etc., multiple synchronised rites. For grades and ancient rituals (Roman, Gallican, and Oriental), see Duchesne, *Les origines du culte chrétien*, pp. 344–78.

[4] F. Kohl, *Die tiroler Bauernhochzeit* ("Quellen und Forschungen zur deutches Volkskunde," III [Vienna, 1908]), pp. 275–81.

nature. During the meal, the presence of aides or sponsors of the parish priest and of clergy who are his friends tends to calm the ritual enthusiasm. As a matter of fact, ecclesiastical authorities have succeeded in eliminating these customs from some dioceses, although they are maintained, for instance, in Salzburg.

I think few present-day groups possess such a clear-cut ritual of the pure and the impure as do the Subba or Sabians, who live in the vicinity of Baghdad.[1] Baptism plays an important part in their ascension from one ecclesiastical grade to another and in all the life of the novices, deacons, priests, and bishops. A novice must be a legitimate son of a priest or bishop, and he must be without physical defect; if he is judged worthy after an examination, he receives a special baptism, studies from seven to nineteen years, and is then ordained deacon. At the end of six months or a year as a deacon, if an assembly of the people wish it, he is ordained a priest. He is confined in a reed hut; for seven days and seven nights he must not soil himself and may not sleep. Each day he changes clothes and must give alms. On the eighth day a funeral is held for him, since he is considered dead. Afterwards, he is accompanied by four priests to the river, where they administer baptism to him. During the sixty days that follow he bathes himself three times a day, and if he has a nocturnal emission that day does not count among the sixty. The days on which either his mother or his wife have their menses are not counted, so that it sometimes takes four or five months to accumulate sixty days free of all pollution. He is subject to dietary taboos and gives alms.

The special function of the priest is the administration of baptism; that of the bishop is the administration of marriage. When a bishop is elected by the priests, he must avoid sexual relations for two months. He is also baptized; he gives a public explanation of the sacred books and must be present at the death of a "good Sabian," who is charged with a

[1] Siouffi, *Études sur la religion des Soubbas*, pp. 66–72.

message for the deity Avather (this rite is obligatory). Three days later, he must pray for the person who died. He performs the benediction at the marriage of a priest (also an obligatory rite), and the final rite of his investiture is a baptism of all the priests.

With the initiation of the magician we enter the category of phenomena of a hybrid nature. Except where magicians form a sort of class or even a caste, as in parts of western North America, they are not subject to rites which unite them into a defined human group. But they must be incorporated into the sacred world and cannot function without the operation of the rites of passage.

For data on the Australian magician, I refer the reader to the sources cited in a monograph by Mauss.[1] They show that the magician changes personality and sometimes simulates dying and subsequent resurrection (removal of organs, dream voyage to the other world, etc.). The Ural-Altaic shaman (1) is nervous and irritable from an early age. (2) He has been "possessed" several times by spirits (hallucinations, phobias, epilepsy, trances, catalepsy, etc.), so that the idea of temporary death arises. (3) He withdraws to the woods, to solitude, to the tundra, etc., and subjects himself to various privations with psychological and neuropathic consequences. (4) Spiritual beings which may be anthropomorphic or animal, malevolent or protective, solitary or numerous, appear to him with increasing frequency and teach him the substance of his profession. (5) Or the shaman dies and his soul departs to the land of the spirits, the gods, or the dead. There he learns its topography and acquires the knowledge necessary to subdue the evil spirits and obtain the assistance of the good ones. (6) The shaman then returns to life, is reborn, and returns home or goes from village to village, and so forth.[2] The important but not

[1] Marcel Mauss, *L'origine des pouvoirs magiques dan les sociétés australiennes* (Paris: Imprimerie Nationale, 1904).

[2] This scheme forms the substance of several chapters of a book which has been in preparation for a long time, *Le shamanisme chez les populations de l'Europe et de l'Asie septentrionale*, especially on the basis of Russian, Finnish, and Hungarian

distinctive fact of shamanism is that in all the shaman's ceremonial actions one finds the recurring series of trances, death, voyages of the soul to the other world return, and application of the knowledge acquired in the sacred world to a particular case (illness, etc.). It is a precise equivalent of the classical sacrifice.

To be initiated as a *peai* among the Caribs, the novice goes to live with an "elder," sometimes for as long as ten years, and for twenty-five to thirty years thereafter he subjects himself to repeated tests, such as a prolonged fast. The old *peais* seclude themselves in a hut, where they whip the novice and make him dance till he falls in a faint; he is "bled" by black ants and made to "go mad" by being forced to drink tobacco juice. Finally, he is subjected to a three-year fast which gradually becomes less rigorous, and from time to time he imbibes tobacco juice.[1] The inner meaning of this sequence of rites emerges from the descriptions by von den Steinen: (1) the novice is exhausted and brought to a state of abnormally high sensitivity; (2) he goes to sleep and dies; (3) his soul rises to the sky and descends again; (4) he awakens and revives as a *peai*.[2]

Among the Barundi of Tanganyika one becomes a *kiranga* (priest-magician-sorcerer) in three ways: by inheritance and ordination—mothers or fathers before their death pass on their role by giving a sacred spear to the eldest son or daughter; from having been struck by thunder; by a sudden calling:

During one of the "ceremonies of the spear" a boy or a girl will rise suddenly and stand opposite the officiating *kiranga* or, rather, opposite the sacred spear; he or she will bend toward the *kiranga* and look at him fixedly with all the energy of his being until he (or she) begins to tremble and finally falls in a faint, as if dead. . . . The person who has fainted is laid on a mat and carried with care into his house, where he

documents. It goes without saying that the variations among these peoples are considerable.

[1] Lafitau, *Mœurs des sauvages amériquains*, I, 330–34; see following pages for other accounts (Moxos, etc.)

[2] K. von den Steinen, *Unter den Naturvölkern zentral Brasiliens* (2d ed.; Berlin: D. Reimer, 1897), pp. 297–98, 300–301 (Bakairí, Aueto, etc.)

or she sleeps for three or four days. When the person comes to himself (or herself), he or she is henceforth a sacred priest or priestess-spouse of the god. Neighbors are called; the "ceremony of the spear" is performed; and the new *kiranga* presides and officiates for the first time.[1]

There is, then, hypnosis, death, a transitional period, and resurrection. Hubert and Mauss correctly note that "the idea of a momentary death is a general theme of magical as well as religious initiation."[2] They cite data from the Eskimos, the Chams, and the Greeks, from Indonesia, Melanesia, and North America. The important point to be noted is that in the detail of these ceremonies there appears a pattern identical to that of many other transitions from one state to another.

All that has been said about priests and magicians also applies to the chief and the king, whose sacred and sometimes divine nature has been clearly brought out by Frazer.[3] The ceremonies of enthronement[4] or crowning show a very great resemblance to ordination ceremonies, both in detail and in their order. Two cases should be considered: the successor may be enthroned either during the lifetime of his predecessor or after the latter's death. Sometimes the succession is opened up only through a special rite during which the predecessor is put to death by his successor. In either case, as in an initiation or an ordination, there is a handing over and an acceptance of the sacra, which here are called "regalia" and which include drums, a scepter, a crown, "relics of the ancestors,"[5] and a special seat; they are at one and the same time the symbol and the receptacle of royal magico-religious power. A transitional period equivalent to the novitiate also recurs here, in the form of a pre-

---

[1] Van der Burght, *Dictionnaire français Kirundi*, p. 107 (see Ethnographic Supplement).

[2] Hubert and Mauss, "Esquisse d'une théorie générale de la magie," pp. 37–39.

[3] Frazer, *The Golden Bough*; *Lectures on the Early History of the Kingship*.

[4] I prefer the term "enthronement" to "crowning" since a special seat is more often the symbol of royalty than a band or crown.

[5] See my *Tabou et totémisme à Madagascar*, pp. 115–17; and on regalia in general as receptacles of royal power, see Frazer, *Lectures on the Early History of the Kingship*, pp. 120–24.

paration and a retreat accompanied by all sorts of taboos and special instruction which sometimes begins in childhood. Another transitional period is the time which elapses between the predecessor's death and the accession to the throne. It is marked by a suspension of social life for all, again reminiscent of the novitiate. This period will be discussed later.

When detailed descriptions are examined, it becomes readily apparent that the conceptual scheme proposed is also applicable to enthronement ceremonies.[1] I shall cite only two cases, the enthroning of the Pharaoh in ancient Egypt and of the *hogon* of the Habé (or Dogon) in the Niger basin. Ceremonies of investiture or of the temporary turning over of powers are among others which fall into the same category. Their operation also requires a separation from the previous surroundings and a gradual or immediate incorporation into a new environment, originally the sacred environment.

The following is the order of rites for the enthronement of the Pharaoh, according to Moret's excellent monograph.[2] The future Pharaoh was born a god,[3] but between his birth and the moment of his enthronement he must have lost his absolute sacredness, for the purpose of the first rite was to make him "pure." He was reincorporated into the sacred world and reidentified with the gods. In one of the rites he was nursed by a goddess. The reigning king then presented him to the people, took him in his arms, and performed the

---

[1] For a good description of the order of rites, see Jean Baptiste Pattas, *Le sacre et couronnement de Louis XVIᵉ, roi de France et de Navarre, dans l'église de Reims 11 Juin, 1745, précédé de recherches sur le sacre des rois de France depuis Clovis, et suivi d'un journal historique de ce que c'est passé a cette Auguste cérémonie*, ed. J. Pichon (Paris: Vente, 1775).

[2] Alexandre Moret, *Du caractère religieux de la royauté pharaonique* (Paris: E. Leroux, 1903), pp. 75–113; and for the same series of rites and details for the inauguration of the temple, see Alexandre Moret, *Le rituel de culte divin journalier en Egypte: D'après les papyrus de Berlin et les textes du temple de Seti 1ᵉʳ à Abydos* (Paris: E. Leroux, 1902), pp. 10–15; see also pp. 25–26 n. 1, 101, 29–32, and Plate I in four pictures corresponding to the four phases of the set of rites.

[3] On theogony, see Moret, *La royauté pharaonique*, pp. 49–52, 59–73. Also see pp. 63–65 and 222 on divine nursing.

motions which gave the breath of life. In the rite that followed, sacred, divine, and royal names were given him; those present "proclaimed" the names and titles of the new Pharaoh and then dispersed themselves with great shouts and leaps (possibly of a ritual nature). The prerogative of these names was displayed so that all should know them. Then the newly proclaimed king "received the crowns of the chiefs of divine places," that is, of the gods; the crowns were held by a sacred headband. At the same time the other regalia (a hook, a whip, a scepter) were given to him; after this rite came the "reunion of the two regions" (Upper and Lower Egypt) by their goddesses, who transmitted them to the new Pharaoh. He took possession of them by a circumambulation, the "circuit of the wall," just as the dead person become a god "took possession" of the habitations of Horus and Set.

The king then went in procession to the sanctuary of the god; the god "embraced him and gave him the breath of life" and affirmed the diadem on his head. That was the final consecration, the equivalent of a transcription of names and titles. These rites date from the earliest times and were maintained up to the time of the Ptolemies, and to some extent also in Ethiopia. They were concluded with pilgrimages to various sanctuaries, public celebrations at the king's expense, religious donations, the repair of temples, and so forth. Thus the ceremony was enacted in stages which began with a rite of separation from the profane, continued with rites of incorporation into the sacred, and ended with rites through which the king took possession of the divine and terrestrial realms. Information on the transitional periods is lacking.

The Habé of the Niger plateau are governed by a *hogon* whose role is simultaneously political, juridical, and religious. He is as much the chief priest as he is the chosen king, and his regalia are also the sacra of the temple in which he lives. They consist of a necklace adorned with an opal, an iron bracelet on his right leg, a copper ring on his right ear, a silver ring on the middle finger of his right hand —the last two obvious signs of incorporation with the deity —a special cane, special clothing, and so forth. He must not be touched, and the name he bore before his enthronement must no longer be pronounced. He is addressed only in the ancient dialect, Sarakolle, is entitled to the first fruits, and has to keep to a special diet. There is a *hogon* for each tribe or clan and a great *hogon*. When a tribal or clan *hogon* is enthroned, the insignia of his position are turned over to him, and he is escorted to the temple that is to serve henceforth as a residence. When the great *hogon* dies, there is a three-year interregnum, during which his death is concealed from the people. This period ends with the announcement of his death, the consultation of the deity, great public feasts and dances, the council's election of a new *hogon*, and the presentation of his insignia. "Accompanied by the crowd of dignitaries and dancing young people, the *hogon* then goes to the temple of the deity, a highly decorated hut which from then on is to be his sacred habitation. This walk is considered the funeral procession of the *hogon*, for from the time of his entrance in the house of the *hogon* and his taking possession of the "symbols of union," the servant and high priest of the deity is considered dead to his family."[1]

The counterpart of initiation rites are the rites of banishment, expulsion, and excommunication—essentially rites of separation and de-sanctification. Those of the Roman Catholic church are fairly well known. It should be noted that, as Smith perceived,[2] excommunication and consecration are based on the same principle, the setting apart of a

---

[1] Augustin-Marie Louis Desplagnes, *Le plateau central nigérien* (Paris: Imprimerie Nationale, 1907), pp. 321–28; in a tribe of the Barasana plains, the Oudio of Ouol, the ceremonies are somewhat different and include, among others, a rite of denial, for which see my *Religions, mœurs et legendes* (Paris: Societé du Mercure de France, 1908–14), pp. 137–54. There also the *hogon* is considered dead to his former environment.

[2] Smith, *Lectures on the Religion of the Semites*, pp. 118–19.

given object or person.[1] Some of the rites performed on the two occasions are therefore identical.

The order in which I have classed the various groups to examine their rites of admission is based not on chance but on a differentiation of the elements which characterize each one. It should be clear that I accept neither the classification nor the theories of Schurtz or Webster. The latter, in particular, finds degeneration where I see incipient forms. As for Schurtz, he was struck by the astonishing similarity among the rites of initiation for totem groups, fraternities, secret societies, and age groups, and from this similarity he deduced an identity of these institutions.[2] One could go far in that direction, but it is the purpose of this volume to show that these cases, like many others, involve a clearly defined category of rites which resemble each other because they have the same purpose, and hence it will be understood that Schurtz's theory does not seem acceptable to me.[3]

During the entire novitiate, the usual economic and legal ties are modified, sometimes broken altogether. The novices are outside society, and society has no power over them, especially since they are actually sacred and holy, and therefore untouchable and dangerous, just as gods would be. Thus, although taboos, as negative rites, erect a barrier between the novices and society, the society is defenseless against the novices' undertakings. That is the explanation —the simplest in the world—for a fact that has been noted among a great many peoples and that has remained incomprehensible to observers. During the novitiate, the young people can steal and pillage at will or feed and adorn themselves at the expense of the community.

---

[1] [William Robertson Smith observed that among primitive societies no sharp line is drawn between the ideas of holiness and uncleanliness, as applied to persons and places, and that even among more advanced societies the two often meet.]

[2] Schurtz, *Altersklassen und Männerbünde*, p. 392.

[3] Frazer's theory (*The Golden Bough*, pp. 344 ff.), taken up by Hubert and Mauss ("Essai sur la nature et la fonction du sacrifice," p. 90), is also not acceptable, since it is too limited. He says that the rites of initiation have as their objective to introduce a soul into a body; but if this were the case, one would find a whole series of special rites for changing the soul, analogous to those of certain medicinal ceremonies.

114

Two examples will suffice for the moment. In Liberia, during the time when the young Vai are being instructed in the legal and political customs of their people, "theft does not seem to be regarded as a misdemeanor for the novices, for, under the guidance of their teachers, they make nocturnal attacks against the villages of the neighborhood and, by trickery or force, steal everything that can be of use (rice, bananas, hens, and other means of subsistence) and bring them back to the sacred wood," although they have in addition special plantations which provide them with the necessary food.[1] Similarly, in the Bismarck Archipelago the members of the Duk-duk and the Ingiet may, during the initiation ceremony, steal and pillage in the houses and plantations as much as they wish, but they must take care to leave intact the goods of other members of the secret society.[2] As a matter of fact, these extortions have taken the form of forced payments in local currency, as they have in all Melanesia.

Moreover, the widespread occurence of the phenomenon under discussion is quite well known.[3] Its dynamics in the instance cited may be understood if one remembers that a suspension of social life also marks interregna and the transition period between provisional and final funerals. The nature of the transitional period may also be at least a partial explanation for the sexual license permitted among a certain number of peoples (in Australia, etc.) between the beginning of the betrothal and the conclusion of the marriage, at which the woman is appropriated by a specific man. A suspension of the usual rules of living does not always bring about such excesses, but such a suspension does constitute an essential element of this phase.

[1] Büttikofer, *Reisebilder aus Liberia*, II, 305–6.

[2] See Parkinson, *Dreissig Jahre in der Südsee*, pp. 609–10.

[3] In French West Africa the mark of initiation is circumcision, and the novice's right to steal lasts from the beginning of the cicatrization of the wound until it is completely healed, or around three weeks. Lasnet, *Une mission au Sénégal*, pp. 50 (Fulah), 65 (Lobi), 77 (Tukulörs), 89 (Malinké), 101 (Soninke), 127 (Khasonke), 145 (Serers), etc.

VII
BETROTHAL AND MARRIAGE

This chapter is concerned with a subject on which an abundance of data has been collected. Explanatory monographs are lacking, however, and the interpretations given have been as diverse as possible. The pattern of rites of passage appears once again, and the necessity of studying rites in their order is strikingly underlined. Unfortunately, theoreticians have been misled into narrow, though often complicated, interpretations by considering isolated segments of rites instead of comparing entire ceremonies with one another.

The rites discussed in the last chapter described the child's admittance to adolescence and social puberty. Maturity follows this stage and is most clearly expressed in the founding of a family. Marriage constitutes the most important of the transitions from one social category to another, because for at least one of the spouses it involves a change of family, clan, village, or tribe, and sometimes the newly married couple even establish residence in a new house. The change of residence is marked in the ceremonies by rites of separation, always primarily focused on the territorial passage.

Furthermore, because of the number and importance of groups affected by the social union of two of their members, it is natural that the period of transition should take on considerable importance. This is the period commonly called the "betrothal."[1] Among a great number of peoples it consists of a special and autonomous part of the marriage ceremonies, including rites of separation and transition and terminating with rites which insure either a preliminary

[1] The best work with which I am familiar on the study of betrothal from a ritual and legal point of view is that by Raffaele Corso, "Gli sponsali popolari," *Revue des études ethnographiques et sociologiques*, November–December, 1908. However, I do not agree with the author that the rites (kissing, presents, veiling, bouquet, waistband, joining hands, ring, shoe, kiss, exchange of bread, of fruit, of wine, etc., going to bed side by side, etc.) have only symbolic value: they bind physically.

incorporation into the new environment or a separation from an autonomous transition period. Then come the rites of marriage, which consist chiefly of rites of permanent incorporation into the new environment but which often include rites of individual union also, though the latter do not occur as frequently as one would at first expect. Thus the pattern of rites of passage is more complicated here than in the ceremonies previously discussed.

The descriptions that follow show not only the dynamics of these series of rites but also the parallels with other types of ceremonies. It will be apparent that marriage is an essentially social act, so that all discussion of Crawley's individualistic and contagionist theory is irrelevant.[1]

Some marriage rites may be classed according to the outline presented in chapter I for pregnancy, birth, etc.; marriage ceremonies also include protective and fertility rites which may be sympathetic or contagious, animistic or dynamistic, direct or indirect, and positive or negative (taboos). Up to now, this aspect of the rites has been studied most often,[2] and it has attracted so much attention that marriage ceremonies have come to be viewed only as rites which are prophylactic, cathartic, and fertility-inducing. A reaction against this simplification is needed, since its narrowness will be apparent to anyone who reads with care a detailed description of the marriage ceremonies of any civilized or semicivilized people, whether they be in Europe or Africa, Asia or Oceania, antiquity or the present.

Since the types of rites mentioned above have been adequately studied, I will not include them in the discus-

[1] See Crawley, *The Mystic Rose*, pp. 321, 350, etc. Hartland understood the collective character of the rites of incorporation; most other family theorists left aside the detailed study of the systemization of ceremonies, especially those of betrothal.

[2] The general attitude of theoreticians is clearly reflected in the following statement by William Crooke (*The Natives of Northern India: Native Races of the British Empire* [London: A. Constable, 1907], p. 206): "Marriage, as we have seen, contemplates that the parties are under the influence of taboo, and the rites are intended to obviate its dangers, and in particular those which may prevent the union from being fertile." I should point out that, on the basis of what was said in chapter I of this volume, the "taboo" cannot be a "danger" but is, in a certain number of cases, a means of protection from danger.

117

sions that follow; and if in this work I focus my attention primarily on the rites of separation and incorporation as such and on their order, I do not mean to imply by so doing that they include all components of marriage ceremonies. I should like to point out that protective and fertility rites actually seem to be inserted somewhat haphazardly among the rites of passage. When one compares the descriptions offered by several observers of the marriage ceremonies of the same people, the pattern of rites of passage emerges with an absolute consistency. The disagreements which occur among observers concern the date, place, and details of rites of protection and fertility. Here again, it is difficult to be certain of the proper interpretation for each particular rite, and the two summations given later in this chapter should be considered highly incomplete. The reader will see that I have rejected the accepted interpretations for several rites, at least in general, though perhaps not absolutely for every particular enactment of a rite. Had I presented the proofs I have collected for each case, this chapter would have become a volume.

The complexity of rites, and the persons and objects involved in them, may vary with the type of family that is to be constituted,[1] but, except in the case of a "common-law marriage," there are always groups of various kinds and sizes which are interested in the union of two individuals. The collectivities in question are: (1) the two sex groups, sometimes represented by the ushers and bridesmaids, or by the male relatives on one hand and the female relatives on the other; (2) patrilineal or matrilineal descent groups;

[1] Here is the classification of Thomas, *Kinship Organizations and Group Marriage in Australia*, pp. 104–9: A. promiscuity: 1. unregulated: (*a*) primary, (*b*) secondary; 2. regulated: (*a*) primary, (*b*) secondary. B. marriage: 3. polygamy, primary or secondary; (*a*) simple, (*b*) adelphic: (i) unilateral, (ii) bilateral; 4. polyandry; 5. polygyny (which falls into the same division but is always unilateral); 6. monogamy: the three forms may be matrilocal, bilocal, and patrilocal. In addition, Thomas notes the existence of "free union," a relationship which does not confer the rights of marriage but is not considered immoral, and "liason," a relationship for which the parties involved are liable to censure or punishment. All these forms may be temporary or permanent. The type of family does not seem to influence the rites of betrothal and marriage.

(3) the families of each spouse in the usual sense of the word, and sometimes families broadly speaking, including all relatives; (4) groups such as a totem clan, fraternity, age group, community of the faithful, occupational association, or caste to which one or both of the young people, their mothers and fathers, or all their relatives belong; (5) the local group (hamlet, village, quarter of a city, plantation, etc.).

One should also remember that marriage always has an economic aspect, of varying importance, and that acts of an economic nature (such as establishing an amount, payment, return of the payment for the girl or the young man, the bride price, the bride service by the young man, etc.) become intertwined with the rites proper. The social groups enumerated above are more or less interested parties in the economic negotiations and arrangements. If the family, the village, or the clan is to lose one of its productive members, whether girl or boy, there should at least be some compensation! This explains the distributions of food, clothing, jewelry, and above all the numerous rites involving the "ransom" of something—especially a free passage to the new residence. These "ransoms" always coincide with rites of separation to such an extent that, at least in part, they may be considered rites of separation in themselves. In any event, the economic aspect is so important that— for instance, among the Turko-Mongols—the rite which is the final conclusion of marriage is not performed until the entire *kalym* (Turkic, *qalin*), or bride price, is paid, although this may occur several years later. In that case, the transition period is extended, though sexual relations between the spouses are not affected by the delay.

Among the Bashkirs,[1] marriages may be decided upon while the spouses-to-be are still small children; the intermediaries (who correspond to the *svaty* of the Slavs) carry out the economic negotiations, settling the amount and date

[1] P. Nazarov, "K etnografii Bashkir," *Etnograficheskoe Obozrenie*, IV (1899), 186–89.

of payment of the *kalym*, or bride price, which legally belongs to the girl.[1] Agreement on the *kalym* is observed by a communal meal, followed by reciprocal visits between the families and an exchange of gifts given by relatives, friends, and neighbors. During these visits the sex groups meet separately in different rooms. When the gift exchange is completed, the young man may freely visit the girl at home and may live in her house if his home is in another village. The only conditions in former times were that he could not show himself to his mother-in-law and that he could not see the face of his betrothed; for that reason he always came at night. A child born during this transition period was placed in the care of the girl's mother. "In short, the relations between the young people are properly those of marriage, and nothing can break them except death," in which case the custom of levirate and sororate operated.

In this connection I should like to point out that the basis of levirate and sororate is not only economic but also ritualistic. A new member has been incorporated into the family, and if he were to leave it special ceremonies would be required. Furthermore, the bonds of marriage have joined not only two individuals but above all the collectivities to whom the maintenance of cohesion is important. This may also be seen in divorce rites.

To continue with the account of marriage among the Bashkirs, when the *kalym* has been entirely paid (sometimes only after several years), the girl's father organizes a feast, for which the young groom bears the expense. All the members of both families and the mullah (Moslem priest) are invited. The couple eat in a separate room which

---

[1] If a detailed study is made of the amount of the *kalym* (Turkic, *qalin*) of the Ural-Altaic, and it is compared to the purchase price of an animal, and then deductions are made for gifts and the wedding expenses which fall on the parents of the girl, and when finally it is noted to whom the *kalym* legally belongs, either as a whole or in part, it becomes clear that the terms "bride price" and "dowry" are inaccurate. It is a system of "compensation" which constitutes special institutions that, for an economist, are equivalent to the system of potlatches of the American Indians or to the large feasts given by African chiefs. There is a centralization and a corresponding decentralization of wealth organized in such a way as to avoid concentration (in Marx's sense).

120

may be entered only by close relatives. In the evening, girls who are friends of the bride take her away and hide her in the court or in the village. The young man will sometimes search for her all night long. When he has found her, he gives her to the girls and returns to the special room, where all the guests have gathered; but before he enters he must break with his foot a red thread which two women hold across the door. If he does not see the thread and falls, everyone makes fun of him. He then sits down, and the guests depart one by one. After he is alone, the bride's friends bring her to him and then depart. She removes his boots, and he tries to kiss her, but she pushes him away. He gives her a silver coin, and it is she who then kisses him. The next morning the bride, in the company of her friends, takes leave of each member of her family, gets on a sled, and is transported to her husband's family, where for over a year she must avoid coming face to face with her father-in-law. The breaking of the thread is a rite of passage; hiding and finding the bride is a separation from the local sex group. It is clear that betrothal includes sexual relations, but the marriage as a social act is not concluded until after the economic stipulations have been fulfilled.

The same conclusions may be arrived at from a study of the ceremonies of a people who are not polygynous but polyandrous. The "stages" are distinctly evident in the Toda ceremonies described by Rivers,[1] but to understand them one should go into all the details of the Toda clan and kinship system, so I shall only mention here that those ceremonies begin before puberty and continue until after pregnancy.[2] Instead of giving a lengthy description of Toda rites, I shall list the order of ceremonies among the Bhotiya,

[1] Rivers, *The Todas*, pp. 502–39.

[2] For another case where the rites of marriage form an organic whole with the rites of initiation and the rites of pregnancy, see Delhaise, "Ethnographie congolaise," pp. 185–207. The sequences fall into the general pattern. Cases of the sort described above are far more numerous and more systematized than I at first believed. They deserve a special monograph, all the more because this phenomenon, which is very important for understanding the functioning of semicivilized societies, has not been studied until now.

who inhabit southern Tibet and Sikkim:[1] (1) Astrologers determine whether the projected marriage will be favorable. (2) Uncles of the girl and the boy act as go-betweens and receive presents of money. They meet in the boy's house and then go with gifts to the girl's, to ask for her in marriage. (3) If the gifts they have brought are accepted (ceremony of *nangchang*), the matter is concluded, and the amount of the dowry is decided upon. (4) The intermediaries are given a feast, and there are prayers to invoke blessings upon the bride and groom (the ceremony is called *khelen*). After the last two ceremonies, which are obviously rites of incorporation of the two families, the boy and girl may see each other in complete freedom. (5) A year later comes the *nyen* ceremony; it is a meal (at the expense of the boy's parents) attended by all the relatives on both sides; the bride price is paid at this time. (6) A year after the *nyen*, the *changthoong* ceremony is held: (*a*) An astrologer is called upon to determine a favorable date for the bride's departure from her parents' home and to decide in detail those arrangements which would be most auspicious. (*b*) A great celebration to which lamas are invited is organized; (*c*) Two men, at that moment called "thieves," force their way into the house, supposedly to steal the girl, and a fight is simulated; the "thieves" are beaten, and half-cooked meat is thrown into their mouths, although they may escape this treatment by giving money to the bride's guardians. Two days later, the "thieves" are honored and named "the happy strategists." (*d*) Guests give presents to the bride and to her parents. (*e*) A retinue departs with rejoicing. (*f*) The boy's mother and father go to meet the retinue and take them to their home; there are celebrations for two or three days. (*g*) The girl and her relatives return home. (7) A year later, the *palokh* ceremony is held; at this time the parents give the bride her dowry (which is double the amount that has been paid for her), and she is escorted to

---

[1] A. Earle, "Polyandry amongst the Bhotia," *Census of India*, 1901 (Calcutta, 1903), VI, Part I, Appendix V, pp. xxviii–xxix.

the boy's home; this time she remains permanently. Thus the betrothal and marriage ceremonies among the Bhotiya last at least three years.

In discussing the rites of separation, it is first necessary to speak of an altogether different class of rites, very similar to each other, which are commonly thought to be survivals of marriage by rape or by capture.[1] The establishment of a *permanent social union* by capture has only very rarely been encountered as an institution, and there are no possible grounds for contesting Grosse's opinion that it is an individual, sporadic, and abnormal form. Furthermore, women obtained in this fashion in large groups, for instance during raids, subsequently remain slaves or concubines. As a rule, they are held inferior to women of the abductor's own clan or tribe, and the ceremonies customarily uniting man and woman are not performed in their case.

However, if two lovers want to get married against the wishes of their families, or against rules of society which seem more or less useless or absurd to them, an accommodation is usually made. Either the union is accepted as a *fait accompli*, or only a portion of the customary ceremonies is performed. But the full pattern of ceremonies continues to exist for all those who conclude marriages conforming to the usual tribal customs. The supposed institution of marriage by rape is founded not on directly observed facts but on the interpretation of a whole category of special rites for which no other explanation was known.

An impartial reading of detailed descriptions, and a comparison of rites of "capture" with analogous rites of initiation, will suffice to show that there is, indeed, an abduction,

[1] Post (*Afrikanische Jurisprudenz*, I, 324) makes the following distinctions: A. abduction against the will of the girl: (1) by war, (2) by a young man and his friends whether in or out of her tribe; B. abduction after an agreement between the interested parties: (1) after the understanding that the marriage will follow, (2) after agreement between the two families; C. as a marriage game. It can be seen that the last three cases are simply rites, that the first two are individual and occasional, and that the first is a method of obtaining slaves rather than wives who will enjoy tribal privileges. Westermarck, in *The History of Human Marriage*, has added nothing to Post's point of view, any more than have other historians of the family; for documents on the rites of marriage in Africa, see Post, pp. 326–98.

but not in the accepted sense. It is not a survival but an actual fact, which is repeated at every initiation, every marriage, and every death, and it expresses a change in the condition and status of specific individuals. To marry is to pass from the group of children or adolescents into the adult group, from a given clan to another, from one family to another, and often from one village to another. An individual's separation from these groups weakens them but strengthens those he joins. The weakening is at once numerical (and therefore a reduction in force), economic, and emotional.

The so-called rites of rape or capture express the resistance of the losing groups. They will vary in intensity according to the value attached to the departing member and the comparative wealth of the parties involved. And those who become stronger compensate in some measure for the weakening of groups linked to them by pre-existing bonds of consanguinity, co-nationality, or real or potential reciprocity. The compensations will be in the form of a dowry, gifts, a feast, public celebrations, and money given in exchange for the removal of one or another of the obstacles which those interested place in the way of departure. The emotions of members of the groups involved should also be taken into account; they are not as fully expressed among the semicivilized as they are in our literature and popular sayings, but they nevertheless exist. When a daughter leaves her mother, tears are shed, and though they may often be ritual tears, they express a real sorrow. The companions of the betrothed may also suffer and express their feelings in ways which are sometimes very different from ours.

At this point I should like to summarize one of the descriptions that has most often been quoted as proof of the theory of an ancient marriage by capture. It is Burckhardt's account of marriage among the Arabs of Sinai.[1] The

[1] John Lewis Burckhardt, *Notes on the Bedouins and the Wahabys* (London: Coburn & Bentley, 1831), I, 263–64. [French translation by J. B. B. Eyries (Paris: A. Bertrand, 1835) was used by van Gennep.]

future husband and two other young men seize the girl in the mountains and take her to her own father's tent; she defends herself on the way, and "the more she struggles . . . the more she is applauded ever after by her companions." The young men force her into the women's quarters, and a relative of the future husband covers her with a cloak and cries, "None shall cover thee but such a one" (that is, the bridegroom). The girl's mother and her female relatives dress her, and she is placed on a camel but continues to defend herself while the groom's friends hold her. She is led three times around his tent in this fashion while her companions shout and exclaim; then she is taken to the women's quarters in the groom's tent, and she is expected to weep all the way to his tent, irrespective of the distance—which may be considerable. It is apparent that at her own home the bride is separated from the girls of her own age group. If the rite were a survival of rape, the girl's whole family or tribe would have to resist the undertakings of the young man's tribe, family, and companions. Instead, only two age groups are represented in the struggle.

In addition to having the help of her own age group, a girl may also be assisted by all the women of her kin or tribe, whether young or old, married or widowed. Where this is the case—as in the Khond practices described later in this chapter—it is no longer the solidarity of an age class that is involved by the solidarity of a specific sex group. I know of no case where an inclusive solidarity of the sexes is expressed—that is, where the girls and women of the young man's family, clan, and tribe oppose the bride's entry. And this fact suffices to upset Crawley's theory; he had seen from the works of Fison, Westermarck,[1] and Grosse[2]

---

[1] He leans toward Spencer's theory that the girl's resistance has become a traditional expression of modesty; this may be true in individual cases, but it does not explain why the parties in conflict are not always the same and why this selfsame struggle has not become an institution as universal as marriage.

[2] E. Grosse, *Die Formen der Familie und die Formen der Wirtschaft* (Freiburg im Breisgau: J. C. Mohr, 1896), pp. 107–8, tries to see in these ceremonies a corrupt survival of real rape in warfare among peoples who have become peaceful but who wish to retain a reputation for bravery.

that the survival of marriage by rape is a fantasy, but he claimed, "This may be called 'capture,' but it is capture from the female sex."[1]

The girl cannot be torn from her sex group either primarily or secondarily, for she does not change her sex. But she leaves a particular restricted sex group, familial as well as local, to be incorporated into another restricted sex group which is also familial and local. This fact is portrayed in the following Samoyed rite: the Samoyeds "look for a girl in a family other than their own" (clan exogamy); an intermediary carries out negotiations for the *kalym*, of which half belongs to the bride's father and half to her other relatives; the father-in-law and the young man eat a meal together; the father prepares "the gift for the day after the wedding." On the date set "the groom, accompanied by several women unknown to the girl's family, comes to fetch his wife. All relatives who have had part of the *kalym* are visited, and they give small gifts to the couple. The women brought by the groom seize the bride, take her by force to a sled onto which they bind her, and depart"; the gifts received are loaded onto the sleds, and the groom rides on the last one. When they arrive at the groom's yurt (a tent of felt stretched over a light framework of wood), the young woman prepares a bed for herself and her husband and they sleep together, but their sexual relations only begin a month

[1] Crawley, *The Mystic Rose*, p. 352. See also pp. 333, 354 ff., 367 ff. The rites concerning the solidarity of sex groups are especially well defined in Islam, where the separation of the sex groups permeates all phases of social life. For North Africa, compare the descriptions given by Maurice Gaudefroy-Demombrynes, *Les cérémonies du mariage chez les indigènes de l'Algérie* (Paris: Petit, 1901), and "Coutumes de mariage: Algérie," *Revue des traditions populaires*, Vol. XXII (1907), Nos. 2, 3; Doutté, *Merrâkech*, *passim* (bibliography in detail for North Africa, p. 334); the *Archives marocaines* and the *Revue africaine*, *passim*; Karl Narbeshuber, *Aus dem Leben der arabischen Bevölkerung, in Sfax (Regentschaft Tunis)* (Leipzig: Staat Museum für Völkerkunde, 1907), pp. 11–16 and notes; Edmond Destaing, *Étude sur la dialecte berbère des Beni-Snous* (Paris: E. Leroux, 1907), I, 287–91. In this last work I read that in order for the bridegroom to enter the room where the bride was waiting, he had to jump over her mother, who was lying on the threshold (p. 289); in all these ceremonies, often highly complicated, the thread of rites of passage can be found underlying numerous rites of protection and fertility. And everywhere, as in other North African ceremonies, there is a combination of elements indigenous to the Berbers, with others that are Moslem or strictly Arabic.

later. The husband gives a present to his mother-in-law if his wife was a virgin. Periodically thereafter the young woman goes to visit her father, and he must each time give her many gifts (in compensation for the *kalym*); in the event of the wife's death or a separation, the father-in-law returns the *kalym*.[1]

It is apparent that the bride price (*kalym*) is amply compensated for by gifts the bride's relatives are required to give her and that the girl's forcible removal from the restricted sex group of her adolescence is effected by representatives of the sex group of which she is about to become a member. Among the Khond of southern India, the girl's group includes not only her friends but the young women of her village in general. When agreement between the families has been reached, the girl is dressed in a red blanket and carried to the groom's village by her maternal uncle in the company of the young women of her village; the retinue carries gifts for the groom, who stands in the road, accompanied by young boys from his village armed with bamboo sticks. The women attack the young men, hitting them with sticks, stones, and clods of earth, and the boys defend themselves with their sticks. Bit by bit they all approach the village, and when they reach it the fighting stops. The groom's uncle takes the bride and carries her into the groom's house. "This fighting is by no means child's play, and the men are sometimes seriously injured."[2] After the bride has reached the village, there is a communal meal at the groom's expense.

This rite is performed among all the Khond tribes, and I mention it because Thurston saw it as an excellent example of the retention, in ceremonial form, of marriage by capture.[3] However, the bride's party pushes back the groom's

---

[1] Peter Simon Pallas, *Voyages dans plusieurs provinces de l'empire de Russie et dans l'Asie septentrionale* (1st ed.; Paris: Maradan, 1788–93; original in German and in Russian, St. Petersburg, 1771–76), II, 171–74.

[2] Thurston, *Ethnographic Notes in Southern India*, pp. 18–23. One can find in this book (pp. 1–131) an excellent detailed monograph on the marriage ceremonies among diverse tribes of Southern India.

[3] *Ibid.*, p. 8.

and the fight is between two groups of different sexes and localities. That is why I see this rite as a separation of the girl from her former sex group, age group, family, and village.

In the ceremonies of Mabuiag (in the Torres Strait Islands) the sexual element of the struggle disappears, and the suitor fights with the girl's collateral relatives (called "brothers," a term which should here be interpreted according to its meaning in the classificatory system— "brothers who represent the totem clan"). The girl proposes marriage to the boy. She makes a grass bracelet, which the boy's sister attaches to his wrist, and in exchange he sends a *makamak*, which the girl fastens to her leg. The young people arrange meetings by day and by night and have sexual relations. The boy performs small services for the girl's mother and father, who pretend not to know anything about his relationship with their daughter. But the brothers engage the lover in a mock battle; first they wound him only on the leg, but finally they hit him on the head with a club. Immediately afterward, one of the girl's brothers takes her by the hand and gives her to the young man.

The young man then amasses all sorts of goods, which on a specified day are piled onto a mat and laid out in a public place around which all the girl's relatives squat. The girl is dressed and painted ceremonially and is accompanied by the wives of two of her elder brothers. The wives take the gifts and give them to the girl, and she distributes them to her brothers. Then all eat a communal meal and the marriage is accomplished. Clearly, the sexual act is independent of the social union. There are individual rites of incorporation, then a transition period, then social rites of separation and incorporation, and finally compensation for the loss sustained by the family group, which is founded on the totemic and classificatory system. However, the wife does not become a member of her husband's clan, and he owns her completely, having "paid for her."[1]

[1] Alfred C. Haddon, ed., *Cambridge Anthropological Expedition to Torres Straits* (Cambridge: University Press, 1903–35), V (1904), 223–24; see also 224–29 and VI

Among the Irtysh Ostyaks, when the nuptial party started for the young man's village, the boy's of the bride's village detained her sled with a cord which they released if the bride threw them a gift of money. For a second and again a third time they caught up with her and received money, and only after the third ransom was the sled allowed to depart.[1] It should be remembered that there is a shortage of women among the Ostyaks, who have been reduced to making common-law unions with Russian women.

I want to draw attention to the fact that the ties of the young man or the girl with the former groups (of age, sex, kinship, and tribe) are often so powerful that several attempts are required before they are broken; therefore there are multiple flights and pursuits in the forest or the mountains; dowry or bride price is paid by instalments; and rites are repeated several times. In the same way, incorporation into the new groups—such as family, the social group of married men or women or of individuals who have lost their virginity, the clan, or the tribe—is not accomplished at once. During a period of varying duration the newcomer is an intruder, especially in relation to the immediate family. That is how I explain the mother-in-law and father-in-law taboos for daughter-in-law and son-in-law, and the uncertain position of the wife until her pregnancy or until the birth of a son.

Sometimes the alliance of the two families, already established by the ceremonies preceding the sexual union of the spouses, must be cemented by further gifts and communal feasts—in short, by a series of ceremonies following the marriage, such as those which in North Africa last seven days. From descriptions given by Gaudefroy-Demombynes for Tlemcen (in Algeria) it appears that there the newly married man or his wife are incorporated into particular groups first by the men of the two families, then by all the

(1908), 112–19. For the idea of a compensation for the loss, see p. 225; for economic compensations, pp. 230–32.

[1] Serafin Keropavich Patkanov, *Die Irtysch-Ostiaken und ihre Volkspoesie* (St. Petersburg: Imprimerie de l'Académie Impériale des Sciences, 1897), I, 141.

men and women of both families, then by all the women. It seems that in Constantine this incorporation is carried out only by the men and women of the two families.[1] A new equilibrium of the sex groups is created in the course of these ceremonies.

In addition to the rites of "rape" already discussed, I should like to mention the following rites of separation: changing clothes; emptying a pot of milk and bursting three berries (the Gallas); cutting, breaking, or throwing away something connected with childhood or bachelorhood; releasing the hair; cutting or shaving the hair or the beard; closing the eyes; removing jewelry; consecrating one's toys, such as dolls, one's jewelry, and one's childhood dress to a deity; preliminary perforation of the hymen and all other mutilations; breaking the so-called chain of virginity; baring the waist; changing food habits and being subject to temporary dietary taboos; distributing toys or jewelry or gifts of "souvenirs" to childhood friends; beating or insulting one's childhood companions or being beaten or insulted by them; washing one's feet or being washed; bathing or anointing oneself; damaging, destroying, or carrying away the hearth, the deities, or the sacra of one's family of origin; closing hands, crossing arms, covering oneself with a veil; enclosing oneself in a litter, a palanquin, a carriage; being pushed or mistreated; vomiting; changing one's name or one's personality; and being subjected to temporary or permanent taboos on work performed by one's sex group.

In addition, I would include among rites of separation two that are more complex than those listed above. The rite of passing over something—performed by the entire retinue, the betrothed pair, or only one of them—can undoubtedly be interpreted in various ways. It appears from descriptions of the rite that acts which on first impression seem identical may not be identically interpreted by the participants. The obstacle may be stepped over, and in that case, if the rite is performed by the girl, it may be a fertility

[1] Gaudefroy-Demombynes, *Les cérémonies du mariage*, pp. 71–76.

rite. The obstacle may be jumped over, perhaps in order to jump from one world to another or from one family to another. It may or may not be touched, and the rite may be one of passage, fertility, or consecration (preservation). It will be a rite of passage if the person is lifted over the obstacle, if an obstacle such as a thread across a door or a barrier on the threshold is broken, or if a door is forced or is made to open by coercive gestures or prayers. In short, this type of rite may be discussed only if detailed documentation is presented.[1]

The ritual substitution of another person for the bride or groom also may vary from people to people in its meaning.[2] In some cases, as Crawley believes, the substitution may be intended to remove the danger of "inoculation." On the evidence of detailed descriptions, however, I think that most often the rite represents an attempt to avoid a weakening of the interested groups (the age and sex group, the family, etc.) by relinquishing or uniting only individuals who are least valuable socially and especially economically (e.g. a little girl, an old woman, or a small boy). This attitude is indicated by the mockery made of the replacements and the furious protests of friends and relatives of the bride and groom.[3]

Now I come to rites of incorporation. Various observers have often noted in their detailed descriptions of marriage ceremonies which rite has the greatest significance and ends the negotiations. As a rule, that rite is either a meal eaten

[1] For documents, references, and theories different from mine, see Hartland, *The Legend of Perseus*, I, 173 ff.; Crawley, *The Mystic Rose*, p. 337; Crooke, "The Lifting of the Bride," pp. 226, 244; Trumbull, *The Threshold Covenant*, pp. 140–43.

[2] For these facts, see among others, Hugo Hepding, "Die falsche Braut," *Hessische Blatter für Volkskunde*, V (1906), 161–64; Thurston, *Ethnographic Notes in Southern India*, pp. 3, 29. It should be noted that here it is the bridegroom who goes to live with his wife, and also that the substitution is made for him.

[3] I mention from memory the taboos relating to the mother-in-law for the son-in-law, the father-in-law for the daughter-in-law, etc., which E. B. Tylor saw as a "cutting" or rite of separation ("On a Method of Investigating the Development of Institutions, Applied to Laws of Marriage and Descent," *Journal of the Royal Anthropological Institute*, XVIII [1888], 245 ff.) but which Crawley classes in the wider category of taboos relating to sex group solidarity.

in common after the last payment of the bride price or the dowry, a communal meal which is not connected with economic stipulations, or else the collective participation in an essentially religious ceremony. Among the rites of incorporation it is possible to isolate those which have an individual meaning and which unite the two young people to each other: giving or exchanging belts, bracelets, rings,[1] or clothes which are worn; binding one to the other with a single cord; tying parts of each other's clothing together; touching each other reciprocally in some way;[2] using objects belonging to the other (milk, betel, tobacco, occupational implements); offering the other something to eat or drink; eating together (communion, confarreation); being wrapped in a single piece of clothing or a veil; sitting on the same seat; drinking each other's blood; eating from the same food or dish; drinking from the same liquid or container; massaging, rubbing, anointing (with blood or clay); washing each other; entering the new house; and so forth. These are essentially rites of union.

However, some rites of incorporation have a collective significance, either in joining one or the other of the individuals to new groups or in uniting two or more groups. Within this category may be included: the exchange of gifts,[3] exchanges of sisters (in Australia, among the Bassa-Komo of West Africa, and elsewhere), participation in collective ceremonies such as ritual dances, betrothal and wedding feasts, the exchange of visits, rounds of visits, putting on the dress of adult or married men and women and, for the woman, being pregnant or giving birth. Some rites are both individual and collective; the acceptance of a gift

---

[1] On the constraining power of the wedding ring as a theme for legend, see E. Nourry (pseud. P. Saintyves), *Les saints successeurs des dieux* (Paris: E. Nourry, 1907), p. 255.

[2] In detail: joining hands, intertwining the fingers, kissing, embracing, pressing one head against the other, sitting one upon the other or against each other, lying down together, etc.

[3] The refusal of a gift is a sign that the proposed union is not accepted; and, in cases of betrothal before birth or in early childhood, the return of the gift is a sign that the arrangements have been dissolved.

places a constraint not only upon the individual who accepts it but also upon the groups to which he belongs. It is often the first rite of the betrothal.

A special rite of incorporation known as the "marriage to the tree" has often intrigued theoreticians; it is readily understood if one remembers that in some cases—as among the Kol of Bengal—marriage is an incorporation into the totem clan and therefore also an initiation rite.[1] At present, marriage is celebrated among the Kol between the ages of sixteen and eighteen for the boys, and between fourteen and sixteen for the girls, but formerly it occurred at a much later age. The following facts should be noted: the Kol believe that the souls of the dead go to a special region, but children possess no soul and cannot even become demons. Until marriage, a child is not subject to the dietary taboos of his clan and may have sexual relations without considering rules of exogamy. It is marriage which gives him a soul and incorporates him into the clan.

The Kol clans are totemic; the principal totems are the mango and the mahua (*Illipe latifolia*). One of the rites of Kol marriage consists of first marrying the boy to the mango and the girl to the mahua by an embrace. On the basis of the foregoing I think that this "fictitious" marriage must be seen not as a transfer of personality to "insure the harmlessness or success of the real ceremony"[2] but as a rite of initiation into the totem clan. It is woven into the marriage ceremonies, which in their entirety are, among the Kol, also the ceremonies for entrance into the clan. An individual who for one reason or another is excluded from the clan may re-enter it if he gathers representatives from different villages and has the priest of his village sacrifice a white goat or a white ox. He drinks some of its blood or sprinkles it on

[1] F. Hahn, *Einführung in das Gebiet der Kolsmission* (Gütersloh, 1907), pp. 74–82, 87–88. The Kol form a section of the Munda.

[2] Crawley, *The Mystic Rose*, pp. 340–44. The rite of tree marriage described by E. T. Dalton in *Descriptive Ethnology of Bengal* (Calcutta, 1872), p. 194, has, according to H. H. Risley (*Census of India*, 1901), fallen into disuse; however, Hahn seems to speak as an eyewitness; see also Thurston, *Ethnographic Notes in Southern India*, pp. 44–47.

the roof of his house, invoking the sun-god, and then the meat is eaten by all the representatives of the clan.[1]

All these rites of incorporation should be understood literally rather than symbolically: the cord which binds, the ring, the bracelet, and the garland which encircles have a real coercive effect. It is very interesting to examine from this point of view the rites of passage across thresholds.[2] In some rites the entry is accompanied by violence; in others the new world is penetrated. In Palestine, for instance, a girl approaches her future husband's house carrying a jar full of water on her head, and he makes the jar fall at the moment when the girl straddles the threshold. This rite is not a libation, as Trumbull thinks, but a separation from the old environment and an incorporation into the new one by a sort of baptism. On the island of Karpathos the breaking of a rod placed across the doorway has the same significance.

Mr. Chavannes has called to my attention an interesting Chinese rite in which the physical passage is accomplished not all at once but in stages.[3] Among a tribe of the ethnic group of Ho-mi (southern Yunnan),[4] when the future son-in-law comes to fetch his wife from the future father-in-law's house, "the father-in-law leads the son-in-law through the second and third hall and makes him cross the pavilion. At each door, an aide loudly announces the rite which must be accomplished, and the son-in-law prostrates himself twice. This procedure is called the 'obeisance to the doors' (*pai men*). The opening of the doors becomes important to the father-in-law because he is about to permit his daughter to be seen; that is why he creates difficulties for the son-in-law."[5]

Among the Cheremiss the retinue which comes to fetch

[1] Hahn, *Einführung in das Gebiet der Kolsmission*, p. 159.

[2] Trumbull, *The Threshold Covenant*, pp. 26–29.

[3] *T'oung-Pao: Ou archives concernant l'histoire, les langues, la géographie, et l'ethnographie de l'Asie orientale*, December, 1905, pp. 602–3.

[4] [This group may be the Ho Nhi or Lolo.]

[5] The translator of the Chinese document sees in this rite, quite incorrectly, a survival of marriage by abduction.

the bride is stopped at the gates leading to the courtyard of her parents' farm. The *sabūs* (director of ceremonies) enters the isba, and the master of the house gives him food and drink. The *sabus* requests the right of entry for the retinue, and the father asks if they have lost anything. "Yes," says the *sabus*, "so-and-so (the groom) has lost one of the sleeves of his jacket, and we have come to see if it is in your home." The father says "No," and the *sabus* leaves, then returns; only on the third time does the father say "Yes." Then the doors are opened and the rites of incorporation begin.[1]

The transition period may or may not have a sexual significance. Among certain peoples the betrothed pair have sexual relations, and children conceived or born during that time are considered legitimate (cf. the cases previously cited). Elsewhere, the separation between the two young people is absolute, and a child born as a result of disobedience of that rule would be denied his proper place in the family or the society. For instance, "The Lapps never permit the betrothed pair to sleep together before their wedding day; if it should happen that they do, a child so conceived would be declared a bastard, even if it were proved that he was conceived after the betrothal and the promise given. The child, whether male or female, would be most contemptible and would always rank lowest among its brothers and sisters. If he grew up and the reindeer should flourish under his care, he would often be thrown out of the house."[3] This last detail is interesting, since it shows that the child retains the qualities and imperfections acquired from his being conceived during the impure (taboo) period.

This attitude is shared also by the Chaga of Tanganyika, whose marriage ceremonies comprise very distinct stages. The young man (aged sixteen) chooses a certain girl and

[1] G. Iakovlev, *Religioznye obriady Cheremis* ("Religious Ceremonies of the Cheremiss") (Kazan, 1887), pp. 55–56.

[2] Johannes G. Scheffer, *Histoire de la Laponie: Sa description, l'origine, les mœurs, la manière de viorses des habitant*, trans. from Latin by Father Aug. Lubin (Paris: V. O. de Varennes, 1678); see p. 395 as complement to p. 275.

135

ascertains her feelings. If she responds favorably, the young man's father goes to find the head of his family and, as authorization for the betrothal, gives him a goat and four pots of fermented drink. He then goes to find the girl's father and asks for his consent as well as the girl's. The young man gives the girl pearls and a bracelet; the young man's mother invites the girl to eat, and the girl stays in her hut overnight; these invitations are repeated frequently. The girl spends the last two months of her betrothal in her mother-in-law's hut. The betrothal lasts several years, during which, bit by bit, the young man pays the bride price to his parents-in-law and their relatives, in accordance with a fixed protocol. The last act of the betrothal consists of the slaughtering of an ox. Its hindquarters and one shoulder go to the girl's father, who is also given a goat which the groom brings, tied with dracaena leaves, to his father-in-law's hut. This goat is the center of the wedding feast, which is attended by all the relatives of the betrothed pair. After the feast everyone goes to the young man's hut, the girl walking behind him with her hands on his shoulders. The relatives of the young girl lament the family's loss of a daughter, sister, etc. This is the rite of separation.

During the next three months the girl is not supposed to do anything, and all the work is done by her mother and her mother-in-law, who teach the girl how to keep house. The young man is similarly instructed by his father and his father-in-law. This period of apprenticeship terminates with the celebration called *wali*, "which alone validates the marriage"; any child born before it is considered illegitimate. This celebration occurs two to five months after the beginning of the couple's life together, depending on the time of the harvest of eleusine (African millet). All relatives, neighbors, and friends are invited to drink a fermented beverage called *wari* and to dance and sing songs which are mostly erotic in nature. The young man gives his wife a heavy copper bracelet, which she puts on her left arm. If she is already pregnant, only old men are invited to the celebration. On the third day goats are killed and eaten; then the feast is ended, and the woman must work. It is apparent that until the *wali* celebration the marriage is an act which is of interest only to two individuals and two restricted (sex and family) groups, and that the feast of *wali* gives the act a general and social significance.[1]

Among the Senufo

who have remained faithful to their national customs, the young man who desires to marry a young girl is careful not to let his intentions be known either to her or to her family. But he watches the comings and goings of the girl's parents, and if he sees the mother going to the bush to bring back dead wood, he awaits her return on the path and must rush to relieve her of her load, which he then carries on his head. Later, he helps the girl's father carry pieces of termite nest for the hens. A few days later, the suitor will himself gather a load of wood and take it to the home of his beloved. Then he brings as gifts to her father kola nuts, a chicken, and finally some cowries. The girl's father than gathers together his family and invites a village elder to the meeting, where the father explains that so-and-so has been very obliging toward him and that he would be happy to reward him by giving him his daughter in marriage. The assembly approves, and the elder informs the suitor that he may consider himself accepted. But the trials of the future husband are not yet at an end. When the cultivating season approaches, he must gather his brothers and his friends and go with them to plow his future father-in-law's field. After the sowing he must come to weed. He buys millet beer and treats the girl's entire family. Only then does the official betrothal begin.

Often the girl is at that time far from marriageable. She remains at her father's home until she is nubile, and, during this waiting period, the groom must continue to assist her family with his labor and resources. When the girl is marriageable, her father gives her to the groom, who makes a gift of five to ten cowrie francs to the father and another of the same value to the mother. When the young couple have lived together for a month, the girl's father brings her home for two or three months, and she is returned to her husband upon payment of ten cowrie francs. The second period of cohabitation again lasts a month, and at the end of it the father again claims his daughter for two or three months, after which she is permanently returned to her husband, who pays another ten francs. If the girl becomes pregnant during this preparatory period, her father is required to give a loincloth to the

[1] M. Merker, *Rechtsverhältnisse und Sitten der Wadschagga* (Petermanns Mitteilungen, Suppl. No. 138 [1902]), pp. 4–6.

137

husband at the time of the child's birth. According to the elders, this custom is designed to give the future spouses ample time to know and appreciate each other and thus to prevent badly matched unions.[1]

In the example that follows, the transitional phases of betrothal and initiation have been merged in such a way that they constitute a single period from the beginning of initiation to the completion of a socialized sexual union. Among the Vai of Liberia the separation of the sexes is reinforced by the fact that a girl sometimes does not leave the *sande* except to marry. The *sande* is a sacred place in the forest to which all girls are taken before or around the age of ten, and where they remain till after their first menses. Like the boys in the *belly* they are considered dead, as are the old women who come to instruct them in domestic and sexual behavior. Their annual coming-out celebration is a rebirth. Often, however, a girl's parents affiance her while she is in the *sande*, and in that case she does not leave it on the annual holiday but must remain there until her first menses.[2] The girl's parents are immediately informed when these occur, and they notify her betrothed, who sends gifts to the *sande*. The girl is rubbed with perfumed oil, adorned with jewels, and so forth, and her parents come and fetch her at the entrance to the sacred forest.

After a ceremonial meal the girl's mother takes her to the hut of her betrothed. Coitus is consummated while the two families and their friends eat a meal together; when the act is terminated, the husband comes out of the hut and participates in the meal. The ceremony is the same if the betrothal occurs after the departure from the *sande*. Thus among the Vai the period of betrothal merges with the initiation period, and the first menses are important for a departure from the *sande* only if the girl is already betrothed. Physiological puberty is a legal prerequisite for marriage among the Vai, as among many other peoples.

[1] Maurice Delafosse, "Le peuple Siéna ou Sénoufo" (a series of articles), *Revue des Études ethnographiques et sociologiques*, 1908, p. 457.

[2] This is proof that here, too, the initiation ceremony has nothing to do with puberty.

Moreover, the sexual separation of the betrothed pair is here guaranteed by the sacred nature of the *sande*.[1]

From the evidence presented in these illustrations it becomes clear that the stages of marriage—and especially the major one, the betrothal—have significant economic aspects. Moreover, every marriage is a social disturbance involving not just two individuals but several groups of varying sizes. A marriage modifies a number of elements in their relationships to each other, and these changes, step by step, bring about a disturbance of equilibrium. This phenomenon is scarcely noticed in our large cities, but it is more apparent in remote corners of our countrysides where weddings are occasions for a stoppage of production, an expenditure of savings, and an awakening from the usual apathy. It is even more noticeable among Turko-Mongol tribes and Arab tribes on the oases, and especially among semicivilized peoples, who always live in small and highly cohesive groups.

The impact of a marriage on a group's daily life seems to me to explain, as adequately as the biological theory advanced by Westermarck and Havelock Ellis, why marriages are held in spring, winter, and autumn—i.e., at the time of little activity and not at the moment when there is work in the fields. I would not go so far as to deny a persistence of the ancient periods of rut or the influence of celestial cycles, which are marked by a renewal of vegetation and a sexual excitation of animals and man. But this influence hardly explains the frequency of marriages in the autumn. It is often said, on the other hand, that this time is chosen because the agricultural work is completed, the granaries and treasuries are full, and there is a good opportunity for bachelors to establish a home for themselves for the winter. The rather widespread interpretation of simultaneous marriages of several couples as a survival either of the rutting period or of an ancient group marriage cannot be accepted, since "primitive promiscuity" is a fantasy.

[1] Büttikofer, *Reisebilder aus Liberia*, II, 304–13.

It seems to me, furthermore, that multiple synchronic marriages at one or two occasions during the year should be compared with other ceremonial synchronisms, such as the celebration of the birthday of all the children born on the same day, or those born the same day, month, or year as the child of a king or prince. Other instances include an annual celebration in honor of all the women who gave birth during the year (among the Ngente of the Lushae Hills); periodic celebrations of return or of the anniversary of an initiation, and especially initiations of several children at the same time, either every year or every two or three years; and commemorations and great annual feasts for the dead.[1] Briefly, since all these acts have a generally social significance, the system under discussion is the extreme form by which their generally social nature is expressed. In place of ceremonies enacted only by restricted groups (the family, the clan, etc.), rituals have been instituted which include all the groups that constitute society. These are to be found, for instance, in the curious marriage ceremonies at Ouargla, carefully described by Biarnay.[2]

For some peoples the period of transition and the betrothal ceremonies are quite simple. Thus among the Herero the young man gives the girl an iron bead which she fastens to her apron; he leaves and is not allowed to see her or to enter her kraal until the marriage. That ceremony typically includes a clearly sacred meal expressing the solidarity of the bride with her companions and with her clan. Neither the young man nor his friends are present at the meal, but when it is finished they come to fetch her and take her to

[1] Annual rededication of the churches among the Sabians in the vicinity of Baghdad; Siouffi, *Études sur la religion des Soubbas*, p. 120.

[2] Mr. Rene Basset was kind enough to show me the proofs of the book by Mr. Biarnay on Ouargla. Marriages take place there each year in springtime, and the series of rites follow a very strict order; at first only the two interested persons and their two sex groups take part in them; then the rites become more and more socialized: the families participate in them, then sections of the oasis, and finally the entire oasis. I regret that I am not even able to give a résumé of these rites, which Mr. Biarnay described in great detail, keeping track of all the variations of persons, locality, magico-religious techniques, etc. See Biarnay, *Étude sur le dialecte de Ouargla* (Paris: Leroux, 1909), Ap. pp. 379–492.

their kraal. Then come rites incorporating the girl into the sacred practices of the new household and the new tribal group. After the meal and therefore before the sexual union (which takes place in the husband's kraal) the girl's mother dresses her in the "hat" and clothing of a married woman. The husband ceremonially brings back to her mother the "girl's apron" of his wife. The Herero have the custom of a bride price and are organized in totem clans.[1]

The fact that marriage ceremonies may be analogous, and are sometimes identical in every detail, to adoption ceremonies, will seem understandable if one remembers that in the last analysis a marriage is the incorporation of a stranger into a group. Among the Ainu, for instance, the husband may go to live in his wife's family or the wife in her husband's and in each case the spouse participates in the sacred practices of the household.[2] His or her entrance into the family is clearly identified with adoption. Furthermore, marriage ceremonies often include details resembling aspects of enthronement: a veil spread over the king or the spouses; a crown; sacred objects peculiar to the betrothed, like the regalia of a future king. The resemblances are especially strong where, as in North Africa and certain parts of India, the groom is called "king," "sultan," or "prince," and the bride "queen," "sultana," or "princess," or where, as in China, the groom is called "mandarin." Although cases where marriage is regarded as a rebirth are rare, those where it is an initiation or an ordination are not. All these resemblances and identifications are expressed in rites of passage, which are always founded on the same idea, the reality of a change in the participants' social condition.

The ceremonies of divorce and widowhood as counterparts to those of marriage deserve brief consideration. The rites of divorce among most peoples seem to be of the simplest kind. Ordinarily it is sufficient if the wife leaves the conjugal home and returns to her parents' house, or

---

[1] Irle, *Die Herero*, pp. 105–9. [2] See Batchelor, *The Ainu*, pp. 224–25.

if the husband physically removes his wife from their common house. It is my impression, however, that if divorce ceremonies seem so simple in ethnographic literature it is because observers either have not been interested in them or have not understood the meaning of certain acts, and, in particular, because they have seen separation and divorce only in their legal and economic aspects. When an individual and collective bond has been established with such care and so many complications, one would not expect that it could be broken one day by a single gesture. We know, for example, that in the Roman Catholic church divorce is not even permitted and that only an annulment of the marriage can be obtained.[1] Moreover, the annulment is preceded by an investigation which does not include any procedures of a really magico-religious nature.

The Jews, on the other hand, have elaborated such a complicated divorce ceremony[2] that it has become an obstacle to many people's desires. A ritualized letter is given to the wife, and it must be written as perfectly as a sacred writ. The rabbi throws this letter into the air, and one of the wife's witnesses must catch it in mid-air; otherwise the proceedings must begin over again. This is the final rite of separation.[3] Among the Habé (or Dogon) of the Niger plateau, as in classical antiquity, if a marriage has been consecrated by a domestic ceremony, the spouse who is leaving must break his or her ties with the family deities by a sacrifice.[4] Among the Eskimo, the husband looks at his wife, then leaves the hut without a word. Among the Chuvash, a husband who is dissatisfied with his wife and wants to part

---

[1] [Under certain conditions an ecclesiastical court can grant an absolute divorce.]

[2] See, among others, Jungendres, *Jüdisches Zeremoniell oder Beschreibung* . . . (Nuremberg, 1726); *Jewish Encyclopedia*; etc.

[3] [According to *The Jewish Encyclopedia*, the *get*, or bill of divorcement, must be written in a prescribed form, in the Talmudic idiom, and attested to by witnesses. The rabbi places it in the wife's hand and then tears it in two and keeps it. The minute regulations are attributed to a desire to avoid misunderstandings. They developed through a gradual restriction of what was originally a husband's absolute right to divorce his wife.]

[4] Desplagnes, *Le plateau central nigérien*, p. 222.

with her tears her veil. This rite is also found among the Cheremiss, the Mordvinians, the Votyaks, and the Voguls.[1]

In Java, "if a man wishes to be divorced, the priest cuts the 'marriage cord' before witnesses, and this simple act severs the nuptial tie."[2] Among the southern Galla, if a woman is mistreated by her husband, her brother may come and fetch her, but he does not have the right to enter the hut or the village if her husband forbids it; he has to wait till his sister comes out—for instance, to draw water—and then he takes her away. A woman divorced in this fashion may not remarry, and her husband does not have the right to reclaim her; but the two interested groups are reconciled through a payment in sheep or goats.[3] Among the Zaramo the husband lets his wife know that he no longer wants her by giving her a special sort of reed, and among the Nyoro the husband cuts a piece of leather in two, keeps one half, and sends the other to his wife's father.[4]

The Islamic rite of separation is verbal: it suffices for the husband to say three times to his wife, "You are divorced" or "I divorce you," and she must go away with her belongings; the husband usually returns one-third of the dowry. But if the woman wants a divorce, she has to have a judgment of the cadi (a minor Moslem judge), whose function and jurisprudence are fundamentally religious in nature. At its origin, the triple repetition was a truly magic formula. It has this character also in India and among the Swahili.[5] Sometimes a tribal council is called, and it settles

---

[1] J. G. Georgi, *Russland: Beschreibung aller Nationen des russischen Reiches* . . . (Leipzig, 1783), I, 42.

[2] Crawley, *The Mystic Rose*, p. 323.

[3] E. S. Wakefield, "Marriage Customs of the Southern Gallas," *Folk-lore*, XVIII (1907), No. 4, 323–24.

[4] Post, *Afrikanische Jurisprudenz*, I, 452.

[5] R. C. Temple, "The Folk-lore in the Legends of the Panjab," *Folk-lore*, X (1899), 409–10; for the formula among the Swahili ("I do not wish to have anything more to do with your nakedness, etc."), see D. Carl Velten, *Sitten und Gebräuche der Suaheli* (translation of *Desturi za Wasuali na Khgbori za Desturi za Sherila za Wasuahela*) (Göttingen, 1903), pp. 237–38. The letter of divorcement is also used among adherents of Islam in Morocco, in Palestine, in Turkey, among the Swahili, and elsewhere.

the divorce to the economic advantage of one or the other of the parties. But the procedure which is much more widespread is neither ceremonial nor ritual; it consists simply in the sending away, or the departure, of one or the other spouse.

The simplicity of divorce rites contradicts neither the conceptual scheme of rites of passage nor the sociological explanation which I propose. The marriage establishes the girl and boy in the category of socially adult women and men, and nothing can take this from them—a fact that also applies to the widower and the widow. Furthermore, the bond between the families is not broken by separation of the spouses since the negotiations which determine the future position of the separated or divorced couple also minimize the threat of a breach. There are, of course, individual exceptions on emotional grounds. Many peoples do not permit divorce if there are children, and under such circumstances the group bond remains intact. In summary, although I do not claim that the pattern and the system of interpretations I have proposed are absolutely rigid or universal, I do not think that the lack of elaborate divorce rituals can be used as an objection against them.

It is remarkable, furthermore, that the bond which can be so easily broken through divorce is hardly affected by death, and not at all in those instances where the widow commits suicide. I know very well that mourning includes many rites which are simply prophylactic or protective. However, funeral ceremonies in which the widowed partipate include more than mourning, and, in theory at least, one must also recognize their social nature.[1] For instance, a Hupa widow, to free herself, need only perform the rite of passing between her husband's legs before he is carried

[1] The following rite practiced among Orthodox Jews may be considered a rite of passage: if a man dies childless and his widow does not wish to become the wife of her dead husband's brother (levirate), she removes his shoe, spits on the ground, and recites a special formula (*Jewish Encyclopedia*, p. 170, *s.v.* "Halizath"; see p. 174 for interpretations which are for the most part not acceptable to the author). It is clearly a matter of separation from the husband's family, and the rite is intended to assure the passage into a category of either free widow or remarried woman.

out of the house. Otherwise she is bound to him for the rest of her life,[1] and all unfaithfulness to the dead man will bring her misfortune.

Marriages of the widowed as well as the divorced are ceremonially greatly simplified, for reasons to be explained.

There do not seem to be any rites of menopause, or of the graying of hair, though these both mark the beginning of a new phase of life which is very important among the semicivilized. In general, either old women become identified with the men and therefore participate in their ceremonies, political activities, and so forth, or they acquire a special position within their own sex group, especially as ceremonial leaders. Old age brings increased social standing for the men.

[1] P. E. Goddard, *Life and Culture of the Hupa* (University of California Publications in American Archeology and Ethnology [Berkeley: University Press, 1903]), Vol. I, No. 1.

VIII FUNERALS

On first considering funeral ceremonies, one expects rites of separation to be their most prominent component, in contrast to rites of transition and rites of incorporation, which should be only slightly elaborated. A study of the data, however, reveals that the rites of separation are few in number and very simple, while the transition rites have a duration and complexity sometimes so great that they must be granted a sort of autonomy. Furthermore, those funeral rites which incorporate the deceased into the world of the dead are most extensively elaborated and assigned the greatest importance.

Once again I must be satisfied with a few brief suggestions. Everyone knows that funeral rites vary widely among different peoples and that further variations depend on the sex, age, and social position of the deceased. However, within the extraordinary multiplicity of detail certain dominant features may be discerned, and some of these I shall class together.

Funeral rites are further complicated when within a single people there are several contradictory or different conceptions of the afterworld which may become intermingled with one another, so that their confusion is reflected in the rites. Furthermore, man is often thought to be composed of several elements whose fate after death is not the same—body, vital force, breath-soul, shadow-soul, midget-soul, animal-soul, blood-soul, head-soul, etc. Some of these souls survive forever or for a time, others die. In the discussion that follows I shall abstract from all these variations, since they affect the formal complexity of rites of passage but not their internal structure.

Mourning, which I formerly saw simply as an aggregate of taboos and negative practices marking an isolation from society of those whom death, in its physical reality, had

146

placed in a sacred, impure state,[1] now appears to me to be a more complex phenomenon. It is a transitional period for the survivors, and they enter it through rites of separation and emerge from it through rites of reintegration into society (rites of the lifting of mourning). In some cases, the transitional period of the living is a counterpart of the transitional period of the deceased,[2] and the termination of the first sometimes coincides with the termination of the second—that is, with the incorporation of the deceased into the world of the dead. Thus among the Habé of the Niger plateau "the period of widowhood corresponds, it is said, to the duration of the journey of the deceased's wandering soul up to the moment when it joins the divine ancestral spirits or is reincarnated."[3]

During mourning, the living mourners and the deceased constitute a special group, situated between the world of the living and the world of the dead, and how soon living individuals leave that group depends on the closeness of their relationship with the dead person. Mourning requirements are based on degrees of kinship and are systematized by each people according to their special way of calculating that kinship (patrilineally, matrilineally, bilaterally, etc.) It seems right that widowers and widows should belong to this special world for the longest time; they leave it only through appropriate rites and only at a moment when even a physical relationship (through pregnancy, for example) is no longer discernible. The rites which lift all the regulations (such as special dress) and prohibitions of mourning should be considered rites of reintegration into the life of society

[1] Van Gennep, *Tabou et totémisme à Madagascar*, pp. 40, 58–77, 88, 100–103, 338–39, 342.

[2] This is what George Alexander Wilken had already seen about Indonesia ("Uber das Haaropfer: Und einige andere Trauergebräuche bei den Völken indonesiens," *Revue coloniale internationale*, 1886 and 1887, see p. 254); he has been followed by Robert Hertz, who generalizes his point ("Contribution à une étude sur la représentation collective de la mort," *Année sociologique*, X [1905–6], 82–83, 101, 105, 120). In reality, the duration of mourning depends more often, as is stated below, on two other factors.

[3] Desplagnes, *Le plateau central nigérien*, p. 221; on beliefs concerning the other world, see pp. 262–68.

as a whole or of a restricted group; they are of the same order as the rites of reintegration for a novice.

During mourning, social life is suspended for all those affected by it, and the length of the period increases with the closeness of social ties to the deceased (e.g., for widows, relatives), and with a higher social standing of the dead person. If the dead man was a chief, the suspension affects the entire society. There is public mourning, the proclamation of holidays, and, following the death of certain petty kings of Africa, a "period of license." At this very moment (1908) in China, new political, economic, and administrative necessities tend to mitigate the considerable effects on the society of the Emperor's and Empress Regent's deaths.[1] Formerly, social life even in the households in China was completely suspended on such occasions for many months— a suspension which in our time would be simply catastrophic.

The transitional period in funeral rites is first marked physically by the more or less extended stay of the corpse or the coffin in the deceased's room (as during a wake), in the vestibule of his house, or elsewhere. But this stay is only an attenuated form of a whole series of rites whose importance and universality has already been pointed out by Lafitau. "Among most savage nations, the dead bodies are only in safekeeping in the sepulchre where they have initially been placed. After a certain time, new obsequies are given them, and what is due them is completed by further funeral duties."[2] Then he describes the rites of the Caribs: "They are convinced [that the dead] do not go to the land of souls until they are without flesh." The existence of a transitional period also interested Mikhailowski.[3] The chief rite of this period consists of either removing the flesh or waiting until it falls off by itself. On this idea are based, for instance, the ceremonies performed by the Betsileos of

[1] [Both died in November, 1908. Van Gennep must be referring to the considerable internal turmoil in China due to economic and political reform and to the often unsatisfactory relations with European powers.]

[2] Lafitau, *Mœurs des sauvages amériquains*, II, 444.

[3] M. M. Mikhailowski, *Shamanstvo*, fasc. 1 (St. Petersburg, 1892), p. 13.

Madagascar, who have a first series of rites while waiting
for the corpse to decompose in its abode (where its putrefaction is accelerated by a great fire) and then a second series
for the burial of the skeleton.[1]

For others, the transition stage is sometimes subdivided
into several parts, and, in the postliminal period, its exten-
sion is systematized in the form of commemorations (a
week, two weeks, a month, forty days, a year, etc.) similar
in nature to rites of the anniversary of a wedding, of birth,
and sometimes of initiation.

Since funeral stages already have been closely studied for
Indonesia,[2] I shall use instances from data pertaining to
other regions. The ceremonies of the Todas are similar to
the Indonesian rites.[3] They include cremation, preservation
of the relics and burial of the ashes, and the erection of a
circle of stones around them. The whole procedure lasts
several months. The dead go to Amnodr, a subterranean
world, and there they are called "Amatol"; the route is not
the same for all the clans, and it is surrounded with obstacles. The "bad" fall from a thread which serves as a
bridge into a stream on whose shores they live for a while,
mingling with individuals from all sorts of tribes. The
buffaloes also go to Amnodr. The Amatol walk a great deal
there, and when they have worn their legs up to the knees
they return to earth. Among the Ostyak of Salekhard,[4] the
house is stripped of all its contents except the utensils of
the deceased, who is dressed and placed in a dugout canoe.

---

[1] See reference in van Gennep, *Tabou et totémisme à Madagascar*, chap. vi,
pp. 277–78.

[2] Hertz, "La représentation collective de la mort," pp. 50–66; a collection of
detailed descriptions of the world beyond the grave, journeys to reach it, etc., may
be found in Kruijt, *Het Animisme in den Indischen Archipel*, pp. 323–85, a work
based on the theories and points of view of Tylor, Wilken, and Le Tourneau.

[3] See Rivers, *The Todas*, pp. 336–404; for a description of Amnodr see pp.
397–400); for a description of the rites, see also Thurston, *Ethnographic Notes in
Southern India*, pp. 145–46, 172–84.

[4] I will keep the name given by the informant, although the Ostyak of Salekhard
are a mixture of true Ostyaks and Samoyeds; see Arnold van Gennep, "Origine et
fortune du nom de peuple Ostiak," *Keleti Szemle: Revue orientale pour les Études
Ouralo-Altaiques* (Budapest), II (1902), 13–22.

A shaman asks the deceased why he has died. He is taken to the burial place of his clan and deposited in the boat on the frozen ground, with his feet facing north, surrounded with all the things he will need in the next world. The deceased is thought to partake of a farewell meal eaten on the spot by the mourners, who then all leave. The female relatives make a doll in the image of the deceased, and they dress, wash, and feed it every day for two and a half years if the dead person was a man, or for two years if it was a woman.[1] Then the doll is placed on the tomb.

Mourning lasts five months for a man and four months for a woman. The dead go by a long and tortuous route toward the north, where the dark and cold land of the dead is located.[2] The length of the journey seems to coincide with the period during which the doll is kept. Thus there is a series of preliminary rites, a transitional period, and a final funeral when the dead person reaches his final abode.

The Northern Ostyaks place the land of the dead beyond the mouth of the Ob, in the Arctic Ocean;[3] it is illuminated only by the light of the moon. Not far from that world the road divides in three forks which lead to three entrances, one for the assassinated, the drowned, the suicides, etc., another for the other sinners, and a third for those who have lived a normal life. For the Irtysh Ostyak, the other world is in the sky. It is a lovely country reached by ascending ladders each three hundred to one thousand feet long, or by climbing up a chain; from it the gods, the sacred bears

[1] Gondatti, *Sledy iazychestva u inorodtsev Severo-Zapadnoi Sibirii* ("Traces of Paganism among the Natives of Northwest Asia") (Moscow, 1888), p. 43; he states that the doll is kept for six months. If the deceased was a man, the widow sleeps next to it; among the Irtysh Ostyak, according to Patkanov (*Die Irtysch-Ostiaken*, p. 146), the doll has in recent times been replaced by the pillow and undergarments of the deceased.

[2] V. Bartenev, "Pogrebalnyia obychai Obdorskikh Ostiakov" ("The Funeral Rites of the Ostyak of Obdorsk [Salekhard]"), *Shivaia Starina*, V (1905), 478–92; Gondatti, p. 44.

[3] I do not understand why Gondatti, followed by Patkanov (*Die Irtysch-Ostiaken*, p. 146), later says of this world that it is underground when it is underwater. Incidentally, there is no doubt that there was some Christian infiltration into the beliefs of the Vogul and the Ostyak (the devil, hell, punishment).

(totems perhaps),[1] and the dead sometimes come back to earth—or so say the ancient legends of the epics.[2] It seems to me that there must be a relationship between the length of time during which the dolls are kept and the supposed duration of the journey into the other world.

The funeral ceremonies of the Kol of India furnish a good example of a combination of known prophylactic rites with rites of passage.[3] Their order runs as follows: (1) Immediately after death the corpse is placed on the ground "so that the soul should more easily find its way to the home of the dead," which is under the earth. (2) The corpse is washed and painted yellow to chase away evil spirits who would stop the soul on its journey. (3) For the same purpose the assembled relatives and neighbors utter pitiable cries. (4) The corpse is placed on a scaffold with the feet facing forward so that the soul should not find the way back to the hut, and for the same reason the procession travels by detours. (5) The cortege must not include either children or girls; the women cry; the men are silent. (6) Each man carries a piece of dry wood to throw on the pyre. (7) Rice and the tools of the deceased's sex are placed there, and in the mouth of the corpse there are rice cakes and silver coins for the journey, since the soul retains a shadow of the body. (8) The women leave, and the pyre is lighted;[4] the litter is also burned to prevent the deceased's return. (9) The men gather the calcified bones, place them in a pot, and bring the pot back to the deceased's house where it is hung from a post. (10) Grains of rice are strewn along the route, and food is placed in front of the door so that the deceased, should he return in spite of all precautions, will have something to eat without harming anyone. (11) All the deceased's

---

[1] See my summary in the *Revue de l'histoire des religions*, Vol. XL (1899), of the monograph by N. Kharouzine, *Le serment par l'ours et le culte de l'ours chez les Ostiak et les Vogoul*.

[2] Patkanov, *Die Irtysch-Ostiaken*, p. 146.

[3] See Hahn, *Einführung in das Gebiet der Kolsmission*, pp. 82–88.

[4] If it is raining too hard, the corpse is buried according to specific rites so that it may be disinterred after the harvest and cremated; in this instance the ceremony takes place in three stages.

utensils are carried far away, because they have become impure and because the deceased may be hidden in them. (12) The house is purified by a consecrated meal. (13) After a certain time the ceremony of "betrothal," or "union of the deceased with the population of the lower world," is performed. Marriage songs are sung, there is dancing, and the woman who carries the pot leaps with joy. (14) A marriage retinue with music, etc., goes to the village from which the deceased and his ancestors have originated. (15) The pot containing the bones of the deceased is deposited in a small ditch, above which a stone is erected. (16) On their return the participants must bathe. All those who have been mutilated or who have died because of a tiger or an accident remain evil spirits and cannot enter the land of the dead. That land is the home of the ancestors to which only persons who have been married can go.[1] They return to the earth from time to time, and when they wish they are reincarnated in the first-born (this holds especially for grandfathers and great-grandfathers).[2]

This is not the place for a comparative description of worlds beyond the grave.[3] The most widespread idea is that of a world analogous to ours, but more pleasant, and of a society organized in the same way as it is here. Thus everyone re-enters again the categories of clan, age group, or occupation that he had on earth. It logically follows that the children who have not yet been incorporated into the society of the living cannot be classified in that of the dead.

[1] On this subject, see p. 133, above.

[2] I mention this document because it provides proof for what has been said above (p. 52) about the rite in which the newborn are placed on the ground (also performed by the Kol; see Hahn, *Einführung in das Gebiet der Kolsmission*, p. 72), as are corpses. Dieterich (*Mutter Erde*, pp. 25–29) has collected parallels for the latter practice, which he explains as "a return to the bosom of Mother Earth"; it can be seen that here, at least, this theory is not acceptable. I would like to add that the Kol bury dead children but do not burn them "because they do not have souls" (the Kol acquire a soul only on their wedding day) and do not have the right to go to the land of their ancestors, the purpose of cremation being to give access to it. Another of Dieterich's theories (*Mutter Erde*, pp. 21–25) also collapses on this point.

[3] See, among others, Tylor, *Primitive Culture*, chap. xiii.

Thus, for Catholics, children who die without baptism forever remain in the transition zone, or limbo; the corpse of a semicivilized infant not yet named, circumcised or otherwise ritually recognized, is buried without the usual ceremonies, thrown away, or burned—especially if the people in question think that he did not yet possess a soul.

The journey to the other world and the entrance to it comprise a series of rites of passage whose details depend on the distance and topography of that world. First I should mention the Isles of the Dead to be found in the beliefs of ancient Egypt,[1] Assyro-Babylonia,[2] the Greeks in various times and regions (cf. Hades of Book XI of the *Odyssey*),[3] the Celts,[4] Polynesians,[5] Australians,[6] and others. These beliefs undoubtedly are the reason for the practice of giving the deceased a real or miniature boat and oars. Some peoples see the other world as a citadel surrounded by walls (such as Sheol, the underworld abode of the dead in Hebrew tradition which has bolted doors[7] or the Babylonian Aralu),[8] as a region with compartments (for instance, the Egyptian Duat), as situated on a high mountain (as do the Dyaks), or in the interior of a mountain (as in Hindu India).

What is important to us in these cases is that, since the deceased must make a voyage,[9] his survivors are careful to

[1] On the subject of the fields and islands of Aaru, the judgment and journey of the dead, see Gaston Maspéro, *Histoire ancienne des peuples de l'Orient classique*, I (Paris: Hachette, 1895), 180 ff., with bibliography.

[2] *Ibid.*, pp. 574 ff.

[3] See, among others, Ervin Rohde, *Psyché* (2d ed.; Tübingen: J. C. Mohr, 1898); Albrecht Dieterich, *Nekyia* (Leipzig: B. C. Teubner, 1893); A. J. Reinach, "Victor Bérard et l'Odyssée," *Les essais*, 1904, pp. 189–93.

[4] K. Meyer, *The Voyage of Bran* (London, 1895).

[5] Johannes Zemmrich, "Toteninseln und verwandte geographische Mythen," *Internationales Archiv für Ethnographie*, Vol. IV (1891).

[6] See Carl Strehlow and Leonhardi, *Die Aranda und Luritja-Stämme in Zentral Australia* (Frankfurt am Main: Völker-Museum, 1907–8), I, 15; II, 6.

[7] See Schwally, *Das Leben nach dem Tode: Nach dem Vorstellung die alter Israel in dem Judentus einschliesslich Volkglaubens in Zeitale Christi* (Giessen, 1892).

[8] Maspéro, *Histoire ancienne*, I, 693 ff.

[9] Regarding the world of the dead according to Sabian beliefs, see Siouffi, *Étude sur la religion des Soubbas*, pp. 156–58; on the roads which lead there and join together, pp. 126–29; and on the corresponding funeral rites, pp. 120, 121 n., 124–26. The soul requires seventy-five days to make the journey, but mourning lasts only sixty days; the communal meal and the meal of commemoration are

equip him with all the necessary material objects— such as clothing, food, arms, and tools—as well as those of a magico-religious nature—amulets, passwords, signs, etc.—which will assure him of a safe journey or crossing and a favorable reception, as they would a living traveler. Thus, in some particulars, these rites are identical with those discussed in chapter III. The Lapps, for instance, took care to kill a reindeer on the grave so that the deceased might ride it during the difficult journey to his final destination.[1] Some believed the journey lasted three weeks, while others said three years.

A great many similar customs could be mentioned. The passage is marked, for instance, by the ancient Greek rite of "the obol (coin) for Charon."[2] This rite has also been encountered in France, where the deceased was given the largest coin available, "so that he would be better received in the other world."[3] The practice persists in modern Greece. Among the Slavs the money for the deceased is intended to pay the expenses of the trip, but among Japanese Buddhists it is given to the old woman who runs the ferry across the Sanzu; the Badaga use it for the passage over the thread of the dead. Moslems cannot cross the bridge formed by a sharpened sword unless they are pure or "good." In the Zend-Avesta dogs guard the bridge of Chinvat just as in the Rig-Veda Yama's dogs, who are spotted and have four eyes, guard the paths that lead to one of the ancient Hindu abodes beyond the grave, a sort of cavern, "a closed and covered enclosure" which is reached through a dark underworld.[4]

absolutely obligatory; the rite of the "last mouthful" provides the deceased in the other world with "something more than his ordinary ration, which is ordinarily insufficient."

[1] N. Kharuzin, *Russkie Lopary* (Moscow, 1890), p. 157, and for more information of the same kind, Mikhailowski, *Shamanstvo*, pp. 19–24.

[2] See Richard Andree, *Totenmünze* (2d ed.; 1889), p. 24. Also *Mélusine*, *passim*.

[3] J. B. Thiers, *Traité des superstitions* (Paris, 1667); for other French parallels, see Sebillot, *Le folk-lore de la France*, I, 419, where information can be found on the crossing of the sea (inside the earth) to reach hell.

[4] See Oldenberg, *La réligion du Véda*, pp. 450–62; another abode is in the sky. Oldenberg is right in believing these two conceptions to be independent and juxta-

Sometimes special powers—magicians, evil spirits, deities —are charged with showing the dead the way, or with leading them in groups. (Those of ancient Greece are known as psychopompoi—guides of souls to the afterworld.) This role of Isis and of Hermes-Mercury is quite well known. Among the Muskwaki (commonly known as Fox) at the lifting of mourning the deceased is guided toward the prairies of the next world by a young warrior who takes the name of the deceased, gallops for several miles, makes a detour, and returns. He retains that name henceforth and is considered the adopted child of the relatives of the deceased.[1]

The Luiseno Indians of California have a dramatic ceremony which has the direct effect of sending the spirits of the dead away from the earth and "attaching," or fastening, them, as if by a physical bond, to the four sections of the sky and particularly to the Milky Way.[2]

Because of the familiar themes combined in the Haida's ideas about the next world, I shall describe them in some detail. The road to the afterworld leads to the banks of a sort of bay; on the other side of it is the land of souls, from which a self-propelled raft is sent by a soul to the deceased. When he has arrived on the other bank, the deceased begins the search for his wife, which takes a very long time, since the villages are scattered like those of the Haida and each dead person has only one wife assigned to him. When he is dying, a man indicates in which village he wants to live, and messengers are sent to guide him on his voyage. Each offering to the deceased multiplies for his use, and the funeral songs help the deceased to enter his village with his head held high. The dead send riches to their poor earthly relatives. In the land of the souls sacred dances are performed, and everyone amuses himself. Beyond that land

posed on one another, but they are not elements in a dualistic system. This coexistence of different beliefs among a people is a frequent occurrence, and when there is localization of some dead in one of these worlds, and others in the other worlds, it is often on a social and magico-religious basis rather than on an ethical one.

[1] Owen, *Folk-lore of the Musquakie Indians*, pp. 83–86.

[2] Du Bois, *The Religion of the Luisenio Indians*, pp. 83–87.

lives a chief called Great Moving Cloud, who is responsible for the abundance of salmon. After some time in the land of souls the deceased equips a canoe, reassembles his belongings, and amid the lamentations of his companions goes away to a country called Xada. This is his second death, and he also goes through a third and a fourth. Upon his fifth death he returns to earth as a blue fly. Some think the four deaths occur only after several human reincarnations. There are different countries for the drowned, for those dead by violent means, for shamans, and so forth.

The funeral rites for a person who dies in the ordinary way are given below. The face of the deceased is painted, a sacred headdress is placed on his head, and he is seated on the bier, where he remains for four to six days. Special magical songs are sung, recited first by the members of the clan and then by those of the opposite clan. All sorts of food and drink and tobacco leaves are thrown into a "crying fire." These become multiplied many times and are taken by the deceased to the other world. Relatives put on the signs of mourning—they shave their heads and stain their faces with pitch. The coffin is carried out through a hole in the wall and is taken to the grave house, where only the deceased of the same clan can be placed.

For ten days the widow fasts, uses a rock in place of a pillow, and bathes daily without washing her face. Then she gathers some children of the opposite clan and serves them a meal. (The Haida are exogamous.) "This feast was called 'causing one's self to marry.' The object of it was that she might marry someone next time who had still more property, and that she herself and her new husband might have long lives and be lucky. Another informant added that the widow went through regulations much like those of a girl at puberty."[1] Briefly, while the purpose of the rites is to unite the corpse with those of members of his clan and to provide him with what he will need during his voyage and

[1] J. R. Swanton, *Contributions to the Ethnology of the Haida* ("Publications of the Jesup North Pacific Expedition," V, Part I [Leiden, 1905]), 52–54; for Haida ideas of the afterlife see pp. 34–37.

in his sojourn beyond the grave, these rites are at the same time prophylactic and animistic (the opening in the wall of the house, the coffin, the vault, etc., prevent a return of the deceased) or prophylactic and contagious (mourning, baths, etc.).

The funeral rites of ancient Egypt furnish a good example of a system of rites of passage whose purpose is incorporation into the world of the dead. Here I shall examine only the Osirian ritual,[1] whose fundamental idea is the identification of Osiris and the deceased on one hand, the sun and the deceased on the other. I think there must at first have been two separate rituals which were unified on the theme of death and rebirth. As Osiris the deceased is dismembered and then reconstituted; he is dead and is born again in the world of the dead, and so there are a series of resurrection rites. As Ra (the sun), the deceased dies each evening upon arrival at the edge of Hades. His mummy is thrown into a corner and abandoned; but the series of rites it undergoes during the night in the sun's barge, revives him little by little, and in the morning he is again alive and ready to resume his daily journey in the light, above the world of the living. These multiple rebirths of the sun ritual have been combined with the single reconstitution of the deceased upon his first arrival in Hades, according to the Osirian ritual, so that this reconstitution has come to take place daily. The performance of the converging rites is in accordance with the general idea that the sacred, the divine, the magical, and the pure are lost if they are not renewed in periodic rites.

The following is the syncretic pattern according to the *Book of What Is in Hades* and the *Book of the Doors*.[2]

---

[1] Gaston Maspéro, *Études de mythologie et d'archéologie égyptienne*, Vol. II: *Compte rendu de les hypogées royaux de Thèbes* (Paris: E. Leroux, 1893), 1–187; G. Jequier, *Le livre de ce qu'il y a dans l'Hadès: Version abregée publié d'après les papyrus de Berlin et de Leyde avec variations et traduction* (Paris: E. Bouillon, 1894); Alexandre Moret, *Le Rituel du culte divin journalier en Égypte*, and *La royauté pharaonique*.

[2] This book was written to conciliate the solar theory with the Osirian theory not taken into account in the *Book of What Is in Hades*; see the summary of it given by Maspéro, *Les hypogées royaux de Thèbes*, pp. 163–79.

Different conceptions of Duat (Hades) were current in different periods and places, but through fusions and combinations the priests of Thebes developed a complete plan. Hades was "like an immense temple, very long, divided into a certain number of rooms separated by doors and having at each end an outside court and a pylon (gateway building) contiguous to both the inside world and the outside world."[1] In the first hour of the night, when the sun was dead, he received in his barge the souls which were "pure," that is, buried in accordance with the proper rites and provided with the necessary talismans, and the doors guarded by baboons and spirits were opened to him. The dead who did not go in the sun's bark had to vegetate eternally in the vestibule.[2]

According to the *Book of the Doors*, the doors were identical to those of fortresses and were guarded at the entrance and the exit by a god in the form of a mummy, at the bend by two uraei (cobras) emitting flames and nine mummy-gods; passage was obtained by an incantation.[3] The journey is described in the *Guide for the Traveller in the Other World*.[4] For details I refer the reader to the works cited, but I want to mention that each compartment was separated from the preceding one by doors whose opening had to be secured by ritual means. The names of the first three and of the last are unknown; the names of the fourth and the doors following it were "the one which hides the corridors," "the pillar of the gods," "the one adorned with swords," "the portal of Osiris," "the one which stands upright, motionless(?)," "the guardian of the flood," "the great one of beings, the begetter of forms," and "the one which incloses the gods of Hades." At the exit there was also a vestibule.

[1] Jequier, *Le livre de ce qu'il y a dans l'Hadès*, p. 19.

[2] *Ibid.*, pp. 20, 39–41; Maspéro, *Les hypogées royaux de Thèbes*, pp. 43–44; note the conversation between the god and cynocephalus (baboon) for the "opening of the doors."

[3] *Ibid.*, Vol. II, pp. 166–68; on the door which opens on the place of judgment, see *Livre des morts* ("Book of the Dead"), chap. cxxv, I, ll. 52 ff

[4] Maspéro, *ibid.*, Vol. I, p. 384.

These "openings of the doors" had a counterpart in the ritual of daily worship—the opening of the doors of the naos (the part of the temple within the walls): the cord was broken, the seal was removed, and the bolts were slid.[1] Then came the dismemberment and reconstitution of the god, a rite which was also part of the funeral (opening the mouth,[2] etc.). The second opening of the naos reaffirmed the first. The god was washed with water and incense, dressed in sacred bands, and anointed with paint and perfumed oils. Then the statue was replaced in the naos and installed on the sand, just like the mummy and the statue of the deceased in the funerary ritual. The ritual closing of the naos which followed was the principal rite of departure from the sanctuary.[3]

Thus the divine worship had for its object the daily revival of Ra-Osiris, just as the funeral rites both (1) revived the deceased and made him a god by mummification and various rites, and (2) prevented a real and final death by a reconstitution and nocturnal rebirth.[4] There are, therefore, parallels among the funeral rites, the daily worship, the inauguration of a temple, and the ritual of enthronement.[5] The death and rebirth, simultaneously, of Ra, Osiris, the king, the priest, and every deceased man who was "pure" certainly constitutes the most extreme case known to me of a dramatic representation of the death and

[1] Moret, *Le rituel du culte divin journalier en Égypte*, pp. 35 ff.

[2] *Ibid.*, pp. 73–83, 87–89; Maspéro, "Le Rituel du sacrifice funéraire," *Les hypogées royaux de Thèbes*, pp. 289–318.

[3] *Ibid.*, pp. 102–212 and Plate III.

[4] Moret, *Le rituel du culte divin journalier en Egypte*, p. 226; cf. pp. 10–15 and pages noted above.

[5] The compartments of Hades belong to at least two originally distinct systems. The final rebirth is secured on the twelfth hour, according to the Theban ritual, by the passage of the sacred barge, from tail to head, across the gigantic serpent "The life of the gods"—symbol, says Jequier, of the renewal due to the serpent's ability to change skins each year (*Le livre de ce qu'il y a dans l'Hadès*, pp. 132–33). But this does not explain the reason for the passage across the two bulls' heads (Maspéro, *Les hypogées royaux de Thèbes*, pp. 169–71); on the subject of the twelfth hour, see pp. 96–101.

rebirth theme. It should be added that birth into life on earth was in itself considered a rebirth.[1]

All these rites of rebirth prevented the deceased from dying again each day. The belief in such a possibility is found among many peoples, sometimes combined with the idea that after each death the deceased passes from one abode to another, as among the Haida. Among the Cheremiss, some groups believe that the deceased dies only once, but others—for example, the Cheremiss of Vyatka—say that a man may die seven times and pass from one world to another and that he is then changed into a fish.[2] The Cheremiss rites consist of feeding the deceased often at first and then periodically through "commemorations." The events of the afterlife explain in part the alimentary and sumptuary rites of the Vogul and the Ostyak, some of whom believe that the soul of the deceased lives for a time in the world under the sea or in the skies,[3] then diminishes little by little until it is only the size of a certain small insect or transforms itself into that insect, and then disappears altogether.[4] The doctrine of worlds superimposed on each other is widespread in Asia and existed in Mithraism. (There were seven planetary worlds and successive initiations.)

Like children who have not been baptized, named, or initiated, persons for whom funeral rites are not performed are condemned to a pitiable existence, since they are never able to enter the world of the dead or to become incorporated in the society established there. These are the most dangerous dead. They would like to be reincorporated into the world of the living, and since they cannot be, they behave like hostile strangers toward it. They lack the means of subsistence which the other dead find in their own world

[1] *Ibid.*, I, 23 ff., 29. It should be noted that the purpose of mummification is precisely to make rebirth, the life beyond the grave, possible.

[2] Ivan Nikolaevitch Smirnov, *Les populations finnoises des bassins de la Volga et de la Kama*, trans. Paul Boyer (Paris: E. Leroux, 1898), I, 138.

[3] See above, p. 150 and the sources cited there.

[4] Gondatti, *Slièdy iazytchestvra u inorodtsev Sièvero-Zapdnoï Sibirii*, p. 39.

and consequently must obtain them at the expense of the living. Furthermore, these dead without hearth or home sometimes have an intense desire for vengeance. Thus funeral rites also have a long-range utility; they help to dispose of eternal enemies of the survivors. Persons included among the homeless dead vary among different peoples. In addition to those already mentioned, this category may include those bereft of family, the suicides, those dead on a journey, those struck by lightning, those dead through the violation of a taboo, and others. What I have said holds in general, but the same act does not have the same consequences among all peoples, and I want to reiterate that I do not claim an absolute universality or an absolute necessity for the pattern of rites of passage.

In this connection, I want to mention the diverse beliefs concerning the fate, in the next world, of persons who have committed suicide. Lasch isolated four categories: (1) Suicide is considered a normal act, and the fate of the person who has committed it is the same as that of the ordinary dead; in case of serious illness, mutilation, etc., suicide may even be a means of insuring that the soul is in good condition and not weakened or mutilated, (2) Suicide is rewarded in the other world (suicide of the warrior, the widow, etc.). (3) The person who has committed suicide cannot be incorporated with the other dead and must wander between the world of the dead and that of the living. (4) Suicide is punished in the next world, and the individual must wander between the two worlds for the duration of the time he would normally have lived, or he is admitted only to a lower region of the world of the dead, or he is punished by tortures, etc. (as in hell).[1] Obviously the character of the funeral rites, those pertaining to prophylaxis and purification as well as rites of passage, differs with each one of the four categories.

The rites of passage are present also in rites of resurrec-

---

[1] R. Lasch, "Die Verbleibsorte der abgeschiedenen Seele der Selbstmörder," *Globus*, LXXVII (1900), 110-15.

tion and reincarnation, for even if a soul has been separated from the living and incorporated into the world of the dead, it can also reverse the direction and reappear among us, either by itself or under the constraint of another person. The means are sometimes very simple. It may be sufficient for the soul to be reincarnated in a woman and to reappear in the form of a child. That is the case, for instance, among the Arunta of Australia, who think that souls lies in wait in stones, trees, etc., and that from there they leap into women who are young, fat, and desirable. The rites of reintegration into the world of the living which ensue are those that have been studied with reference to birth and naming.

The ceremonies of the Lushae tribes of Assam furnish a good example of the "eternal return."[1] The deceased is dressed in his best clothes and tied in a sitting position on a scaffold of bamboo, while next to him are placed the tools and weapons of his sex. A pig, a goat, and a dog are killed, and all the relatives, friends, and neighbors divide the meat; the deceased is also given food and drink. At nightfall he is placed in a grave dug right next to the house. His nearest relative says goodbye and asks him to prepare everything for those who will come and join him. The soul, accompanied by those of the pig, the goat, and the dog—without whom it would not find its way—goes dressed and equipped to the land of Mi-thi-hua, where life is hard and painful. But if the deceased has killed men or animals on the hunt, or if he has given feasts to the whole village, he goes to a pleasant country on the other side of the river, where he feasts continuously. Since women can neither fight nor hunt nor give feasts, they cannot go to this beautiful country unless their husbands take them there. After a certain time, the soul leaves one or the other of these regions and returns to earth in the form of a hornet. After another lapse of time it is transformed into water and evaporates in the form of dew, and, if a dewdrop falls on a man, that man will beget a

[1] Major Shakespear, "Typical Tribes and Castes," p. 225.

child who will be a reincarnation of the deceased.[1] When the child is born, two chickens are killed, and the mother washes herself and the child. The child's soul spends the first seven days perched like a bird on the clothes or the bodies of his parents; for this reason they move as little as possible, and during this time the household god is appeased with sacrifices. All sorts of ceremonies follow, and during one of them the nearest maternal relative gives a name to the child—that is, the child is permanently incorporated into the clan.

Sometimes the souls of the dead are reincarnated directly into animals, vegetables, etc., especially into the totems. In that case there are rites incorporating the deceased into totemic species.

There is not always a special place beyond the grave for the dead. At least it frequently happens that their abode is in the environs of the house, the tomb (called "the isba of the dead" by the Votyak), or the cemetery (called "village of the dead" by the Mandan). In that case the burial is the real rite of incorporation in the world of the dead. This is very clear among the Cheremiss. Perhaps as a result of the Moslem influence of the Tatars, the Cheremiss also believe in a next world, analogous to the Ostyak heaven, which is reached by a pole forming a bridge over a cauldron, or by a ladder. The Mordvinian dead also have their abode in the tomb or the cemetery.[2] The bond with the living, and therefore the transition, lasts for a longer time in these instances, since, as has been pointed out, it is periodically renewed by the living, either by communal meals or by visits or by feeding the deceased (through a hole in the ground and in the coffin, with a reed, by depositing food on the tomb, etc.). But a moment always comes when this tie is broken, after being loosened bit by bit. The last commemoration or the last visit completes the rites of separation in relation to

[1] This is one of the very rare cases of reincarnation through the father.
[2] See Smirnov, *Les populations finnoises*, I, 133–44, for the Cheremiss; pp. 357–76 for the Mordvinians.

the deceased and the reconsolidation of the society or restricted group of the living.

The following is a list of rites of passage considered in isolation; I make no claim that it is complete, any more than other lists given in this volume.

Among rites of separation, some of which have already been reviewed, it is appropriate to include: the various procedures by which the corpse is transported outside; burning the tools, the house, the jewels, the deceased's possessions; putting to death the deceased's wives, slaves, or favorite animals; washings, anointings, and rites of purification in general; and taboos of all sorts. In addition, there are physical procedures of separation: a grave, a coffin, a cemetery, a wicker mat, places in the trees, or a pile of stones is built or used in a ritual manner; the closing of the coffin or the tomb is often a particularly solemn conclusion to the entire ceremony. There are periodic collective rites expelling souls from the house, the village, and the tribe's territory. There are struggles for the corpse, widespread in Africa, which correspond to the bride's abduction. Their true meaning seems not to have been understood up to now: it is that the living do not want to lose one of their members unless forced to do so, for the loss is a diminution of their social power. These struggles increase in violence with the higher social position of the deceased.[1] As for the destruction of the corpse itself (by cremation, premature putrefaction, etc.), its purpose is to separate the components, the various bodies and souls. Only very seldom do the remains (bones, ashes) constitute the new body of the deceased in the afterlife, whatever Hertz may think on the matter.[2]

Among rites of incorporation I shall first mention the meals shared after funerals and at commemoration celebrations. Their purpose is to reunite all the surviving members of the group with each other, and sometimes also with the

---

[1] For references, see Hertz, "La représentation collective de la mort," p. 128 n. 2.

[2] *Ibid.*, p. 78; Hertz here presents a modification of Kleinpaul's theory, which is too absolute.

deceased, in the same way that a chain which has been broken by the disappearance of one of its links must be rejoined. Sometimes a meal of this sort also takes place when mourning is lifted. When the funerals are observed in two stages (provisional and permanent), there is usually a communion meal for the relatives at the end of the first, and the deceased is thought to partake of it. Finally, if the tribe, clan, or village is involved, convocation by drum, crier, or messenger gives the meal even more of the character of a collective ritual.

As for rites of incorporation into the other world, they are equivalent to those of hospitality, incorporation into the clan, adoption, and so forth. They are often alluded to in legends whose central theme is a descent to Hades or a journey to the land of the dead, and they are mentioned in the form of taboos: one must not eat with the dead, drink or eat anything produced in their country, allow oneself to be touched or embraced by them, accept gifts from them, and so forth. On the other hand, drinking with a dead person is an act of incorporation with him and the other dead, and it consequently enables one to travel among them without danger, as does the payment of a toll (coins, etc.). There are other special rites such as a club blow administered by the dead on a newcomer's head,[1] the Christian sacrament of extreme unction, or the custom of placing the deceased on the earth. Finally, the "dances of the dead" performed by certain American Indians, by the Nyanja of Africa,[2] by members of secret societies, and by other special magico-religious groups should perhaps be included in this category.

[1] Haddon, *Cambridge Anthropological Expedition to Torres Straits*, V, 355; this same rite is among those performed at marriage (see above, p. 128).

[2] See F. A. Werner, *The Natives of British Central Africa* (London: A. Constable, 1907), p. 229; R. Sutherland Rattray, *Some Folk-lore, Stories, and Songs in Chinyanja* (London: S.P.C.K., 1907), p. 179.

IX OTHER TYPES OF RITES OF PASSAGE

It would be fitting at this point to examine each rite of passage and to demonstrate that it is really a rite of either separation, transition, or incorporation. But to do so would require several volumes, since almost any rite may be interpreted in several ways, depending on whether it occurs within a complete system or in isolation, whether it is performed at one occasion or another.[1] I have therefore limited myself to an enumeration of rites for several of the categories discussed.[2]

All the rites which include the act of cutting, on the one hand, and of tying, on the other, hardly present material for discussion. I have explained circumcision as a rite of separation. In rites of incorporation there is widespread use of the "sacred bond," the "sacred cord," the knot, and of analogous forms such as the belt, the ring, the bracelet, and the crown. All these are particularly common in rites of marriage and enthronement, and their origin may be traced to the kerchief. I should explain briefly, however, why I have included certain practices among rites of passage. Among these are rites pertaining to hair, to veiling, to the use of special languages, sexual rites, practices of flagellation, seasonal rites, and some others.

Rites involving hair have been the subject of a monograph by Wilken,[3] whose opinions have been accepted and elaborated by Smith,[4] Hartland, and others. In reality, what is called "the sacrifice of the hair" includes two distinct operations: cutting the hair, and dedicating, consecrating, or sacrificing it. To cut the hair is to separate oneself from the previous world; to dedicate the hair is to bind oneself to the sacred world and more particularly to a deity or a spirit

[1] In this connection, the rites mentioned by Eugène Monseur in "La proscription religieuse de l'usage récent," Revue de l'histoire des Religions, LIII (1906), 209–305.

[2] See above, pp. 15–17, 27–30, 38–39, 47–48, 52–54, 62, 130–32, 134, 164.

[3] Wilken, "Uber das Haaropfer"; see, among others, Frazer, The Golden Bough, I, 368–89, for a good collection of facts.

[4] Smith, Lectures on the Religion of the Semites, pp. 324–25.

with whom kinship is in this way established. But such a dedication is only one of the ways of handling hair which has been cut off. In the shorn hair, as in the foreskin and in nail parings, there resides a portion of the personality, but very often such a concept is absent and nothing at all is done with these scraps. Where the concept is present, the hair may be buried, burned, saved in a sachet, or placed in a relative's keeping. The rite of cutting the hair or of a tonsure is also used in many different situations: a child's head is shaved to indicate that he is entering in to another stage, that of life; a girl's head is shaved at the moment of marriage to indicate a change from one age group to another widows cut their hair to break the bond created by marriage, and the rite is reinforced by placing the hair on the tomb; sometimes the same purpose is achieved by cutting the hair of the deceased.

Now there is a reason why a rite of separation should affect the hair. In its form, color, length, and arrangement it is a characteristic distinguishing an individual as much as a group, and it is easily recognized. "While they are very young, the little girls among the Rahūna (in Morocco) go about with their heads shaved except for the front hair and a tuft on the crown; when they reach puberty, they let their hair grow, leaving loose that which is on the forehead and rolling the rest on their heads; when they are married, the hair is divided into two braids which are allowed to hang in back; but when they become mothers they bring those two braids forward over their shoulders on to their breasts."[1] Thus for the Rahūna the hair style serves to signify the stages of their life and their membership in one or another group of women. It would be easy to cite many other documents of the same order, but what I wanted to point out is that the handling of the hair very often falls into the category of rites of passage.[2]

---

[1] Doutté, *Merrâkech*, I, 314–15.
[2] Smith (*Lectures on the Religion of the Semites*, pp. 327–28) saw clearly that cutting or tonsuring the hair is a common rite of initiation, but he identified it with a

With reference to the veil, Plutarch inquired, "Why do people veil their heads when worshiping the gods?" The answer is simple: to separate themselves from the profane and to live only in the sacred world, for seeing is itself a form of contact, as was pointed out with reference to the Shammar. In worship, sacrifice, and marriage rites, for example, the veiling is temporary. But in other cases the separation or the incorporation, or both, are permanent. For example, Moslem women and Jewish women of Tunisia, who belong on the one hand to their sex group and on the other to a given family group, must isolate themselves from the rest of the world by covering themselves with a veil. Similarly in Catholicism, to pass from a liminal stage (novitiate) to the stage of permanent incorporation into the community is to "take the veil." This rite was also present in the initiation to the Mysteries, and the same explanation applies in both cases. Among certain peoples a widow may wear a veil, either during mourning only or permanently, to separate herself from her husband or from other married women and from men. Socrates covered himself with a veil after drinking the hemlock, thereby separating himself from the world of the living to be incorporated in the world of the dead and of the gods; but, having asked Crito to sacrifice a cock to Aesculapius—that is, wishing once again to act like a living man, he uncovered his face and covered it again immediately afterward.[1] Similarly, when the Romans "dedicated" to the gods, they intended, by veiling the designated victims, to separate them from this world in order to incorporate them into the other, the divine and sacred.

consecration; it might be more accurate to state that the same rite is found both in the rituals of passage and in the rituals of consecration.

[1] There is no reason to introduce, as does Reinach in his study on "the veil of oblation" (*Cultes, mythes, et religions*, I, 299), the idea that "the sight of a corpse would have soiled the heavenly light." Farther on (p. 309), he offers an explanation similar to mine but does not follow through with his argument: "the correlation between purification, penance, and mourning," and then between the veiling of the initiate and the use of a common veil in Roman and Christian marriage, should have shown him the meaning of the practices in question as rites of both separation and incorporation.

During most of the ceremonies which have been discussed, and especially during the transition periods, a special language is employed which in some cases includes an entire vocabulary unknown or unusual in the society as a whole, and in others consists simply of a prohibition against using certain words in the common tongue. There are languages for women, for initiates, for blacksmiths, for priests (liturgical language), etc. This phenomenon should be considered of the same order as the change of dress, mutilations, and special foods (dietary taboos), i.e., as a perfectly normal differentiating procedure. I shall not dwell on this point, since I have discussed it elsewhere in greater detail.[1]

A prohibition of the sex act is a component of most sets of ceremonies and should not be classed separately any more than should special languages. Among peoples for whom coitus does not imply either impurity or magico-religious danger, the taboo in question does not occur; but, where such an implication exists, the presence of the taboo is natural, since an individual who wishes to enter the sacred world and, having entered it, to act in it must place himself in a condition of "purity" in order to remain there. On the other hand—and this is one of the forms of the pivoting of sacredness which I discussed in chapter I—though it is impure, coitus is "powerful"; that is why it is sometimes used as a rite of great efficacy. It is clear that coitus with a prostitute who is consecrated to a deity is only one of the means, similar in nature to communion, of being incorporated with the deity or even identified with it.[2] The physical impact of the act—that of penetration—should be borne in mind.

Other rites, such as that of Mylitta (in which every girl

---

[1] Arnold van Gennep, "Essai d'une théorie des langues spéciales," *Revue des Études ethnographiques et sociologiques*, 1908, pp. 327–37.

[2] I believe that it would be useless to discuss all the earlier theories of Crawley, Frazer, and others. It is difficult to find a better procedure to express a close and intimate incorporation; the communal meal itself seems complicated when compared to coitus.

must once offer herself to a stranger and receive a coin from him), require more complex explanations. The best interpretation of this rite has been given by Westermarck, who thinks that, because of the sacred power of the stranger, it was a means to insure the girl's fertility.[1] She was not, strictly speaking, a sacred prostitute; but the act was performed on sacred ground, and it is possible that its purpose also included the incorporation of the stranger into the deity or the city. Coitus as the final act in initiation ceremonies I interpret also as a rite of incorporation. In Australia, coitus is a rite of this sort, intended in some cases to incorporate a messenger into the tribe, in others to insure the proper course of ceremonies in progress,[2] and in yet others as an act of friendship (lending and exchanging wives, sisters, etc.).

As for the "sexual license" following initiation ceremonies—practiced, for example, by certain Russian sects which allow men and women to unite according to their pleasure or to chance on such occasions—it appears to me not at all as a survival of the supposed "primitive promiscuity" but as a complete expression of that same idea of incorporation. It is the precise equivalent of a communal meal participated in by all members of a particular group. Should one derive from the universal existence of communal meals an argument in favor of the communistic ownership of food in former times? At these occasions, too, the rights of personal property are forgotten and, at a simple picnic, for instance, each person eats of the food brought by the others. All are united to all, so that a complete and profound union is effected among the members of the group, which may be constituted about a totem or a heresy, or on some other basis. Mutilations affecting the sex organs have no sexual significance strictly speaking, as I have shown many times. This statement holds true even with reference to the

[1] Westermarck, *The Origin and Development of Moral Ideas*, II, 445–46; on Australia, see pp. 47–48.

[2] See my *Mythes et légendes d'Australie*, pp. lvi–lvii.

perforation of the hymen through coitus preliminary to marriage.

Everything that has just been said about heterosexual practices is equally true for those of a homosexual nature. But since discussions of the latter have been more confused and the documents less detailed, a few examples should be cited. At the initiation into certain Ingiet groups (see p. 83, n. 1), an elderly member of the group strips and covers himself with lime from head to foot. He holds the end of a plaited mat in his hand and gives the other end to one of the novices. They alternately pull and struggle until the old man falls on the novice and the act is carried out. All the novices must submit in turn to this operation, for pederasty is considered not a vice but an amusing act by these Melanesians.[1]

Furthermore, it is known that homosexuality was normal among the ephebi[2] of antiquity and still constitutes a pact of friendship among the Albanians. It is also practiced by the inhabitants of "communal houses" where boys and girls do not live together,[3] and in such cases the first homosexual intercourse is a rite of friendship. There is no necessity for Reinach's idea that the act constitutes "a transfer of the male force of the powerful warrior to the ephebus who is attached to him to receive a military and civic education."[4] Among the ancient Jews the *kedeshim*, men who were dedicated to the deity and who submitted to passive pederasty, corresponded to the sacred prostitutes, *kedeshot*;[5] here again the act was a rite of incorporation.

[1] Parkinson, *Dreissig Jahre in der Südsee*, p. 611; sodomy is likewise practiced as a rite of initiation in New Guinea: Rev. James Chalmers, "Notes on the Bugilai, British New Guinea," *Journal of the Royal Anthropological Institute*, XXXIII (1903), 108–10.

[2] [Young men in ancient Greece who had just been admitted to citizenship.]

[3] For facts and references, see Ellis, *Studies in the Psychology of Sex*, Vol. II; Westermarck, *The Origin and Development of Moral Ideas*, II, 456–89; and the periodical of Friedrich S. Krauss, *Anthropophyteia: Jahrbücher für folklorische Erhebung und Forschungen zur Entwicklungs Geschichte des geschlechtlicher Moral* (Leipzig), Vols. I (1904), II (1905), III (1906).

[4] Reinach, "La lutte de Jacob et de Moïse avec Jahvé," p. 356, n. 5.

[5] [The *kedeshot* were priestesses of Ashtoreth, or Astarte, whose worship was introduced by Solomon; the *kedeshim* were their male counterparts. The Old Testament

The phenomenon of transvestites need not concern us here, although the rite practiced on the island of Kos should be mentioned. There the priests of Hercules wore women's clothing, and a groom greeted his bride dressed as a woman.[1] The similarity between these two practices can be easily explained if one accepts that the priests were the wives of Hercules and therefore that incorporation with this god comprised homosexuality, and that the groom acted entirely like Koryak shaman couples, among whom the husband is the wife and the wife the husband.[2] The parallel in question is thus but a coincidence unless it is assumed that the marriage rite influenced the rite of the temple, and in that case, whatever the reason for the disguising of the groom, the rite of the temple still can be nothing but a rite of incorporation with the deity.[3] Ritual pederasty may be found also among the Pueblo Indians,[4] who intentionally make certain young men (*mujerados*) effeminate and then employ them in the course of various ceremonies,[5] undoubtedly for the same purpose as that of the Arunta when they ritually avail themselves of women. In both cases the act might be called a "magical lubricant."

records the subsequent presence of both groups and the attempts made to expel and abolish them. For references, see *The Jewish Encyclopedia*.]

[1] Frazer, *Adonis, Attis, Osiris*, p. 433.

[2] See Waldemer Iochelson, *The Koryak* ("Publications of the Jesup North Pacific Expedition," Vol. VI, Part I, Memoir of the American Museum of Natural History [Leiden: E. J. Brill, New York: G. E. Stechert, 1908]), pp. 52–54.

[3] The customs of priests and magicians dressing in women's clothes is so common that we should perhaps look for further explanations; see Iochelson's interesting notation, *The Koryak*, p. 53; Van der Burght, *Dictionnaire français Kirundi* p. 107; Frazer, *Adonis, Attis, Osiris*, Appendix, pp. 428–35. The idea behind the priest's adoption of woman's dress may be that he believes himself possessed by a female spirit or goddess with whom he wishes to become identified. Frazer cites (p. 434) this rite as a rite of marriage and thinks that it is intended to assure the birth of male children. This interpretation is not acceptable. If it were correct, the groom would give birth to girls or procreate only girls! In my opinion, it is a matter of the young man's becoming incorporated into the family of the bride, and the girl into the family of the groom, or, more probably, just a simple rite of union between the two individuals identical to the exchange of rings, foodstuffs, etc.

[4] [Although men do impersonate women in Pueblo ceremonies, there is no reference in ethnographic sources to the custom described above.]

[5] F. Karsch, "Uranismus oder Päderastie und Tribadie bei den Naturvölkern," *Jahrbuch für sexuelle Zwischenstufen*, III (1901), 171–75.

Similarly, a few facts will suffice to show that intercourse with an animal may in particular cases be a rite of incorporation. The rite appears in a very clear-cut form in Madagascar. Among the Antaimoro, a man can have sexual relations with a woman only after having had intercourse with a heifer which has been specially cared for and which is adorned with flowers and garlands; the nickname of the Antaimoro is "cows' suitors," and the rite is perhaps related to totemism. Among certain tribes of British New Guinea, bestiality[1] is one of the rites in the initiation ceremonies.[2] The dramatic representation of animal intercourse, if not the act itself, plays an important part in initiation among at least some Australians and American Indians, as well as among the Bushmen of the Kalahari Desert; the latter perform the dance of the bull and the cows, the turkey, or the porcupine, simulating the coitus of these animals with great precision.[3]

The magical efficacy of coitus with animals emerges from the following prescriptions, noted in Dalmatia by Mitrovics. To be freed of consumption, a man should have intercourse with a hen or a duck; to get rid of gonorrhea, with a hen, cutting her throat during the act; to become master of the black art, one should have intercourse with a cow; to have good fortune, with a hen; to learn the language of the animals, with a female snake; to keep Vilas (bad fairies) from harming animals, with a mare; to steal without being caught, with a cat; to have good fortune in the house, one should have intercourse with a goat, collect the sperm, and rub the door of the house with it.[4] The custom of intercourse with hens, ducks, etc., which is so widespread in Annam that a European must never eat one of these fowl if it has

[1] See my *Tabou et totémisme à Madagascar*, pp. 249–51, 280–81, 343.

[2] Chalmers, "Notes on the Bugilai," p. 109.

[3] Siegfried Passarge, *Die Buschmänner der Kalahari* (Berlin: D. Reimer, 1907), pp. 101–4.

[4] Friedrich S. Krauss and R. Reiskel, *Die Zeugung in Glauben: Sitten und Bräucher der Völker* (Leipzig: Deutsche Verlagsaktie Gesselschaft, 1909), trans. with supplements by J. A. Dulaure, *Des divinités génératrices: Ou du culte de phallus chez les anciens et les modernes* (Paris: Dertu, 1805).

not been killed in his presence, undoubtedly springs from opinions of the same kind.

Among the acts which may be interpreted in several ways, even if they are only ritually enacted, is the practice of flagellation. Its importance in the psychology of sex is known: it is one of the most powerful means of erotic stimulation. But even its role in that context, like the occurrence of flagellation in rites, should be placed within the larger category of beatings, given singly or repeatedly, and all should be regarded as one of the forms of sadism. Ritually, whipping and beating may sometimes have a sexual effect. Where they do not, it is necessary to supplement the interpretations, accepted up to now, that the rite is simply intended to expel an evil spirit or an impurity. Reinach has gathered data on ritual flagellation in ancient times and has explained Mannhardt's theory that in the Lupercalia evil spirits are sent away by whipping.[1] Frazer sees flagellation as a rite of purification.[2] Thomson considers it a means of transferring into the body of the patient the force and vitality of the tree (a hazel tree) or the animal (a billy or nanny goat), parts of which are used for the whip. Reinach adopts this theory and sees the rite as one of communion—what I call a rite of incorporation. This interpretation also should be accepted for the Lupercalia and for the flagellation on the altar of Artemis Orthia.

Whipping is an important rite in many initiation ceremonies (the Zuñi practice has been noted[3]) and is equivalent to the New Guinea rite of hitting a person over the head with a club to incorporate him into the totem clan, the family, or the world of the dead.[4] It must be noted, however, that the administration of a whipping or beating serves in some cases (e.g., in Liberia and in the Congo) as a

---

[1] Reinach, "La flagellation rituelle," in *Cultes, mythes, et religions*, I, 173–83.

[2] Frazer, *The Golden Bough*, II, 149 ff.

[3] See above, pp. 77–78, and for another typical case, Webster, *Primitive Secret Societies*, p. 113.

[4] See above, p. 165.

physical rite of separation from the previous world; striking is then the equivalent of cutting or breaking. Finally I want to mention that the rite of hitting an object is fairly widespread and that there exists a rite of appropriation which consists of "striking the ground" or "striking the boundaries."[1]

There is a popular saying that only the *first time* counts; it is an interesting fact that this idea is truly universal and that it is everywhere expressed to some extent through special rites. That the rites of passage do not appear in their complete form, are not greatly emphasized, or do not even exist except at the time of the first transition from one social category or one situation to another has been shown repeatedly. Therefore, in order not to overload a book which is too full of details already, I will content myself here with a few suggestions. I should mention first that what has been said above applies to all rites of founding and of inauguration (of a house, temple, village, or town); these comprise ceremonies of separation from the ordinary or the profane, and an appropriation or a consecration. Founding ceremonies include individual rites of prophylaxis, propitiation, and so forth, but the pattern of rites of passage is basic to their organization and especially apparent in the rites of the first entrance. For a stranger there are also rites on the occasion of his first entry; then he is free to go out again and to re-enter.

The first pregnancy and the first childbirth are ritually the most important, though hygienic and medical considerations tend to reduce the differences between the first time and the others. The birth of the first child, and especially of the first son, is a more important event than the delivery of later children, and the point of view involved is legally expressed in birthright and primogeniture.

[1] See J. Brand, *Observations of Popular Antiquities: Origins of Our Customs, Ceremonies, and Superstitions* (London: Chatto, 1900), chap. xxxvi; Fowler, *The Roman Festivals*, p. 319, etc.

The first haircut, the first tooth, the first solid food, the first step, the first menses—all are occasions for ceremonies which are multiple in form, but based on one fundamental idea and parallel in their patterns. The first betrothal is more important than any that come later, and we know how a girl whose engagement has been broken falls into disgrace. A woman's first coitus has a ritual character which gives rise to a whole series of rites pertaining to the loss of virginity. The first marriage is the most important, and the reason for its primacy is not simply the loss of virginity, since among many peoples there is either a preliminary period of relations with young men (e.g., the communal house in the Philippines) or a defloration before the girl is delivered to her husband. Marriage ceremonies are simplified (or even parodied) in the case of remarriage by a divorcée or widow. In this connection I want to cite Biarnay's observations at Ouargla, because they are valid in a general way:

Four categories of marriage (at Ouargla) should be distinguished:

(1) A marriage between two young people, neither of whom has been married before; during the feasts and ceremonies which accompany or precede the marriage, and which as a whole are known as *islan*, the young man is called *asli* and the girl *taslet* or *taselt*; (2) a marriage between a man who has been widowed, divorced, or is already married to one or more other wives, and a virgin; this is the marriage of a *boumaoud* and a *taselt*; (3) the marriage of a young man who has never been married (*asli*) with a widow or a divorcée (*tamet'out*); (4) the marriage of two people who both have been married before.

The celebrations and feasts occasioned by the marriage diminish in number and in importance beginning with the marriages of the first category, which might be called complete marriages, and ending with those of the fourth category, considered banal formalities of interest only to the future spouses.[1]

Among polygynous peoples the first wife has definite prerogatives over the others. The first paternity among the polyandrous Todas[2] governs several succeeding paternities,

[1] Biarnay, *Étude sur le dialecte de Ouargla*, Appendix.
[2] Rivers, *The Todas*, pp. 322, 517.

and among the polygynous Sakalava[1] a husband performs a special rite to make sure that he is the father of the first child in order that he may also be the father of those to follow. The birth of the first child is often the terminal point of the marriage ceremonies or, as in the Cameroons, the event which enables the young wife to enter the group of full-fledged women.[2]

The rites of initiation are also, as the term indicates, the most important, since they secure for the individual a permanent right to attend or to participate in the ceremonies of fraternities and the mysteries. To see a sacred object for the first time is universally an act of very great import; the magic circle is broken for the first time, and, for that individual, it can never again be completely closed. The special nature of a Brahman's first sacrifice and a Catholic priest's first Mass is expressed in a number of special rites. The first funeral is more complicated than the second, and the funeral of the child which is the first in a family to die sometimes has a special complexity or significance. Finally, the best offerings are those of the first-born, the first fruits, and so forth.

It is apparent from this brief enumeration that an explanation of "rites of the first time" should have a generality which Schurtz hardly suspected when he studied them in relation to initiation rites.[3] He considered the gradual simplification of rites to be a consequence of the fact that secrecy was no longer necessary with the rise to higher degrees and that the members of the higher degrees were in control "behind the scenes"—an interpretation which obviously is not acceptable for all the other cases cited. These rites are simply rites of entry from one domain or situation into another, and it is natural that, once the new domain or situation has been entered, the repetition of the

[1] A. Walen, "The Sakalava" (4th in a series of articles), *Antananarivo Annual* VIII (1884), 53–54.

[2] Girls and women are naked until the birth of their first child; Hutter, *Wanderungen und Forschungen*, p. 421.

[3] Schurtz, *Altersklassen und Männerbünde*, pp. 354–55.

first act has a decreasing importance. Furthermore, psychologically, the second act no longer presents anything new;
it marks the beginning of habituation.

Those rites which accompany and bring about the change
of the year, the season, or the month, should also be included in ceremonies of passage. These cycles have been
examined by various authors, especially by Mannhardt and
Frazer, but their studies have been made from a special
point of view, and they seem not to have related the
essential significance of the ceremonies to that of other rites
of passage. The ceremonies of the end of the year and the
new year are so well known that it is unnecessary to stress
them.[1] In Peking, on the last day of the year, a meal brings
all members of the family together, even those ordinarily
separated by differences. The rite of "forgiving" is secondary in importance; it is a preparatory rite whose object is
to make the whole group cohesive. All take leave of the
departing year, and all members of the family kowtow
before the ancestors, the elders going first (the daughters
are exempt, since they will enter another family). The
eldest son makes farewell visits to related families, and so
forth.[2]

The length of the transition from the old to the new year
varies among different peoples. It may last the entire night,
from midnight to one o'clock in the morning, or sometimes
only the few minutes at the time of the change itself. In Peking
the gate between the Mongol and Chinese sections is closed
for half an hour. Pieces of red paper and similar items are
fastened to house doors and cupboards. Then rites are performed to welcome the new year; these include a sacrifice
to the ancestors and deities and a meal at which all the
relatives gather. The transitional period takes the form of
a day, week, or month of festivity or vacation. One such
example is the month during which administrative func-

---

[1] See, among others, Fowler, *The Roman Festivals*, pp. 35–43, 48–50.
[2] Grube, *Zur pekinger Volkskunde*, pp. 93, 97–98.

tions are suspended in China—known as "the sealing up of his (the mandarin's) seal of office."[1] New Year's Day is among many peoples a day when the routines of daily life are broken, and in Indochina this interruption is carried to such a point that even the dead leave their abodes and come to have a taste of earthly life.[2] The period of the Twelve Days or the Twelve Nights (between Christmas and Epiphany) is also a transitional period whose study is extremely instructive from the point of view of rites of passage.

Rites of passage which conform to the usual pattern are found in the ceremonies pertaining to the seasons which often fall at the time of the summer and winter solstices (the latter being combined in Europe with the ceremonies of the end of the year), and at the spring and fall equinoxes. Often the expulsion of winter is a rite of separation, bringing summer into the village a rite of incorporation; in other cases the winter dies and the summer or spring is reborn.[3]

The seasons are of no concern to man except for their economic repercussions on the more or less industrial life of winter and the primarily agricultural and pastoral life of spring and summer. It follows that an exact parallel to purely seasonal rites of passage may be found in rites intended to assure the rebirth of vegetation after the transitional period of winter dormancy. These rites also insure the resumption of animal sex life and the resultant increase in herds. All these ceremonies include both rites of passage and sympathetic rites—direct or indirect, positive or negative—for fertility, multiplication, and growth. It is strange that only the sympathetic rites attracted the attention of Mannhardt, Frazer, and those, like Hoffmann-Krayer,[4] who continued their work; but, since these scholars published their data in considerable detail, it is easy for anyone to see that

[1] See Doolittle, *Social Life of the Chinese*, II, 38–40, and Grube, *Zur pekinger Volkskunde*, pp. 98–99.

[2] For further facts, see Frazer, *Adonis, Attis, Osiris*, pp. 306 ff.

[3] Frazer, *The Golden Bough*, III, 70 ff.; I, 208; II, 91 ff.

[4] Hoffmann-Krayer, "Die Fruchtbarkeitsriten im schweizerischen Volksbrauch," pp. 239–68.

within these ceremonies the pattern of rites of passage clearly coexists alongside the category of sympathetic rites.

The most prominent element in the pattern, when the seasonal and economic power is personalized (e.g., in the case of Osiris, Adonis, etc.), is the dramatization of the idea of death, expectation, and rebirth.[1] Adonis is given a solemn funeral, mourning is worn, and all social life is suspended; he is reborn, the bond that united him with society is reestablished, and social life recommences. Finally, I must mention a fact emphasized by Beuchat and Mauss:[2] among the Eskimos social life is organized on a different basis in summer than in winter, and the transition from one seasonal form of life to the other is expressed through definite rites of passage.

There is another whole category of rites which has been incorrectly interpreted because the rites of passage were not understood. These are the ceremonies related to the phases of the moon. Frazer collected and described a great number of them but saw only one of their components, the sympathetic rites.[3] The correspondence between the phases of the moon and the growth and decline of plant, animal, and human life is one of humanity's oldest beliefs. As a

[1] See Frazer, *The Golden Bough*, almost all the second volume, and III, 138–200; *Adonis, Attis, Osiris*, pp. 187–93, 219–30, 254–59, 299–345; Cumont, *Les religions orientales*, pp. 300, 310; Reinach, *Cultes, mythes, et religions, passim*.

[2] Marcel Mauss and M. H. Beuchat, "Essai sur les variations saisonnières des sociétés eskimos: Étude de morphologie sociale," *Année sociologique*, IX (1905), 39–132. The authors did not devote any special study to the practices pertaining to the change of residence (dismantling, procession, various acts of propitiation, etc.), but it is possible to find these described in the sources cited. They are comparable to the rites making the passage from the life of the valley to that of the mountains (spending the summer in Savoy, Switzerland, the Tirol, the Carpathian Mountains, etc.). The departure and return always include communal meals, village celebrations, processions and benedictions, and so forth. We might place all similar rites into this category. There is, for instance, the Russian custom of making the animals step over a bar placed over the threshold when they leave the barn for the first time at the end of the winter. (Trumbull, *The Threshold Covenant*, p. 17); this act apparently separates them from a domestic enclosure and incorporates them into the outdoors.

[3] See Frazer, *The Golden Bough*, I, 156–60; *Adonis, Attis, Osiris*, pp. 369–77. For Sin, the Assyrian-Babylonian moon god, see Étienne Combe, *Histoire du culte de Sin en Babylonie et en Assyrie* (Paris: Geuthner, 1908).

matter of fact, these beliefs express an approximate correspondence with reality in the sense that the phases of the moon are themselves an element in the great cosmic rhythms to which everything is subject, whether it is the movement of celestial bodies or the circulation of blood.[1] But I should point out that, when there is no moon, a cessation not only of physical life but also of life within the larger society or restricted group comprises a transitional period.[2] The purposes of the ceremonies under discussion is precisely to end that period, to insure the coming of the expected vital fulness, and—when the moon is waning—to make the decline temporary rather than permanent. That is why the idea of a renewal, a periodic death and rebirth, is present in these ceremonies and why rites relating to the moon in all its phases, or only to the full moon, have the character of rites of separation, rites of entry, transition rites, and rites of departure.

Since the week is nothing more than a subdivision of the month, it is not marked by rites of passage except as it may be related to market days (especially in Africa). But rites of passage are sometimes performed in connection with the passage of a day. The many ceremonies in ancient Egypt[3] that were intended to insure the daily course of the sun, conformed to the pattern of rites of passage.

All those rites whose purpose is the multiplication of animals and plants, the periodicity of fertilizing floods, the fertilization of the earth, the normal growth and ripening of grains and fruits, and so forth, are only a means of securing a desirable economic position. The same holds true for rites pertaining to fishing and hunting, ceremonies for the multiplication of the totem (*intichiuma* in central Australia), and to some extent for rites of war and marriage ceremonies. But this is not the place to study the economic aspect of certain ceremonial cycles or to go into those

[1] See Ellis, *Studies in the Psychology of Sex*, pp. 85–160.
[2] Cf. departure of members of the Duk-duk from the forest before the last quarter of the moon (Webster, *Primitive Secret Societies*, p. 114).
[3] See above, p. 157, and below, p. 187.

external features of a transition which involve no magico-religious elements.

The phenomenon of a *transition* may be noted in many other human activities, and it recurs also in biological activity in general, in the applications of physical energy, and in cosmic rhythms. It is necessary that two movements in opposite directions be separated by a point of inertia, which in mechanics is reduced to a minimum by an eccentric and exists only potentially in circular motion. But, although a body can move through space in a circle at a constant speed, the same is not true of biological or social activities. Their energy becomes exhausted, and they have to be regenerated at more or less close intervals. The rites of passage ultimately correspond to this fundamental necessity, sometimes so closely that they take the form of rites of death and rebirth.

A few pages back I said that one of the most striking elements in seasonal ceremonies is the dramatic representation of the death and rebirth of the moon, the season, the year, vegetation, and the deities that preside over and regulate vegetation. But this same element is to be found in many other ceremonial cycles, and the parallels need not be explained by contamination or a borrowing from another cycle. The idea is suggested or dramatized in seasonal ceremonies, rites of pregnancy and delivery,[1] rites at birth among peoples who believe in reincarnation,[2] rites of adoption,[3] puberty,[4] initiation,[7] marriage,[5] enthronement,[6] or-

[1] In Madagascar pregnant women are considered "dead" and congratulated after delivery for being "resurrected" (see van Gennep, *Tabou et totémisme à Madagascar*, p. 165.
[2] See above, p. 53.   [3] See above, p. 38.
[4] See above, p. 67, and the very clear case cited by Frazer, *The Golden Bough*, III, 210 (Borneo).
[5] See above, pp. 138, 141.   [6] See above, pp. 112–13.
[7] See above, pp. 91–92. There is in Frazer's *The Golden Bough* (III, 422–66) a good collection of cases where death and resurrection are used as a part of initiation ceremonials. The explanation given by Frazer, however, is not acceptable. He thinks that in this rite the soul is externalized so that it may become identified with the totem. Not only is this theory inapplicable to identical rites used in the ceremonials I have enumerated, but there is nothing to prove that the union or identification with the totem has an essentially animistic basis. It could come about directly, for

dination,[1] sacrifice,[2] and funeral rites among peoples who believe in the survival of the individual or, more especially, in reincarnation.[3] Perhaps it may also be found in the vow and the pilgrimage. The "logical idea" behind these parallels, some of which Schurtz observed, is one he was unable to find and whose existence he even seems to deny:[4] the transition from one state to another is literally equivalent to giving up the old life and "turning over a new leaf."

It is difficult to decide, however, whether the introduction of the idea of death and rebirth is a cause or a consequence. It seems to be a consequence in the ceremonies of initiation and ordination, which, among other elements, include ecstasies, externalizations,[5] or, as among many American Indians, a dream or simply sleep. For instance, among the Fox on the last evening of the initiation (which lasts nine years) the novices lie down on the floor of the dance houses, go to sleep, and awaken as men.[6] The presence of the idea of death and rebirth in the ritual is a consequence also in seasonal ceremonies, when "nature goes to sleep" and "awakens"; but it is the cause of special dramatic rituals customary in the worship of Osiris, Adonis, and Attis, for example, and it has an existence of its own in Christianity

example, through ritualistic eating of the totem (the totemic communion of Robertson Smith), as in central Australia. On the subject of death and resurrection in rites of initiation, see M. Kulischer, "Die Behandlung der Kinder und der Jugend auf der primitiven Kulturstufen," *Zeitschrift für Ethnologie*, XV (1883), 194 ff.; Webster, *Primitive Secret Societies*, pp. 38 ff.; Goblet d'Alviella, "De quelques problèmes relatifs aux mystères d'Éleusis"; Harrison, *Prolegomena to the Study of Greek Religion*, p. 590 (Orphism); Farnell, *The Evolution of Religion*, p. 57 and n. Dieterich, *Eine Mithrasliturgie*, pp. 157–58; Schurtz, *Altersklassen und Männerbünde*, pp. 98, 99–108 for generalities, and *passim* for details; Schurtz failed to see that the rites dramatizing death and resurrection fall in with the other rites of initiation according to a necessary sequence.

[1] See above, pp. 108–10.

[2] See Hubert and Mauss, "Essai sur la nature et la fonction du sacrifice," pp. 48, 49, 71, 101 of the special edition (Paris: Alcan, 1899).

[3] See above, *passim*, as well as Hertz, "La représentation collective de la mort," p. 126.

[4] Schurtz, *Altersklassen und Männerbünde*, pp. 355–56.

[5] O. Stoll, *Suggestion und Hypnotismus in der Völkerpsychologie* (Leipzig: Veit & Co., 1903), pp. 289 ff.

[6] Owen, *Folk-lore of the Musquakie Indians.*

(the death and resurrection of the Saviour, which serves as a point of departure for interpreting the symbolic death and rebirth of novices). From the very fact that this idea occurs not only in initiation rites, the conclusion should be drawn that it is not an interpretation of hypnotic states, catalepsies, temporary amnesias, and other pathological phenomena. The idea in question becomes simple and normal if one accepts the following view: the transition from one state to another is a serious step which could not be accomplished without special precautions.[1] In some cases a ritual death and rebirth may result from an association of the stages of human life with the phases of the moon, for among a great many peoples[2] the origin or introduction of death is attributed to the moon.

The typical series of rites of passage (separation, transition, and incorporation) furnished the pattern for ceremonies of sacrifice, and in this connection it was systematized down to the last detail in ancient Hindu and Jewish rituals,[3] as well as sometimes in the pilgrimage and the *devotio*. It is known that the Catholic pilgrim must follow a certain number of rules of preliminary sanctification before his departure, so that he can be removed from the profane world and incorporated into the sacred world. The external signs of the pilgrim's state include the wearing of amulets, a rosary, pilgrim's cockles, etc., and restriction by taboos such as abstention from meat, sexual and sumptuary abstentions, and temporary asceticism.

Among Moslems[4] the pilgrim who has pledged to go to

[1] Some cases of interment in a crouching position might be an expression of the idea of rebirth in a world beyond the grave, but that this rite does not everywhere carry that meaning and that it is not fundamental to the practice has been well demonstrated by Richard Andree, "Ethnologische Betrachtungen über Hockerbestattung," *Archiv für Anthropologie*, N.S. IV (1907), 282–307, in contradiction to Dieterich and many other theorists.

[2] See, among others, my *Mythes et légendes d'Australie*, pp. 183–84; Hollis, *The Masai*, p. 271, etc.

[3] Hubert and Mauss, "Essai sur la nature et la fonction du sacrifice."

[4] See, among others, Smith (*Lectures on the Religion of the Semites*), whose interpretations must be supplemented by ours; for the orthodox Moslems see Ciszewski, *Künstliche Verwandschaft bei den Südslaven*, pp. 4 ff.

Mecca is in a special state called *iḥrām* from the moment he enters the limits of the sacred territory (Mecca and Medina). But, according to ancient custom, he was invested with sacredness, with *iḥrām*, as soon as he left his home, so that every pilgrim, from the time of his departure until his return, was outside ordinary life and in a transitional state. The same is true in Buddhism. At departure there are, of course, rites of separation, and upon arrival at the sanctuary there are special rites of pilgrimage, including rites of incorporation into the divine (touching the Black Stone, and perhaps originally the rite of stone throwing); these are followed by rites of separation from the sanctuary and return into the life of society and the family. The *devotio*, considered as a sacrifice in itself or as a special form of the usual sacrifice, operates in the same manner. Incidentally, its dynamics are related to those of initiation rites.[1]

Though I make no attempt to be completely exhaustive in this first essay on the various occasions in which the pattern of the rites of passage plays a part, I must point out certain instances where the transition possesses an autonomy of its own as a secondary system inserted within a ceremonial whole. For example, carrying and being carried is one of the practices which is found more or less universally in the various ceremonies through which a person passes in the course of a lifetime. The subject of the ceremony must not touch the ground for a specific length of time. He is carried in someone's arms or in a litter, placed on a horse, an ox, or in a carriage; he is placed on a mat which is movable or fastened, on a scaffold or an elevated seat, or on a throne. This rite is basically different from that of straddling something or being transported over something, although the two are sometimes combined. The idea is that the person should be raised above or lifted onto something.

[1] See Charles Daremberg and Edmond Saglio, *Dictionnaire des antiquités grecs et romains d'après les textes et les monuments* (Paris: Hachette, 1877–1906), for sources; P. Huvelin, *Les tablettes magiques et le droit romain* (Extrait des annales internationale d'histoire [Mâcon, 1901]).

Contrary to the view commonly accepted, the rite is not intended to prevent the earth, as sacred object or as the Earth Mother, from being touched by an impure being who would pollute her. Since this rite is used at birth, puberty, initiation, marriage, enthronement, ordination, funerals, and the travels of sacred personages (such as a king or priest), a general explanation must be found for it, and the simplest is, I think, that it should be viewed as a transition rite. It is intended to show that at the moment in question the individual does not belong either to the sacred or to the profane world; or, if he does belong to one of the two, it is desired that he be properly reincorporated into the other, and he is therefore isolated and maintained in an intermediate position, held between heaven and earth, just as the deceased on his bier or in his temporary coffin is suspended between life and true death.

Vengeance is sometimes the occasion for a highly complicated ritual, and it is generally true that a group which goes on an expedition of revenge is subject during its pursuit and at its return to specific observances in which the pattern of rites of passage recurs. There is a consecration, a transition, and a de-sanctification. This group of facts will be studied elsewhere, for its own interest and in relation to the right of asylum. I simply want to mention here that in Australia and Arabia the pattern emerges very clearly.

The various rites of appropriation, which include the imposition and lifting of taboos, and so forth, and whose purpose is to remove a person from the common domain in order to incorporate him into a special domain, also include the essential elements of the pattern. In Arabia, for example, the rites of sacred appropriation (by a deity, etc.) of new lands were followed by a transitional period, and only at the expiration of that period could the lands be cultivated.[1] Undoubtedly this fact can also be observed in Oceania and in Africa.

The transfer of relics also includes a transitional period

[1] See Smith, *Lectures on the Religion of the Semites*, p. 124 and n.

between the departure from wherever they are first preserved and the arrival at the place where they will be permanently housed. In the Catholic church there is a special
ritual for this occasion, since the transition places all those
participating in the transfer in a special sacred position.
The situation is similar when statues of gods or saints are
moved, or when a king-priest-god makes a journey; the act of
carrying is in this context the performance of a transition rite.

The pattern of the rites of passage thus recurs not only at
the foundation of the sets of ceremonies which accompany,
facilitate, or affect the transition from one stage of life to
another, or from one social position to another, but also at
the base of several autonomous systems which are employed for the benefit of whole societies, restricted groups,
or individuals. Parallels among these systems thus may be
found not simply in some of their forms but in their very
structures. As a matter of fact, these parallels were consciously developed by the Egyptians in keeping with their
tendency toward systematization. In Egypt during the
Theban epoch, the same fundamental elements of ritual
were used for the enthronement of the Pharaoh,[1] for the
divine service performed by the Pharaoh in his capacity as
a priest, and for the incorporation of a deceased person into
the world of the dead and the gods. In each instance there
was an identification with Horus, according to a prescribed
order, just as in another system of ritual there was identification throughout with Osiris. The latter included another
divine service, another procedure of incorporation into the
world of the dead,[2] and a ritual related to celestial movements which required the sun to rise each morning, to follow its usual path without eclipse until it set in the west,
and then to return through the land of the dead to the east.

The distinction between these two basically different
ritual systems apparently was not seen by Moret,[3] un-

---

[1] Described above, pp. 111–12.　　　[2] See above, pp. 157–59.

[3] For his descriptions, see Moret, *La royauté pharaonique*, pp. 209–33, 150–67,
176–83, 98, and *Le rituel du culte divin journalier en Égypte*, pp. 95, 100, 228–29, 91.

doubtedly because of the similarity of their fundamental themes,[1] the one being "dismemberment of Horus" and the other "dismemberment of Osiris."[2] Both these rituals concern a transition from one state to another, and the individual rites—sanctification, nursing, naming, "going up to the sacred chamber," passing from one room or region to another, acquiring special dress and insignia, eating a communion meal, etc.—are those which have come up continually in our study of the rites of passage.

There is one situation in which the whole series of rites of passage pertaining to the various periods of life may be seen enacted in a rather short span of time: when a man who has been thought dead returns home and wants to be reintegrated into his former position. He is required to pass through all rites pertaining to birth, childhood, and adolescence. He must again be initiated, and he has to remarry his own wife (e.g., in Greece, in India). An ethnographer should be present at such a rapid succession of a number of the ceremonies discussed here and should describe the various phases with the greatest care. His account would provide the best direct evidence that the present systematization is not a sheer construction of logic; it corresponds at once to the facts, to underlying tendencies, and to social necessities.

[1] I do not know whether this distinction has already been proposed by some Egyptologist, and I am unable to give the exact date of the moment of convergence.
[2] The third ritual is that of the sun (Ra).

X CONCLUSIONS

Our brief examination of the ceremonies through which an individual passes on all the most important occasions of his life has now been completed. It is but a rough sketch of an immense picture, whose every detail merits careful study.

We have seen that an individual is placed in various sections of society, synchronically and in succession; in order to pass from one category to another and to join individuals in other sections, he must submit, from the day of his birth to that of his death, to ceremonies whose forms often vary but whose function is similar. Sometimes the individual stands alone and apart from all groups; sometimes, as a member of one particular group, he is separated from the members of others. Two primary divisions are characteristic of all societies irrespective of time and place: the sexual separation between men and women, and the magico-religious separation between the profane and the sacred. However, some special groups—such as religious associations, totem clans, phratries, castes, and professional classes —appear in only a few societies. Within each society there is also the age group, the family, and the restricted politico-administrative and territorial unit (band, village, town). In addition to this complex world of the living, there is the world preceding life and the one which follows death.

These are the constants of social life, to which have been added particular and temporary events such as pregnancy, illnesses, dangers, journeys, etc. And always the same purpose has resulted in the same form of activity. For groups, as well as for individuals, life itself means to separate and to be reunited, to change form and condition, to die and to be reborn. It is to act and to cease, to wait and rest, and then to begin acting again, but in a different way. And there are always new thresholds to cross: the thresholds of summer and winter, of a season or a year, of a month or a night; the

189

thresholds of birth, adolescence, maturity, and old age; the threshold of death and that of the afterlife—for those who believe in it.

I am certainly not the first to have been struck by the resemblances among various components of the ceremonies discussed here. Similarities have been noted between entire rites, as well as among minor details. Thus, for example, Hartland[1] observed the resemblances between certain initiation rites and some rites of marriage; Frazer[2] perceived those between certain puberty rites and funerals; Ciszewski,[3] those among certain rites of baptism, friendship, adoption, and marriage. Diels[4] followed by Dieterich[5] and Hertz,[6] pointed out similarities among certain ceremonies of birth, marriage, and funerals, and Hertz added to the list rites for the opening of a new house (but did not present evidence) and rites of sacrifice. Goblet d'Alviella[7] pointed out the resemblance between baptism and initiation; Webster,[8] that between initiation into secret societies and the ordination of a shaman.

Hertz[9] was interested in the order of funeral rites and alluded to what he called the "transitory stage"—the period that lasts from marriage to the birth of the first child and that corresponds to the "transitory stage" of the dead in Indonesia (especially in Borneo). But except for him, all these scholars, including Crawley,[10] saw only resemblances in particulars. For instance, the communal meal (Smith's "communion sacrifice"), union through blood, and

[1] Hartland, *The Legend of Perseus*, II, 335–99.
[2] Frazer, *The Golden Bough*, pp. 204–7, 209, 210 ff., 418, etc.
[3] Ciszewski, *Künstliche Verwandschaft bei den Südslaven*, pp. 1–4, 31, 36, 53, 54, 107–11, 114, etc.
[4] Hermann Diels, *Sibyllinische Blätter*, p. 48.
[5] Dieterich, *Mutter Erde*, pp. 56–57.
[6] Hertz, "La représentation collective de la mort," pp. 104, 117, 126–27.
[7] Goblet d'Alviella, "De quelques problèmes relatifs aux mystères d'Éleusis," p. 340.
[8] Webster, *Primitive Secret Societies*, p. 176.
[9] Hertz, "La représentation collective de la mort," p. 130, n. 5.
[10] Crawley (*The Mystic Rose*) points out the precise similarities in the rites of marriage and funerals (p. 369) and rites of marriage and initiation (p. 326); on the last point, see also Reinach, *Cultes, mythes, et religions*, I, 309.

a number of other ties of incorporation furnished the subject matter for several interesting chapters by Hartland. Certain rites of separation, like temporary seclusion and dietary and sexual taboos, Frazer and Crawley found recurring in a great many sets of ceremonies. Diels, Dieterich, and, in general, all those who have been concerned with classical religions have demonstrated the importance in these religions of the so-called rites of purification (anointing, lustration, etc.). It was inevitable that marked resemblances would appear when a specific rite, such as the exchange of blood, was isolated for analysis in a monograph and when contexts were superimposed.

A host of ethnographers and folklorists have demonstrated that among the majority of peoples, and in all sorts of ceremonies, identical rites are performed for identical purposes. In this way, and thanks first to Bastian, then to Tylor, and later to Andree, a great many unilateral theories were destroyed. Today their orientation is of interest because, in the long run, it will make possible the delineation of cultural sequences and the stages of civilization.

The purpose of this book is altogether different. Our interest lies not in the particular rites but in their essential significance and their relative positions within ceremonial wholes—that is, their order. For this reason, some rather lengthy descriptions have been included in order to demonstrate how rites of preliminary or permanent separation, transition, and incorporation are placed in relation to one another for a specific purpose. Their positions may vary, depending on whether the occasion is birth or death, initiation or marriage, but the differences lie only in matters of detail. The underlying arrangement is always the same. Beneath a multiplicity of forms, either consciously expressed or merely implied, a typical pattern always recurs: *the pattern of the rites of passage.*

The second fact to be pointed out—whose generality no one seems to have noticed previously—is the existence of transitional periods which sometimes acquire a certain au-

191

tonomy. Examples of these are seen in the novitiate and the betrothal. It is this concept of transition that provides an orientation for understanding the intricacies and the order of rites preliminary to marriage.

Third, it seems important to me that the passage from one social position to another is identified with a *territorial passage*, such as the entrance into a village or a house, the movement from one room to another, or the crossing of streets and squares. This identification explains why the passage from one group to another is so often ritually expressed by passage under a portal,[1] or by an "opening of the doors." These phrases and events are seldom meant as "symbols"; for the semicivilized the passage is actually a territorial passage. In fact, the spatial separation of distinct groups is an aspect of social organization. The children live with the women up to a certain age; boys and girls live separated from married people, sometimes in a special house or section or in a special kraal; at marriage one of the two spouses, if not both, changes residence; warriors do not keep company with blacksmiths, and sometimes each professional class has its assigned place of residence.[2] In the Middle Ages the Jews were isolated in their ghettos, just as the Christians of the first centuries lived in remote sections. The territorial separation between clans may also be very definite,[3] and each Australian band camps in a specific place when on the march.[4] In short, a change of social categories involves a change of residence, and this fact is expressed by the rites of passage in their various forms.

As I have said several times, I do not maintain that all

[1] Trumbull has even noted (*The Threshold Covenant*, pp. 252–57)—among the Chinese, the Greeks, the Hebrews, and others—an identification of the woman and the door.

[2] [The reader will note that all these instances are not equally applicable to all societies.]

[3] See the separation of the clans in the Pueblo villages as described, among others, by Cosmos Mindeleff, *Localization of Tusayan Clans* (Nineteenth Annual Report of the Bureau of American Ethnology [1897–98], Part II [Washington, D.C.: Government Printing Office, 1900]), pp. 635–53.

[4] See, among others, Howitt, *The Native Tribes of South East Australia*, pp. 773–77 (on camping rules).

rites of birth, initiation, etc., are rites of passage only, or that all peoples have developed characteristic rites of passage for birth, initiation, and so forth. Funeral ceremonies in particular, since they depend on local beliefs concerning man's fate after death, may consist primarily of defensive procedures against the soul of the deceased and rules of prophylaxis against the contagion of death; in that case they present only a few aspects of the typical pattern. Nevertheless, it is always wise to be careful about such conclusions; the pattern may not appear in a summary description of the funeral ceremonies of a particular people, although it is clearly evident in a more detailed account. Similarly, among some peoples who do not consider the woman impure during her pregnancy and who allow anyone to be present at delivery, childbirth is only an ordinary act, painful but normal. But in that case the pattern will be transposed to the rites of childhood, or it may be included in the rites of betrothal and marriage.

The units of ceremonial life among certain peoples sometimes differ from those which are prevalent in our own and most other societies and those around which the chapters of this book have been organized. It has been pointed out, for example, that among the Todas there is a single set of ceremonies extending from the parents' adolescence to the birth of the first child and that it would be arbitrary to divide this set into ceremonies preliminary to puberty, pertaining to puberty, to marriage, to pregnancy, to delivery, to birth, and to childhood. This amalgamation recurs among many other groups, but in the last analysis this effort at synthesis is not affected by it. Although the pattern of the rites of passage occurs in a different form in these instances, it is present nonetheless, and it is clearly elaborated.

Another general observation seems pertinent. The preceding analysis has shown variations in the internal division of societies, the relation of the diverse sections to one another, and the breadth of the barriers between them, which range from a simple imaginary line to a vast neutral

193

region. Thus it would be possible to draw a diagram for each people in which the peaks of a zigzag line would represent recognized stages and the valleys the intervening periods. The apexes would sometimes be sharp peaks and sometimes flattened lines of varying length. For example, among certain peoples there are practically no betrothal rites except a meal shared at the moment of the preliminary agreement; the marriage ceremonies begin immediately afterward. Among others, on the contrary, there is a whole series of stages from the time of the betrothal (at an early age) until the newly married couple's return to ordinary life, and each of these stages possesses a certain degree of autonomy.

Whatever the intricacies of the pattern, the order from birth until death must often consists of successive stages best represented in rectilinear form. Among certain peoples like the Lushae, however, it is circular, so that all individuals go through the same endless series of rites of passage from life to death and from death to life. This extreme cyclical form of the pattern has acquired in Buddhism an ethical and philosophical significance, and for Nietszche, in his theory of the eternal return, a psychological significance.

Finally, the series of human transitions has, among some peoples, been linked to the celestial passages, the revolutions of the planets, and the phases of the moon. It is indeed a cosmic conception that relates the stages of human existence to those of plant and animal life and, by a sort of pre-scientific divination, joins them to the great rhythms of the universe.

INDEX